A
Food Lover's
Companion

Books by Evan Jones

Hidden America (with Roland Wells Robbins)
The Father: Letters to Sons and Daughters
The Minnesota: Forgotten River
Trappers and Mountain Men
Citadel in the Wilderness
American Food: The Gastronomic Story
The World of Cheese
A Food Lover's Companion

A Food Lover's Companion

Evan Jones

Illustrated by Lauren Jarret

Harper & Row, Publishers
New York, Hagerstown, San Francisco, London

Acknowledgments are due to the following publishers, authors, and representatives for permission to use material included in this book:

The New Yorker:
"Brigade de Cuisine" by John McPhee, reprinted from an article in the February 19, 1979 issue of *The New Yorker*. Reprinted by permission; © 1979 The New Yorker Magazine, Inc. From "Good Cooking" by Calvin Tomkins in the December 23, 1974 *New Yorker*. Reprinted by permission; © 1974 The New Yorker Magazine, Inc. From *Old Mr. Flood* (Duell, Sloan and Pearce). © 1944, 1972 Joseph Mitchell. Originally in *The New Yorker*. Reprinted by permission.

Copyright acknowledgments are continued on pages 379–386.

FIRST EDITION

Designer: Gloria Adelson

Library of Congress in Publication Data
Jones, Evan, 1915-
  A food lover's companion.
  1. Gastronomy—Addresses, essays, lectures.
I. Title.
TX631.J66   1979   641'013'08   79–1668
ISBN 0-06-012288-9

79 80 81 82 83 10 9 8 7 6 5 4 3 2 1

In memory of
Russell Jones
1918–1979

*Next to eating good dinners, a healthy man
with a benevolent turn of mind must like,
I think, to read about them.*

                        —THACKERAY

Contents

3 Wolf at the Door

4 Worth a Special Journey

5 "Cookery Is Become an Art"

6 Chefs de Cuisine

7 Hosts and Hostesses

8 Potpourri

11 "A New Creation Glows!"

12 Gastronomic Extravaganzas

INTRODUCTION

This is a book of memories and delights that spring from the thought of food. In the pages that follow are to be found hors d'oeuvres and entremets, main courses and snacks, a kind of larder of good things that have been written about hunger and greed, the appreciation of culinary style, and most of all, perhaps, about the art (or at times the lack thereof) of eating.

Like some tempting things to eat, this book is a sort of hybrid —the result first of my research for other kinds of books that dealt in history and second of the hunting down of background for gastronomic essays on contemporary subjects. "Tell me what you eat; I will tell you what you are," said Brillat-Savarin. History helps to make peoples of past eras more understandable when it tells how they lived and what they ate as well as how they fought their wars and chose their leaders.

Fiction has similar uses. Even a novelist like John Updike, whose pages reveal only a modest interest in gustatory pleasure, brings some of his characters together at a dinner party of "plain country fare" to highlight the fact that one protagonist comes from "a region of complicated casseroles and Hungarian goulashes and garlicky salads and mock duck and sautéed sweetbreads." Taste-buds may twitch a little as one reads the sentence and one knows a little more about the social terrain of Tarbox. In turn, one feels the reality of homesickness when Charlotte Brontë describes the longing to be back in the kitchen "cutting up hash . . . you standing by, watching that I put enough flour, not too much pepper. . . ." And, again, it isn't hard to recognize Dickens as the author when reading that "glimpses were caught of a roast leg of pork bursting into tears of sage and onion in a metal reservoir full of gravy, of an unctious piece of beef and blisterous Yorkshire pudding, bubbling hot in a similar receptacle. . . ."

Historians just as nimble at evoking time and temptation can also make a reader salivate. Here is Macaulay on a dinner given in Belgrave Square: "A huge haunch of venison on the sideboard; a magnificent piece of beef at the bottom of the table; and before my Lord himself smoked not a *dindon aux truffes,* but a fat roasted goose stuffed with sage and onions." It seems almost certain that, even as he wrote, Macaulay was filled with appetite for the viands he described. I know those feelings—when I was digging for material about an American fort that was, for a time, the most northwesterly point of U.S. settlement, I came across a paragraph on the niceties of military provisions so far from civilization. "There is an abundant store," a young lieutenant had written, "of cold boiled ham, of the true Virginia flavor—of corned beef, and of chickens: and the buffalo tongue should not be forgotten. Our coffee—not used with the stinting hand of a frugal *housekeeper*—was made after the most approved method, and with extreme care and attention; it was drawn with boiling water, like tea, and not suffered to boil afterwards. But who shall do justice to the venison, roasted in bits on a stick, with alternate pieces of salt pork? . . . 'O let me die eating ortolans, to the sound of soft music.' Bah!"

So far from luxurious living, anyone might cast a cold eye on more frivolous menus, or more heady ambiances. But for a curious reader it seems satisfying to picture that young soldier relishing the bounty of the frontier and not above a glancing blow at gastronomic flourishes he has left behind. Good writing about food tells much, even when it is not so appetizing. I doubt that anyone who has ever read Lillian Hellman's *Scoundrel Time* will be able to forget her setting the scene of a dinner with Henry Wallace and his wife; the meal consisted of two poached eggs for the host put on two shredded wheat biscuits, "a horrid sight, made more insulting by one egg on shredded wheat for me and one for Ilo."

I may have turned away from that passage less hungry than I had been before. Far more often, I've found myself nourished, in an unconscious way, by many of the selections that appear in the following pages. When my wife and I first saw Switzerland together it was from a bus that took us from the airport near Geneva to the Lausanne Palace Hotel. It was a bright day, the mountain air lucid as we sought out points of interest across the lake that separates Switzerland and France, and in the distance we glimpsed the slopes above Vevey. It was a moment of transcendence in which the awareness grew that we were in a place we already knew without ever having entered it before—it had become real for us in M. F. K. Fisher's *An Alphabet for Gourmets,* for it was in "P Is for Peas," which appears early in this book, that we had read about the best small chickens ever roasted, by Madame Doellenbach of Vieux Vevey, which were served "cooled in their own intangibly delicate juices" with the season's first tiny green peas to come from the terrace above the lake.

Much reading about food seems to heighten the experience of travel. This book also contains a piece by William Sansom that should be read before or after—better, both—a return to Provence. In this story of an authentically provincial restaurant there is, I think, much to whet the appetite for sights and sounds and fragrances, as well as the perceptions of another to add, on leaving Provence, to one's own memories. In Eleanor Clark's "On Tasting Oysters" there is not only a feeling of Brittany and its sea-oriented well-being but marvelous, graphic understanding of what food means to a Frenchman. Colette takes one into the French past and conjures, in "The Kicked Fish," mysteries of one of the still untrammeled regions. And for me, at least, not even Colette is more joyous in her evocation of country pleasures than is Jane Grigson in her appreciation of the mushrooms of the Bas-Vendômois.

James Michener reiterated a common sentiment when he said that "to dine in harmony with nature is one of the gentlest and loveliest things we can do. Picnics are the apex of sensible living and the traveler who does not so explore the land through which he travels ought better to stay at home." A lot of us, long before reading that defense of picnicking, have scurried to get to the nearest *charcuterie* or *fromagerie* ahead of noon-hour closings, just to have the kind of *déjeuners sur l'herbe* described in "Moveable Feasts" by James Beard, Simone Beck, or—thousands of feet off the ground, to be sure—Calvin Trillin.

After the publication of her book *Cross Creek,* during World War II, the late Marjorie Kinnan Rawlings wrote that a chapter called "Our Daily Bread" had brought her mail from servicemen in Hawaii, the Philippines, Australia, Ireland, and Egypt, all of which contained "wistful comment on my talk of foods," and one letter, she said, warned that "the chapter on foods, if read by many soldiers, will wreck the morale." She concluded, smilingly, I'm sure, that the world is hungry for food and drink "—not so much for the mouth as for the mind; not for the stomach, but for the spirit." Just as such appetites are more often stimulated by reminders of the simplest food of rural childhoods, words about food that touch the heart are also often simple words. It doesn't always take a poet to rouse the blood, and some of the most appreciable pieces in this collection are as unaffected as the eating pleasures they bring to life—there is Richard Bissell's tongue-in-cheek description of a traveler's first encounter with chili and Edna Lewis's understated memory of her mother's preparations for dining under the trees on Revival Sunday.

It is often a relief to find humor in Americana, as Bissell did, or in the foibles of W. C. Fields, as his biographer Robert Lewis Taylor recognized in chronicling the comedian's prandial pleasures. There is similar entertainment to be had in relishing the preposterous as Art Buchwald so clearly did—once more—in writing "Dinner Guest for Rent." *A Food Lover's Companion* would have been less fun for me had I not discovered these contributions in the years of reading and making subconscious mental notes about memorable gastronomic passages. Mimi Sheraton's "I Had Not Underestimated This Man" is another example of the sort of titillation I mean. And then there is the experience, irresistibly described by Ralph Ellison, of wolfing down roasted yams on a New York street. "I'll never again cook a sweet potato," a friend said, "without thinking of that. I can almost taste it right now, it's so real."

The best writing about food has been, at times, both light-hearted and serious since man got the hang of cooking and turned away from a primarily animal existence toward one we now call human. Since Petronius's satire titled "Trimalchio's Feast," there have been food lovers who preserved such bits of literature, and in the last couple of centuries there has been many an anthology. In all cases, including this one, selections have had to be made arbitrarily. To establish some sort of rationale for *A Food Lover's Companion,* I've diminished the emphasis on material cited in the past which is still easily accessible to average readers. Some of the selections here are complementary. In addition to a sampling of Brillat-Savarin himself, there is a fine portrait of Belley's imperishable gastronomer by that signal writer on food of the twentieth century, Joseph Wechsberg. There also is word of Dr. William Kitchiner, whose name alone warrants a passing glance and who, since his *The Cook's Oracle,* published in 1816, was unearthed by M. F. K. Fisher, has contributed more than his due of quotations to various tomes.

As in a felicitously planned meal, a book of this sort can't have everything and, in this bill of fare, sacrifices have been made to allow space for a few long entertainments (James Laver's "Déjeuner de Rupture," "A Hunting Weekend in the Haute Savoie" by Escoffier himself, and Phyllis Feldkamp's "Carême, the Kitchen Monarch," for example.) Other selections (Calvin Tomkins' glimpse of Julia Child) are here because they help to show that no period of change in American social history has been as radical as the recent years in which some of us have seemed to grow slightly giddy over such once specific expressions as the word "gourmet"; more people than ever before have been dazzled by the mastery of culinary arts, and their interest in fine cooking is serious—that, of course, is good.

I trust that many of these selections reflect that spirit, even though I cannot hope that everything here will be new to every reader. In the past many Americans, including Thomas Jefferson, Mark Twain, and such frequenters of Delmonico's Restaurant as Sam Ward, were proud of their enthusiasm for good food, but never before was it really fashionable to be fascinated by its preparation and dedicated to mastering the wizardry of the kitchen. Recently many men and women have made such gains. Cookbooks stand at attention on their shelves, and they have found splendid wonders in the world of food. Such pleasures, I think, can be extended by some of the contributors to *A Food Lover's Companion.*

EVAN JONES

New York, 1979

PURE MILK

1
Country Pleasures

Maybe it's because the pleasures of rural life are rarer than they once were. There are fewer hills in northern Vermont where once you could go with no more than a hat or an apron and pick as many blueberries as you could handily carry home. In the Middle West few pastures still have blackberry patches and fewer woods are laden with wild grapes to be picked in lazy solitude. But the rewarding leisure of the outdoors still beckons a reader and sometimes evokes a real hunger, which is all the more reason to sample the vicarious fulfillment in Marjorie Kinnan Rawlings' oyster roast, for instance. A food lover's country pleasures are various and often spurred on by nostalgia, as in Waverley Root's New England memory, or by the tingling of the palate aroused by William Humphrey's barbecue. To be hungry in the country is to have a sharper sense of appreciation.

What wond'rous Life is this I lead!
Ripe Apples drop about my head;
The Luscious Clusters of the Vine
Upon my Mouth do crush their Wine;
The Nectaren and curious Peach
Into my hands themselves do reach;
Stumbling on Melons, as I pass,
Insnar'd with Flow'rs, I fall on Grass.
                    —Andrew Marvell

P Is for Peas

M. F. K. FISHER

. . . Naturally! and for a few reasons why the best peas I ever ate in my life were, in truth, the best peas I ever ate in my life.

Every good cook, from Fannie Farmer to Escoffier, agrees on three things about these delicate messengers to our palates from the kind earth-mother: they must be very green, they must be freshly gathered, and they must be shelled at the very last second of the very last minute.

My peas, that is, the ones that reached an almost unbelieveable summit of perfection, an occasion that most probably never would happen again, met these three gastronomical requirements to a point of near-ridiculous exactitude. It is possible, however, that even this technical impeccability would not have been enough without the mysterious blending, that one time, of weather, place, other hungers than my own. After all, I can compare bliss with near bliss, for I have often, blesséd me, eaten superlative green peas.

Once, for instance, my grandmother ran out into her garden, filled her apron with the fattest pods, sat rocking jerkily with a kind of nervous merriment for a very few minutes as she shelled them—and before we knew it she had put down upon the white-covered table a round dish of peas in cream. We ate them with our spoons, something we never could have done at home! Perhaps that added to their fragile, poignant flavor, but not much: they were truly *good*.

And then once in Paris, in June (what a hackneyed but wonderful combination of the somewhat overrated time-and-place motif!), I lunched at Foyot's, and in the dim room where hot-house roses stood on all the tables the very month roses climbed crazily outside on every trellis, I watched the headwaiter, as skilled as a magician, dry peas over a flame in a generous pan, add what looked like an equal weight of butter, which almost visibly sent out a cloud of sweet-smelling hay and meadow air, and then swirl the whole.

At the end he did a showy trick, more to amuse himself than me, but I sat open-mouthed, and I can still see the arc of little green vegetables flow up into the air and then fall, with a satisfying shush, back into the pan some three or four feet below and at least a yard from where they took off. I gasped, the headwaiter bowed faintly but with pride, and then we went about the comparatively mundane procedure of serving, tasting, and eating.

Those petit pois au beurre were, like my grandmother's, à la crème mode d'Iowa, good—*very* good. They made me think of paraphrasing Sidney Smith's remark about strawberries and saying, "Doubtless God could have made a better green pea, but doubtless He never did."

That was, however, before the year I started out, on a spring date set by strict local custom, to grow peas in a steep terraced garden among the vineyards between Montreux and Lausanne, on the Lake of Geneva.

The weather seemed perfect for planting by May Day, and I had the earth ready, the dry peas ready, the poles ready to set up. But Otto and Jules, my mentors, said no so sternly that I promised to wait until May 15, which could easily be labeled Pea-Planting Day in Swiss almanacs. They were right, of course: we had a cold snap that would have blackened any sprout about May 10. As I remember, the moon, its rising, and a dash of hailstones came into the picture too.

And then on May 15, a balmy sweet day if ever I saw one, my seeds went into the warm, welcoming earth, and I could agree with an old gardening manual which said understandingly, "Perhaps no vegetable is set out in greater expectancy . . . for the early planting fever is impatient."

A week later I put in another row, and so on for a month, and they did as they were meant to, which is one of the most satisfying things that can possibly happen to a gardener, whether greenhorn and eager or professional and weatherworn.

Then came the day with stars on it: time for what my grandmother would have called "the first mess of peas."

The house at Le Pâquis was still a-building, shapes of rooms but no roof, no windows, trestles everywhere on the wide terrace high above the lake, the ancient apple tree heavily laden with button-sized green fruit, plums coloring on the branches at the far end near the little meadow, set so surprisingly among the vineyards that gave Le Pâquis its name.

We put a clean cloth, red and white, over one of the carpenters' tables, and we kicked wood curls aside to make room for our feet under the chairs brought up from the apartment in Vevey. I set out tumblers, plates, silver, smooth, unironed napkins sweet from the meadow grass where they had dried.

While some of us bent over the dwarf-pea bushes and tossed the crisp pods into baskets, others built a hearth from stones and a couple of roof tiles lying about and made a lively little fire. I had a big kettle with spring water in the bottom of it, just off simmering, and salt and pepper and a pat of butter to hand. Then I put the bottles of Dézelay in the fountain, under the timeless spurt of icy mountain water, and ran down to be the liaison between the harvesters and my mother, who sat shelling peas from the basket on her lap into the pot between her feet, her fingers as intent and nimble as a lacemaker's.

I dashed up and down the steep terraces with the baskets, and my mother would groan and then hum happily when another one appeared, and below I could hear my father and our friends cursing just as happily at their wry backs and their aching thighs, while the peas came off their stems and into the baskets with a small sound audible in that still high air, so many hundred feet above the distant and completely silent Leman. It was suddenly almost twilight. The last sunlight on the Dents du Midi was fire-rosy, with immeasurable coldness in it.

"Time, gentlemen, time," my mother called in an unrehearsed and astonishing imitation of a Cornish barmaid.

They came in grateful hurry up the steep paths, almost nothing now in their baskets, and looks of smug success upon their faces. We raced through the rest of the shelling, and then while we ate rolled prosciutto and drank Swiss bitters or brandy and soda or sherry, according to our various habits, I dashed like an eighteenth-century courier on a secret mission of utmost military importance, the pot cautiously braced in front of me, to the little hearth.

I stirred up the fire. When the scant half-inch of water boiled, I tossed in the peas, a good six quarts or more, and slapped on the heavy lid as if a devil might get out. The minute steam showed I shook the whole like mad. Someone brought me a curl of thin pink ham and a glass of wine cold from the fountain. Revivified, if that were any more possible, I shook the pot again.

I looked up at the terrace, a shambles of sawed beams, cement mixers, and empty sardine tins left from the workmen's lunches. There sat most of the people in the world I loved, in a thin light that was pink with Alpen glow, blue with a veil of pine smoke from the hearth. Their voices sang with a certain remoteness into the clear air, and suddenly from across the curve of the Lower Corniche a cow in Monsieur Rogivue's orchard moved her head among the meadow flowers and shook her bell in a slow, melodious rhythm, a kind of hymn. My father lifted up his face at the sweet sound and, his fists all stained with green-pea juice, said passionately, "God, but I feel good!" I felt near to tears.

The peas were now done. After one more shake I whipped off the lid and threw in the big pat of butter, which had a bas-relief of William Tell upon it. I shook in salt, ground in pepper, and then swirled the pot over the low flames until Tell had disappeared. Then I ran like hell, up the path lined with candytuft and pinks, past the fountain where bottles shone promisingly through the crystal water, to the table.

Small brown roasted chickens lay on every plate, the best ones I have ever eaten, done for me that afternoon by Madame Doellenbach of the Vieux Vevey and not chilled since but cooled in their own intangibly delicate juices. There was a salad of mountain lettuces. There was honest bread. There was plenty of limpid wine, the kind Brillat-Savarin said was like rock-water, tempting enough to make a hydrophobic drink. Later there was cheese, an Emmenthaler and a smuggled Roblichon . . .

. . . And later still we walked dreamily away, along the Upper Corniche to a café terrace, where we sat watching fireworks far across the lake at Evian, and drinking café noir and a very fine *fine.*

But what really mattered, what piped the high unforgettable tune of perfection, were the peas, which came from their hot pot into our thick china plates in a cloud, a kind of miasma, of everything that anyone could ever want from them, even in a dream. I recalled the three basic requisites, according to Fannie Farmer and Escoffier . . . and again I recalled Sidney Smith, who once said that his idea of Heaven (and he was a cleric!) was paté de foie gras to the sound of trumpets. Mine, that night and this night too, is fresh green garden peas, picked and shelled by my friends, to the sound of a cowbell.

An Alphabet for Gourmets

"FULL OF FOOD, AND CONTENT"

For lunch twelve snails, black puddings, cider (which is made here, as well as wine), and a *barquette,* under the lime tree. The temperature is right, there is a little wind, the shadowed side of the tree isn't over warm. I become too sleepy to eat, see white clouds approaching over the cliff behind sprays of elm, and shall soon be fast asleep. J. remarks that this is the way babies fall asleep on breasts, warm, full of food, and content.

—GEOFFREY GRIGSON

"ALL ONE CAN EAT FOR FIFTY CENTS"

South of St. Augustine on the Matanzas River, an old Negro fisherman lives in a shack that would delight the soul of an artist. He "raises" his own oysters, feeding the beds and gathering only the mature oysters. We like to go to Gene's on a moonlight night for an oyster roast—all one can eat for fifty cents. Gene swears he makes a profit, but I do not see how. We take our own butter for melting, condiments, bread or crackers, salad and beer or coffee.

We turn down a narrow sand road between scrub palmettos, and around a bend in the river the orange glow from Gene's fire lights the live oaks and the long pine tables. Sheet iron the size of a double bed lies over blazing fatwood. Gene brings baskets of oysters from the river bed, dumps them out on the hot sheet iron, rakes them flat, and throws over them crocus sacks wrung out of cold water. Steam rises, the oysters sizzle, and at the right mysterious moment known only to himself, Gene removes the sacks, rakes the oysters to one side with a flourish, and piles them along the tables.

"Don't hold back," Gene says. "There's more where them came from!"

Each of us is provided with an oyster knife for one hand and a large white glove for the other. The oysters open easily and we shuck them into our individual ramekins of melted butter and condiments. They are small, but with a fine tangy flavor. We eat incredible dozens.

—MARJORIE KINNAN RAWLINGS
Cross Creek Cookery

Mme. Denis will eat your oysters tomorrow; I might eat some too provided they were roasted; I feel there is something barbarous in eating such a pretty little animal raw.

—VOLTAIRE, IN A LETTER

"THE KIND OF CRABBING MY WIFE LIKES TO DO"
EUELL GIBBONS

I have proved to my own satisfaction that Rock and Jonahs can be caught legally by amateur methods as easily as any crabs anywhere. On a recent trip along the coasts of Connecticut, Massachusetts, New Hampshire and Maine, I was able to catch all the crabs I wanted, and these New England crabs are so good that I wanted a great many of them. . . . While poking around the shore and tide pools at low tide, I discovered the easiest way of all of catching . . . simply to scoop them from the bottom with a dip net. Every time I tried it, I got all the crabs I could use during the hour or so of lowest water. . . .

My wife and I are both fond of crab meat, but she would rather not see the crabs while they're still in the shell. Each day when the tide practically bared the bottom, I would go out and capture a bushel of crabs, sneak into the kitchen of our cottage and boil them for 10 minutes, then take them to a shady place and extract the meat with nutcracker and nutpick. These crabs have a surprising amount of meat in the first joints of their large walking legs, and on very large Jonahs, even the second joints are worth opening. I would take the meat back to the kitchen, add a bit of salt and 1 slightly beaten egg, and shape it into little balls with damp hands. The kind of crabbing my wife likes to do is to return from an afternoon's swim or sunbathing session, open the refrigerator door, and find a generous plate of Crab Cakes all ready to cook. We cooked them in a variety of ways. They were good just baked on a cookie sheet or fried in deep or shallow fat. Once we made a Crab Gumbo with frozen okra and instead of merely adding loose crab meat we dropped small Crab Cakes into it and boiled it for an extra 6 minutes. Served on a helping of wild rice, this made a dinner that could not soon be forgotten.

Stalking the Blue-Eyed Scallop

THE KICKED FISH
COLETTE

In the forest of the Dom there is an auberge—no need to name it; such places are famous enough. It's a beautiful spot, deep in the forest, and the road is romantic enough to remind us of coaches. On summer nights two or three tables are set out beneath the acacia trees, awaiting lovers of game, and lovers of that delicacy I call "kicked fish."

Is there a recipe? No. It's a primeval culinary arrangement, as old as olive trees and spear fishing. No form of cooking needs less equipment—it takes only practice.

Begin with—a Provençal forest; at least a southern one. Select your wood carefully: twisted olive logs, bundles of cistus, laurel roots and laurel branches, round pieces of pine sticky with golden resin, a scant gathering of terebinth, almond, and of course a few vine-cuttings. Build your fire right on the ground, between four great chunks of granite, and light it. While it burns—red, white, cherry, licked with golden blue—you have nothing to do but watch it burn. The greenish Provençal sky overhead will turn a deep lake blue.

The flames grow lower, die down; and of course you have a few beautiful Mediterranean fish, don't you, already cleaned? You bought an ugly rockfish in St. Tropez, with a dragon mouth; or a few thin dark-backed mullets in Toulon; and while you were cleaning them you haven't forgotten to slip a piece of fat bacon into their hollow inside? Good. Now get your broom—that's what I call the fragrant bundle of laurel, mint, thyme, rosemary and sage that you've tied together while you were watching your fire burn. Get the broom ready—dunk it, I mean, in a pot of good olive oil mixed with wine vinegar—and the only allowable vinegar is pink, and soft. Garlic—did you think you could do without it? How naïve. Garlic, pounded to the consistency of cream, gives the mixture the finish it needs. A little salt, quite a bit of pepper.

Be careful now. Your fire will soon be nothing but embers. A thick bed of embers humming softly, flaming up a bit now and then; a light translucent smoke carries the very soul of the forest to your nostrils—but now is the moment to give the whole thing an authoritative kick, one that sends sparks and smoke and embers flying, that exposes the burning pink coals, levels them, uncovering the pure heart of the fire, above which hovers a tiny blue flame, a wisp of fiery ghost.

Take an old grill, three feet high, twisted by ancient fires, lay the fish upon it, baptize it with the sauce, and plant the whole thing in the middle of your fiery inferno. There! But you haven't quite got the skill of the old man from the Dom, the man whose silhouette you make out around the fire, his blackened arm wielding the broom, his blackened arm constantly sprinkling, dousing, turning the fish on the grill for—how long? The old man knows. He doesn't count, he has no watch, he doesn't taste, he simply knows. It's a matter of experience, of magic. If you aren't up to a little magic occasionally, you shouldn't waste time trying to cook.

The "kicked fish" leaps from the grill onto your plate. You see how firm it is, how its skin crackles, splits, and reveals the white flesh whose taste recalls the ocean and the odor of the forest. The pine-scented night begins to fall, and a flickering candle on the table illuminates the pomegranate color of the wine in your glass. The moment is full of happiness. Drink to it.

Prisons et Paradis

Mushrooms of the Bas-Vendômois
JANE GRIGSON

Our first guide to that secret countryside, the key to our explorations, and our great friend, was a local vineyard-owner called Maurice. With a gentle humour at our French and our ignorance —"Pauvres paysans," he would say—he initiated us into the two main occupations of the neighbourhood, wine-making and mushroom-hunting. . . .

Sunday is the occasion. Woods which have been silent most of the week, come alive. The crackling of dry twigs announces our presence to all the others whom we cannot see, a more frequent shushing up of dead leaves, then the triumphant shout of our daughter, who has found the first girolles of the day. Maurice's dog squawks as we all close in swiftly on the fruitful corner, with encouraging noises for the sharp-eyed novice. Then we all spread out again, and a busy silence returns. One is isolated, all sense of time goes in the velvet warmth of the young trees. Suddenly some more girolles appear, or the moist brown head of a cep. . . .

Days in the wood end early. Even the thin, leafless copse subdues a flaring sunset. We are glad to come out into the less somber light of the road, glad to see our car against the skyline. [Then, at home,] we light the lamp quickly, and pour out a drink. One of us separates out the picking, the *cueillette*. Someone else gets down the mushroom book. I go into the large old fireplace which is now my kitchen, light the candles because it is nearly dark, assemble butter, oil, garlic; onions, cream—the things we are going to need for the mushroom feast. . . .

This is the point—good eating. The best of wild mushrooms— ceps, girolles, morels, field mushrooms—have the highest place in grand cookery, particularly in France but in other countries of mainland Europe as well. They have become part of the classic dishes of this tradition—and by classic I mean the very best of their kind, which because of their quality remain untouched through generations of changing taste. The flavour of such mushrooms rises above the main ingredients, like a fine descant which turns a familiar carol into something new, something more enjoyable than one had ever thought possible. . . .

The Mushroom Feast

A HUNTING WEEKEND IN THE HAUTE-SAVOIE
AUGUSTE ESCOFFIER

Although it is already a long time ago, I well remember a shooting party given by one of my friends who owned a vast property in an exquisite valley of the Haute-Savoie. . . . About ten guests were assembled on the Thursday evening, and it was decided that at dawn the following morning we should all set out, dispersing as chance directed, in search of a few coveys of partridge.

Our meal, that evening, was composed of a cream of pumpkin soup with little croutons fried in butter, a young turkey roasted on the spit accompanied by a large country sausage and a salad of potatoes, dandelions and beetroot, and followed by a big bowl of pears cooked in red wine and served with whipped cream.

Next morning at the agreed hour, we were all ready, and furnished with the necessary provisions and accompanied by local guides, we climbed the rocky paths, real goat tracks, without too much difficulty; and before long the fusillade began. It was those members of the party who had gone ahead who were opening the shoot by bagging two hares; the day promised to be fairly fruitful. And indeed so it turned out, since we were back at the house by about four o'clock, somewhat tired, but proud to count out: three hares, a very young chamois, eleven partridges, three large grouse, six young rabbits and a quantity of small birds.

After a light collation, we patiently awaited dinner contemplating the while the admirable panorama which lay before us. The game which we had shot was reserved for the next day's meals.

Our dinner that evening consisted of a cabbage, potato and kohl-rabi soup, augmented with three young chickens, an enormous piece of lean bacon and a big farmhouse sausage. The broth, with some of the mashed vegetables, was poured over slices of toast, which made an excellent rustic soup. What remained of the vegetables was arranged on a large dish around the chickens, the bacon and the sausage; here was the wherewithal to comfort the most robust of stomachs, and each of us did due honour to this good family dish.

To follow, we were served with a leg of mutton, tender and pink, accompanied by a purée of chestnuts. Then, a surprise—but one which was not entirely unexpected from our host, who had an excellent cook—an immense hermetically sealed terrine, which, placed in the middle of the table, gave out, when it was uncovered, a marvellous scent of truffles, partridges, and aromatic herbs.

This terrine contained eight young partridges, amply truffled and cased in fat bacon, a little bouquet of mountain herbs and several glasses of *fine-champagne* cognac. All had been lengthily and gently cooked in hot embers. At the same time was served a celery salad. As for wines, we had first the excellent local wine, then Burgundy, and finally a famous brand of champagne. The dinner ended with beautiful local fruit, and fine liqueurs. . . .

The next day, Saturday . . . luncheon was composed partly of the trophies of the previous day's shooting; the pure mountain air had advantageously taken the place of the apéritif; nor did we have any hors-d'oeuvre but instead, some *ombres-chevaliers* [a kind of char] from Lake Bourget, cooked and left to get cold in white wine from our host's own vineyards. These were accompanied by a completely original sauce, and here is the recipe: Grated horseradish, mixed with an equal amount of skinned walnuts finely chopped; a dessertspoon of powdered sugar, a pinch of salt, the juice of two lemons, enough fresh cream to obtain a sauce neither too thick nor too liquid. . . .

After the char, we had eggs scrambled with cheese, enriched with white truffles which a shepherd had brought in from the boundaries of the Savoie, close to the frontier of Piedmont.

Then came an excellent civet of hare *à la bourgeoise,* assuredly far superior to all the fantasies known as *à la royale.* . . . The majestic roast consisted of the grouse in the center of a great dish, surrounded by the partridges and the tiny birds of which we had killed so many the day before.

A superb *pâté de foie gras,* sent direct from Nancy, was scarcely touched; on the other hand, we did considerable justice to the dessert: the season's fruits and excellent little cream cheeses. . . .

Having risen from table at six o'clock, we once more found ourselves there, as if by chance, three hours later, for a little cold supper; have I not already said that the air of the mountains is the best of apéritifs? . . .

The following day, which was Sunday, we were obliged, not without regret, to take leave of our hosts and return home. As we had two good hours of driving before arriving at the railway station, where we should not in any case have found a decent inn, we had a final lunch before our departure. It was composed of eggs and bacon, little galettes of maize flour fried in butter, a terrine of rabbit and cold meats. . . .

We all carried away with us the happiest memory of this beautiful country of Savoie and of the very hospitable welcome which we had received. For my part, I have never forgotten the sauce of horseradish and walnuts.

Le Carnet d'Epicure, January 15, 1912

A WILD BOAR BARBECUE
WILLIAM HUMPHREY

The oaks in the front lawn were just leafing out, and in their flickering and lacy shade a long trestle table had been set up on sawhorses. Four large unopened cartons labeled *Potato Chips* were spaced along it, alternating with shiny new number 3 galvanized washtubs filled to the brim with creamy white potato salad dotted with green specks of chopped pickle. On four big turkey platters in the center of the table there must have been six grosses of deviled eggs, yellow as a bed of buttercups in blossom. There were columns of paper plates; as for silver, each family was to come bringing its own. Underneath the table, with their rims touching, were tubs packed with ice, sweating cold already, some filled with bottled beer, some with colored soda water for the children. Your mouth watered and your teeth were set on edge so that you knew from a distance of ten feet that the two barrels beneath the biggest tree were full of sour pickles. On the outdoor fireplace a washpot of pork-and-beans slowly bubbled. Rows of folding chairs belonging to the Baptist Church were stacked spoke-wise against trees. Half the ice cream freezers in town had been borrowed for the occasion and half the Negro boys hired to crank them. The freezers were covered with wet towsacks. The boys took turns cranking. Two boys went from freezer to freezer sprinkling rock salt from a bag onto the ice. Two others brought buckets from the garage, where a man was busy chipping the second hundred pound block in a flying spray.

The barbecue pit—eight feet long, three wide, and six feet deep, to judge by the mound of dirt alongside—had been dug the day before; the fire had been lighted and through the night fed half a cord of green hickory, so that now a close view gave you the sensation of looking into the crater of a live volcano. Two tall slingshot-shaped poles had been driven into the ground at the ends of the pit.

At seven A.M. six men brought the boar down from the garage. He was spitted on a length of water pipe to which at one end was fitted a crank. The ends of the pipe were lowered into the crotches on the two posts. The carcass sagged over the fire. The skin at once puckered and shriveled in the heat, and in another moment the fat began to drip onto the coals, sending up little explosions of smoke.

Then down from the house came two more assistants carrying a washtub between them. Behind them came Chauncey in a chef's hat made from a grocery sack, carrying a floor mop over his shoulder. The tub seemed to be full of fresh blood; it was the barbecue sauce, Chauncey's recipe, famous at every Juneteenth, as the Negroes called Emancipation Day, for thirty years. He dipped the new mop into the tub, and while a boy turned the crank, he gave the boar his first basting. When he was turned belly-up he was seen to be stuffed and sewn with wire. Some said he was stuffed with the parts of a dozen chickens, some said with a barrelful of sausage meat and bread crumbs. Chauncey smiled knowingly; he wasn't saying.

Home from the Hill

"The Most Memorable Lobster Salad"

Lobster! I have eaten it in many countries but nowhere has it surpassed, or even equaled, the lobster of New England. No doubt the reputation of Maine lobster is justified, but it happens that the two places in my memory that are connected with superb lobster are both in Massachusetts. One is the island of Cuttyhunk, where I enjoyed the most memorable lobster salad of my life. While the wife of the family with which I was staying went into the garden to pick lettuce, her husband and I rowed out to a lobster pot and pulled up the main ingredient. Lettuce dewy from the garden, lobster dripping from the sea.

—Waverley Root

"Yankee Doodle in a Kettle"

A New England clam chowder, made as it should be, is a dish to preach about, to chant praises and sing hymns and burn incense before. To fight for. The Battle of Bunker Hill was fought for—or on—clam chowder, part of it at least; I am sure it was. It is as American as the Stars and Stripes, as patriotic as the national anthem. It is "Yankee Doodle" in a kettle.

—Joseph C. Lincoln

A FISH FEAST AT BLACKWALL
THOMAS LOVE PEACOCK

All day we sat, until the sun went down—
'Twas summer, and the Dog-star scorched the town—
At fam'd Blackwall, O Thames! upon thy shore,
Where Lovegrove's tables groan beneath their store;
We feasted full on every famous dish,
Dress'd many ways, of sea and river fish—
Perch, mullet, eels, and salmon, all were there,
And whitebait, daintiest of our fishy fare;
Then meat of many kinds, and venison last,
Quails, fruits, and ices crowned the rich repast.
Thy fields, Champagne, supplied us with our wine,
Madeira's Island, and the rocks of Rhine.
The sun was set, and twilight veiled the land:
Then all stood up,—all who had strength to stand,
And pouring down, of Maraschino, fit
Libations to the gods of wine and wit,
In steam-wing'd chariots, and on iron roads,
Sought the great city, and our own abodes.

SUNDAY REVIVAL DINNER
EDNA LEWIS

My mother never started her cooking until late on the eve of
Revival Sunday. By this time she would have everything gathered
in and laid out that she would need, and, I guess, a carefully
planned schedule laid out in her mind as well. When we were
bathed and turned into bed, no pies or cakes had yet been made.
But when we came hurrying down on Sunday morning, the long
rectangular dining-room table would be covered with cakes ready
to be iced and pie dishes lined with pastry dough to be filled and
baked. While we counted them and excitedly discussed our favorites and how many slices of each we could eat, my mother was out

in back feeding her fowl. When she came in she would make us breakfast, standing at the stove with her everyday calm. Then she would help us dress, tie on our ribbons, and send us to sit on the porch until noontime with firm warning to sit quietly so that our new clothes would not get mussed. It would seem a very long morning.

Mother would return to the kitchen to continue her cooking. Because she liked to arrive at the church with the food piping hot, my father would attend the morning service alone and then come back for us as soon as it was over. . . . The churchyard would be filled with people as we drove up; I felt as though everyone was looking at us. My father would drive straight up to one of the long tables that were stretched out in a line under the huge, shady oak trees alongside the church. My mother would spread out a white linen tablecloth before setting out the baked ham, the half-dozen or more chickens she had fried, a large baking pan of her light, delicate corn pudding, a casserole of sweet potatoes, fresh green beans flavored with crisp bits of pork, and biscuits that had been baked at the last minute and were still warm. The main dishes were surrounded with smaller dishes of pickled watermelon rind, beets and cucumbers and spiced peaches. The dozen or so apple and sweet potato pies she had made were stacked in tiers of three, and the caramel and jelly layer cakes placed next to them. Plates, forks, and white damask napkins and gallon jars of lemonade and iced tea were the last things to be unpacked.

All along the sixty-foot length of tables, neighbors were busy in the same way, setting out their own specialties. There were roasts and casseroles, cole slaw and potato salads, lemon meringue, custard, and Tyler pies, chocolate and coconut layer, lemon cream, and pound cakes. . . . My mother and the other ladies were eager to see that all of the guests were served, and there was always a special plate for a special friend.

A Taste of Country Cooking

2
Moveable Feasts

Dining while in transit once had as much elegance as could be found anywhere else. In The New York Times, in fact, Craig Claiborne once said in so many words that the best of all restaurants in 1969 was a floating one, the dining salon of the S.S. France. Things sometimes seemed almost as good aboard America's Twentieth Century Limited, or the Brighton Belle between London and the Channel. But a moveable feast doesn't have to be served to you in the sway of a passenger carrier. It can be found at the end of a processional picnic outing in the mountains of India, or on a Caribbean beach that is barren of sunbathed transient bodies but more rewarding because of the solitude—and the homemade chutney to spruce up a boiled fish, and rum from Barbados and local lime juice to spice a canteen of water. Here, the feasts that follow may have more reality than that outdoor repast in Paradise described by Milton:

> *In ample space under the broadest shade,*
> *A table richly spread in regal mode,*
> *With dishes piled and meats of noblest sort*
> *And savour—beasts of chase, or fowl or game. . . .*

CAPTAIN HORNBLOWER DINES WITH THE ADMIRAL
C. S. FORESTER

A door, thrown open in the midships bulkhead, revealed a dining-room, an oblong table with white damask, glittering silver, sparkling glasses, while more stewards in white ducks were ranged against the bulkhead. There could be little doubt about the precedence when every captain in the Royal Navy had, naturally, studied his name in the captains' list ever since his promotion; Hornblower and the single-epauletted captain were headed for the foot of the table when Pellew halted the general sorting-out.

"At the Admiral's suggestion," he announced, "we are dispensing with precedence today. You will find your names on cards at your places."

So now everyone began a feverish hunt for their names; Hornblower found himself seated between Lord Henry Paulet and Hosier of the *Fame,* and opposite him Cornwallis himself.

"I made a suggestion to Sir Edward," Cornwallis was saying as he leisurely took his seat, "because otherwise we always find ourselves sitting next to our neighbours in the captains' list. In blockade service especially, variety is much to be sought after."

He lowered himself into his chair, and when he had done so his juniors followed his example. Hornblower, cautiously on guard about his manners, still could not restrain his mischievous inner self from mentally adding a passage to the rules of naval ceremonial to the lines of the rule about the officer's head reaching the level of the maindeck—"when the Admiral's backside shall touch the seat of his chair—".

"Pellew provides good dinners," said Lord Henry, eagerly scanning the dishes with which the stewards were now crowding the table. The largest dish was placed in front of him, and when the immense silver dish cover was whipped away a magnificent pie was revealed. The pastry top was built up into a castle, from the turret of which flew a paper Union Jack.

"Prodigious!" exclaimed Cornwallis. "Sir Edward, what lies below the dungeons here?"

Pellew shook his head sadly. "Only beef and kidneys, sir. Beef stewed to rags. Our ship's bullock this time, as ever, was too tough for ordinary mortals, and only stewing would reduce his steaks to digestibility. So I called in the aid of his kidneys for a beefsteak and kidney pie."

"But what about the flour?"

"The victualling officer sent me a sack, sir. Unfortunately it had rested in bilge water, as could only be expected, but there was just enough at the top unspoiled for the pie-crust."

Pellew's gesture, indicating the silver bread barges filled with ship's biscuit, hinted that in more fortunate circumstances they might have been filled with fresh rolls.

"I'm sure it's delicious," said Cornwallis. "Lord Henry, might I trouble you to serve me, if you can find it in your heart to destroy those magnificent battlements?"

Paulet set to work with a carving knife and fork on the pie, while Hornblower pondered the phenomenon of the son of a Marquis helping the son of an Earl to steak and kidney pie made from a ration bullock and spoiled flour.

"That's a ragout of pork beside you, Captain Hosier," said Pellew. "Or so my chef would call it. You may find it even saltier than usual, because of the bitter tears he shed into it. Captain Durham has the only live pig left in the Channel Fleet, and no gold of mine would coax it from him, so that my poor fellow had to make do with the contents of the brine tub."

"He has succeeded perfectly with the pie, at least," commented Cornwallis. "He must be an artist."

"Well, sir. . . . This ship has a complement of six hundred and fifty men. Every day thirteen fifty-pound bread bags are emptied. The secret lies in the treatment of those bags."

"But how?" asked several voices.

"Tap them, shake them, before emptying. Not enough to make wasteful crumbs, but sharply enough. Then take out the biscuits quickly, and behold! At the bottom of each bag is a mass of weevils and maggots, scared out of their natural habitat and with no time allowed to seek shelter again. Believe me, gentlemen, there is nothing that fattens a chicken so well as a diet of rich biscuit-fed weevils. Hornblower, your plate's still empty. Help yourself, man."

Hornblower had thought of helping himself to the chicken, but somehow—and he grinned at himself internally—this last speech diverted him from doing so. The beefsteak pie was in great demand and had almost disappeared, and as junior officer he knew better than to anticipate his seniors' second helpings. The ragout of pork, rich in onions, was at the far end of the table.

"I'll make a start on this, sir," he said, indicating an untouched dish before him.

"Hornblower has judgment that puts us all to shame," said Pellew. "That's a kickshaw in which my chef takes particular pride. To go with it you'll need these puree potatoes, Hornblower."

It was a dish of brawn, from which Hornblower cut himself moderately generous slices, and it had dark flakes in it. There was no doubt that it was utterly delicious; Hornblower diving down into his general knowledge came up with the conclusion that the black flakes must be truffles, of which he had heard but which he had never tasted. The puree potatoes, which he would have called mashed, were like no mashed potatoes he had ever sampled either on shipboard or in a six-penny ordinary in England. They were seasoned subtly and yet to perfection—if angels ever ate mashed potatoes they would call on Pellew's chef to prepare them. With spring greens and carrots—for both of which he hungered inexpressibly—they made a plateful, along with the brawn, of sheer delight. He found himself eating like a wolf and pulled himself up short, but the glances that he stole round the table reassured him, for the others were eating like wolves too, to the detriment of conversation, with only a few murmured words to mingle with the clash of cutlery.

"Wine with you, sir." "Your health, Admiral." "Would you give the onions a fair wind, Grindall?" and so on.

"Won't you try the galantine, Lord Henry?" asked Pellew. "Steward, a fresh plate for Lord Henry."

That was how Hornblower learned the real name of the brawn he was eating. The ragout of pork drifted his way and he helped himself generously; the steward behind him exchanged his plate in the nick of time. He savoured the exquisite boiled onions that wallowed in the beatific sauce. Then like magic the table was cleared and fresh dishes made their appearance, a pudding rich with raisins and currants, jellies of two colours; much labour must have gone into boiling down the bullock's feet and into subsequent straining to make that brilliant gelatine.

"No flour in that duff," said Pellew apologetically. "The galley staff has done its best with biscuit crumbs."

That best was as near perfection as mind could conceive; there was a sweet sauce with it, hinting of ginger, that made the most of the richness of the fruit. Hornblower found himself thinking that if ever he became a post captain, wealthy with prize money, he would have to devote endless thought to the organization of his cabin stores. And Maria would not be of much help, he thought ruefully. He was still drifting along with thoughts of Maria when the table was swept clear again.

"Caerphilly, sir?" murmured a steward in his ear. "Wensleydale? Red Cheshire?"

These were the cheeses being offered him. He helped himself at random—one name meant no more to him than another—and went on to make an epoch-making discovery that Wensleydale cheese and vintage port were a pair of heavenly twins.

Hornblower and the Hotspur

"Some of the Food on the Ship Was Good Enough"

On Monday, May 1, various games were being played on deck with each nation keeping to itself. Seven tenths of the emigrants are German, one fifth Irish, and one tenth Welsh and English. We the Welsh are small in number but greater in our morality.

It is strange what appetites the Germans have. They feast on black bread . . . as black as the conscience of Beelzebub. They have terribly unhealthy looking meat, bacon and herrings all eaten together with delight. At other times they ate herrings without cleaning them. Even the Irish were surprised at them.

We reached New York on Monday 8 May, and the doctor came aboard to see that everyone was vaccinated. What a dinner we had today! Beef and rice! No potatoes! Some put treacle on top of the rice and beef! A nice mess, wasn't it? Although some of the food on the ship was good enough, the way it was cooked and put before us did not make it very tasty. . . .

—Hiram James
From a letter to a Welsh newspaper, July 1882

LIVING HIGH ON THE NO-FRILLS FLIGHT
CALVIN TRILLIN

My decision to take a rather elegant picnic along on my no-frills flight to Miami was solidly based on a theory of economics known as Alice's Law of Compensatory Cashflow, which holds that any money not spent on a luxury one considered even briefly is the equivalent of windfall income and should be spent accordingly. If you decide, for instance, that buying a $500 color television set would be, all things considered, an act of lunacy, you have an extra $500 that you "saved" on the television set available to spend on something else. Or, to cite the only application of Alice's Law that ever struck me as perfectly sensible, saving $33 over coach or $71 over first-class fare by doing without the affliction of an airline meal on no frills calls for spending at least $33 and perhaps $71 on a decent picnic lunch to see you through the flight. All of which is to explain how I happened to climb on board a flight to Miami carrying, among other necessities, a small jar of fresh caviar, some smoked salmon I had picked up at a "custom smokery" in Seattle the week before, *crudités* with *pesto* dipping-sauce, tomato-curry soup, butterfish with shrimp stuffing *en gelée,* spiced clams, lime and dill shrimp, tomatoes stuffed with guacamole, marinated mussels, an assortment of pâtés, stuffed cold breast of veal, a bottle of Puligny-Montrachet, a selection of chocolate cakes, some praline cheesecake and a special dessert, Italian cheese-in-the-basket with fresh strawberries and Grand Marnier, concocted by my wife, Alice.

I think I am as generous as the next person about sharing certain kinds of food; if trapped by an avalanche in a mountain shack, I'm sure I would split my last few pieces of, say, packaged white bread or institutional roast beef with my fellow survivors, figuring that a natural disaster was always a good opportunity to take off a pound or two. I had, however, taken pains not to include in my no-frills picnic any of the type of food I would share, and therefore planned to carry it in a squat briefcase once given to me by a part-time peddler of home-improvement business courses—a briefcase that has always caused people on subway platforms to edge away from me, as if I were about to whip out an *Encyclopedia Americana* and tell them that they owed their children a home filled with culture and learning, suitably bound. As it turned out, though, my eyes were bigger than my briefcase. By the time everything was packed, I found myself carrying a sort of annex to the briefcase in the form of a shopping bag from my purveyor of caviar (and, on other occasions, chopped herring), Russ & Daughters Appetizer Store, and casually trying to keep my newspaper over the part of the bag that carried their irresistible motto, "Queens of Lake Sturgeon."

I need not have worried. Even when I offered the man sitting behind me some caviar—an uncharacteristic gesture prompted by his loan of a nail clipper to pry open the caviar jar—he declined. The woman in the aisle seat across from mine gazed longingly at my marinated mushrooms, but only shook her head nervously when I offered her one. I finally realized that my fellow passengers —chewing away at what people unfamiliar with Alice's Law would think of as a sensible lunch of, say, a chicken sandwich and a Tab—assumed they were in the presence of a maniac, a man who might get a kick out of slipping giggle powder into some spiced clams before he offered them to an innocent traveler. While I was eating my caviar and smoked salmon course, the woman sitting at the window two seats away from me (the seat between us being empty except for two cartons of my food) glanced over now and then with a suspicious although not unfriendly look, the way someone might look at the fellow at the Fourth of July picnic who insists, after a few beers, that everyone form a pyramid on the table he has balanced on his stomach.

She turned out to be a good-humored lady named Mrs. Eva Infeld who, after attending to some family business in New York, was returning to Miami Beach, where her husband, who is semiretired, works part-time in the garment trade. She did not speak to me until we became co-conspirators—the stewardess's reminder about a regulation against drinking out of one's own bottle on an airliner having forced me, after some token resistance ("Are you sure that rule is meant to apply to Puligny-Montrachet?"), to secrete the bottle between my briefcase and Mrs. Infeld's shopping bag and fill my glass covertly whenever the stewardess was busy serving the coach passengers up forward with balsa-wood rolls and whatever other delicacies they were getting for their $33.

"Do you always eat so lavish?" Mrs. Infeld finally asked me.

"Only on no frills," I said, explaining Alice's Law of Compensatory Cashflow.

"If you spent all that money on food, why didn't you go first class?" Mrs. Infeld asked.

"Because the food's no good in first class," I said.

"You're right," she said.

Mrs. Infeld seemed less suspicious after that, but a few minutes later, while I was attacking a salad of roasted peppers and eggplant that I had snared the previous evening from a new Greenwich Village restaurant called Tito's, she fixed me with an accusing look and said, "You must be a gourmet eater."

I denied it, of course. I pointed out that except for a mix-up the main course of my picnic would have been some cold fried chicken from another Village restaurant called The Pink Teacup—a no-frills spot that has the look of a Harlem café transplanted to Bleecker Street as a service to Harlem expatriates and Harlem commuters in the area, the way a McDonald's or a Burger King might appear off Piccadilly Circus to be of comfort to American tourists who feel the deprivation of being thousands of miles away from what they consider the real article. How could she make such accusations, I asked, about someone who was planning to eat, as the main course of his dessert course, a delicacy that can only be described as the classic chocolate chip cookie?

I do think Mrs. Infeld and I gradually became allies of sorts, although all I could persuade her to share with me was something that both she and I took for a deviled egg, but turned out to be what a wildcat East Village caterer named Montana Palace describes, quite accurately, as "Eggs Stuffed with Shrimp and Horseradish." I don't mean she was without criticism: when I got out Montana Palace's *pesto* sauce and started shoveling it onto some celery, she said, "Listen, with that garlic, they're going to throw you off the plane." And she did not, I think it's fair to say, have a natural community of interest with someone who ate tomatoes stuffed with minted mussels out of a business-course briefcase. ("If you put an egg salad sandwich in front of my husband, he's happy," she said, as I was eating some pistachio pâté.) But she did not turn me in for flouting the authority of the Federal Aviation Administration, or whichever agency it is that forbids free-lance boozing on high, and she did, after all, accept from me an egg stuffed with shrimp and horseradish.

As we started our descent into Miami, I was feeling a bit like an egg stuffed with shrimp and horseradish myself. I had been eating pretty steadily for an hour and a half. By pro-rating furiously in my head, I calculated that I had still spent a few dollars less on the trip than the coach passengers who were sitting only a row or two away, still looking sour from memories of the mess-hall rations they had suffered at the hands of the airline. I felt a bit guilty about that, so I had one last piece of chocolate cake to revive my spirits.

Mrs. Infeld was telling me that her friends would never believe her. "I want you to know I had a very interesting trip," she said, when we touched down. "Usually it's boring, but it wasn't boring."

"Thank you, Mrs. Infeld," I said. "It really is amazing how time passes when you keep busy."

Travel and Leisure, Gourmet Magazine

ROADSIDE MEMORIES
JAMES BEARD

I can recall my very first automobile ride, and for this I was indebted to the Hamblets. We drove in a huge touring car, Mother and Grammie Hamblet all done up in veils, and picnicked beside the road. It was an exciting day for all of us, for picnicking in a car was relatively rare, and to drive out of town with a hamper of food was a great adventure. I remember this picnic especially, because it had been suggested on the spur of the moment, which added to the fun. Most of our food came from a Portland establishment known as the Royal Bakery. Some of its offerings were superb and some mediocre. But it did make clubhouse sandwiches so well that the memory of them still lingers on my palate as a standard of perfection. . . .

When . . . I wandered about the world as a young man, there were few chances for really good picnics till I lived in England, where picnicking is one of the greatest of outdoor pleasures. I remember being taken to the races at Epsom and having my first introduction to a Fortnum and Mason hamper, complete with raised pie, cold birds, wine, cheese, fruit and all sorts of elegantly prepared items which looked as if they had just left the kitchen. All of this was enjoyed at a table set with good china and glasses, and then and there my whole idea of picnics came into focus. I knew that a picnic worth doing at all was worth doing with a hell of a lot of care, and this belief has remained with me ever since. Even when I have carside picnics in Europe and in America, there are good glasses along, good forks and knives, and if possible, china plates. I would rather smuggle a few dirty plates into my hotel to wash, wherever I happen to be, than eat food on paper plates. I suppose the new ones with plastic coatings are all right, but there is something aesthetically satisfying about a handsome plate and a linen napkin when you are sitting beside your car, or by a stream, eating sausage and cheese and drinking a pleasant red wine of the country.

Several years ago when I was doing a lot of traveling to and from the Eastern Shore of Maryland, two friends of mine, Henry and Bettina McNulty, with whom I had shared some lovely picnics in France, decided to join me on a few of my trips. On one occasion we reminisced about our French picnics and notably one when Alice Toklas roasted as delicious a chicken as I ever ate, and I, who was settled in a hotel, had searched around early on Sunday morning for the best treats the markets offered. I had found a *pâté* of duckling *en croûte* that Alice praised as the best she had ever eaten, some remarkably good cooked ham from Milan, a selection of cheese and salad greens. The McNultys contributed stuffed eggs, various tidbits for hors d'oeuvre, a superb *gâteau* and two magnums of champagne. Equipped with oversized linen napkins and Baccarat glasses, we settled down in a peaceful meadow about 30 kilometers from Paris and ate with the greatest of delight for hours, consuming both magnums of champagne. . . .

The McNultys and I re-created much the same kind of picnic on our Maryland journeys, some of them, I confess, enjoyed in stolen corners of the Howard Johnson reserves on the New Jersey Turnpike. But we had our Baccarat, our good damask, our china—and we ate filet of beef, salad, bread and cheese. . . .

Delights and Prejudices

ON A TRINIDAD BEACH
ARCHIE CARR

When I had passed nobody for nearly a mile and came to a track leading out toward the beach, I turned and drove through the coral to the seaside edge and stopped. It was a beautiful place—the endless singing palm strand and the wide, open sea and the straight strip of white sand between.

I got out of the car and found my chuck box and arranged a lunch. I had blown myself to a chunk of Stilton cheese in Port of Spain, and I had some pieces of cold boiled wahoo, which sounds dismal but smeared with chutney was good. The wahoo is a fish that fights like a fiend on a line but is thought by many to be poor eating. They are wrong—if there is any chutney around. I had bought the chutney at a bazaar held to raise funds to finish a mosque in St. Augustine. My landlady at the pension there, a Moslem woman of character and charm, was a member of the bazaar committee, and she selected the chutney for me from at least a dozen kinds. I carried it with me in the car, and whenever the fare was under par, like cold boiled wahoo, I uncorked it and things looked up. I had a couple of long, yellow Indian mangoes, too, and a canteen of water and lime juice and Barbados rum, and a Thermos bottle of coffee. Altogether, the lunch was good, or at least the kind of lunch I like; and with a little breeze and the shade there under the coco palms and the view out over the Orinoco water toward the places beyond the horizon, it was a good stop I made.

The Windward Road

Dejeuner Sur L'Herbe
XICO

There are several reasons why a picnic is something at which
    I am apt to look askance,
And the least of them is ance.
Because the eventual discovery of a strip of sward that would
    brighten the eye of a Keith Miller or a Henry Cotton
Is almost immediately followed by a further discovery,
    i.e., that something has been forgotten.
And if there are picnic parties at which it is less common
    to hear a rebuke for forgetfulness than a gracious
    encomium,
Then shomium.
Furthermore, I prefer eating from a chair, be it tubular,
    contemporary, or Windsor,
And I object to postures normally adopted by the kind of
people
    who do their shopping on the Ginza.
So although I am dummer than my fellows in many ways,
    in one respect I am cannier,
And that is my aversion to the Thermos flask and the pannier.

The Basket Lunch of Boule de Suif
GUY DE MAUPASSANT

The coach went so slowly that by ten o'clock in the morning they had not made ten miles. The men had got out three times to climb hills on foot. They began to grow anxious, for they were to have lunched at Tôtes, and now they despaired of reaching the place before night. Everybody was on the lookout for some inn by the way. Once the vehicle stuck fast in a snowdrift, and it took two hours to get it out. . . .

Boule de Suif had several times stooped down as if feeling for something under her skirts. She hesitated a moment, looked at her companions, and then composedly resumed her former position. The faces were pale and drawn. Loiseau declared he would give a thousand francs for a ham. His wife made a faint movement as to protest, but restrained herself. It always affected her painfully to hear money being thrown away, nor could she ever understand a joke upon the subject. . . .

At last, at three o'clock, when they were in the middle of an interminable stretch of bare country without a single village in sight, Boule de Suif, stooping hurriedly, drew from under the seat a large basket covered with a white napkin.

Out of it she took, first of all, a little china plate and a delicate silver drinking-cup, and then an immense dish, in which two whole fowls ready carved lay stiffened in their jelly. Other good things were visible in the basket: patties, fruits, pastry—in fact provisions for a three day's journey in order to be independent of inn cookery. The necks of four bottles protruded from between the parcels of food. She took the wing of a fowl and began to eat daintily with one of those little rolls which they call "Régence" in Normandy.

Every eye was fixed upon her. As the odor of the food spread through the carriage nostrils began to quiver and mouths to fill with water, while the jaws, just below the ears, contracted painfully. The dislike entertained by the ladies for this abandoned young woman grew savage, almost to the point of longing to murder her or at least to turn her out into the snow, her and her drinking-cup and her basket and her provisions.

Loiseau, however, was devouring the dish of chicken with his eyes. "Madame has been more prudent than we," he said. "Some people always think of everything."

She turned her head in his direction. "If you would care for any, Monsieur—? It is not comfortable to fast for so long."

He bowed. "By Jove!—frankly I won't refuse. I can't stand this any longer—the fortune of war, is it not, madame?" And with a comprehensive look he added: "In moments such as this we are only too glad to find anyone who will oblige us." He had a newspaper which he spread on his knees to save his trousers, and with the point of a knife which he always carried in his pocket he captured a drumstick all glazed with jelly, tore it with his teeth, and then proceeded to chew it with satisfaction so evident that a deep groan of distress went up from the whole party.

Upon this Boule de Suif in a gentle and humble tone invited the two Sisters to share the collation. They both accepted on the spot, and without raising their eyes began to eat very hurriedly, after stammering a few words of thanks. Nor did Cornudet refuse his neighbor's offer, and with the Sisters they formed a kind of table by spreading out newspapers on their knees.

The jaws opened and shut without a pause, biting, chewing, gulping ferociously. Loiseau, hard at work in his corner, urged his wife in a low voice to follow his example. She resisted for some time, then, after a pang which gripped her vitals, she gave in. Whereupon her husband, rounding off his phrases, asked if their "charming fellow traveler" would permit him to offer a little something to Madame Loiseau.

"Why, yes, certainly, Monsieur," she answered with a pleasant smile, and handed him the dish.

There was a moment of embarrassment when the first bottle of claret was uncorked—there was but the one drinking-cup. Each one wiped it before passing it to the rest. Cornudet alone, from an impulse of gallantry no doubt, placed his lips on the spot still wet from the lips of his neighbor.

Then it was that, surrounded by people who were eating, suffocated by the fragrant odor of the viands, the Count and Countess de Bréville and Monsieur and Madame Carré-Lamadon suffered the agonies of that torture which has ever been associated with the name of Tantalus. Suddenly the young wife of the cotton manufacturer gave a deep sigh. Every head turned towards her; she was as white as the snow outside, her eyes closed, her head fell forward —she had fainted. Her husband, distraught with fear, implored assistance of the whole company. All lost their heads until the elder of the two Sisters, who supported the unconscious lady, forced Boule de Suif's drinking-cup between her lips and made her swallow a few drops of wine. The pretty creature stirred, opened her eyes, smiled and then declared in an expiring voice that she felt quite well now. But to prevent her being overcome again in the same manner, the Sister induced her to drink a full cup of wine, adding, "It is simply hunger—nothing else."

At this Boule de Suif, blushing violently, looked at the four starving passengers and faltered shyly, "*Mon Dieu!* if I might make so bold as to offer the ladies and gentlemen—" She stopped short, fearing a rude rebuff.

Loiseau, however, at once threw himself into the breach. "*Parbleu!* under such circumstances we are all companions in misfortune and bound to help each other. Come, ladies, don't stand on ceremony—take what you can get and be thankful: who knows whether we shall be able to find so much as a house where we can spend the night? At this rate we shall not reach Tôtes till tomorrow afternoon."

They still hesitated, nobody having the courage to take upon themselves the responsibility of the decisive "Yes." Finally the Count seized the bull by the horns. Adopting his most grandiose air, he turned with a bow to the embarrassed young woman and said, "We accept your offer with thanks, madame."

The first step only was difficult. The Rubicon once crossed, they fell to with a will. They emptied the basket, which contained, besides the provisions already mentioned: a pâté de foie gras, a lark pie, a piece of smoked tongue, some pears, a slab of gingerbread, mixed biscuits, and a cup of pickled onions and gherkins in vinegar —for, like all women, Boule de Suif adored pickles.

They could not well eat the young woman's provisions and not speak to her, so they conversed—stiffly at first, and then, seeing that she showed no signs of presuming, with less reserve. Mesdames de Bréville and Carré-Lamadon, having a great deal of *savoir vivre,* knew how to make themselves agreeable with tact and delicacy. The Countess, in particular, exhibited the amiable condescension of the extremely high-born lady whom no contact can sully, and was charming. But big Madame Loiseau, who had the soul of a gendarme, remained unmoved, speaking little and eating much.

Boule de Suif

A Picnic in the Himalayas
MADHUR JAFFREY

Summer vacations saw us in the Himalayas. . . . All relatives would meet in Delhi, and half a train would be booked to take us from Delhi to the foothills of the towering mountains. A fleet of cars was hired to transport us from there to six, seven, or eight thousand feet above sea level, where several houses were rented to accommodate us.

Once settled, we were left pretty much to ourselves: The only organized activity was the picnic. For this event preparations were begun several weeks in advance, with rickshaws or palanquins arranged for the old and the infirm and horses for the riders. The ladies of the house, as well as numerous servants, spent many days preparing the food. Baskets of mangoes were ordered from various North Indian cities: *langras* from Varanasi for those who liked their mangoes tart; *dussehris* from Lucknow for those who liked them sweet and smooth; and *chusnis,* small sucking mangoes, for those who preferred not to eat the fruit but rather to suck the juice straight from the skin. Litchis, those succulent fruits with sweet white flesh, were sent from Dehra Dun. Most of the packing, including pots and pans, the kettle to make Darjeeling tea, portable charcoal stoves, charcoal, disposable earthenware cups, cotton rugs, blankets, towels, serving spoons, and plates, was done the night before, and at sunrise, when the mountains were still shrouded in an icy mist, porters, rickshaws, palanquins, and horses were all assembled. First the porters were loaded with baskets of food and sent off with a party of servants. The walkers, led by my middle uncle, who had a passion for hiking, were the next lot. Third were those who rode in the rickshaws and palanquins, and the last group consisted of those on horseback.

The picnic site was carefully chosen weeks in advance—by the same middle uncle, who also acted as majordomo. Sometimes it was a distant mountain peak several ranges away; at other times it was a thunderous waterfall; once it was a mountain stream rushing through a remote gorge. (Ordinary picnic spots, where most mortals went, were never considered good enough.) Our spots were picked not only for their grandeur but for their inaccessibility in terms of distance or the climbing required.

Clad in heavy sweaters, mufflers, and shawls, our large party moved slowly, making numerous stops along the way. If we passed an orchard, a halt would be called and the farmer was asked if, for a certain sum, we might pick plums or apricots. My favorite groves were those of almond trees. I loved the green almonds, slit open and robbed of their tender white flesh.

We would generally arrive at our picnic spot around midday. If it was beside a waterfall or stream, the children were permitted to swim while lunch was unpacked. The mangoes were placed in the stream to cool, fires were lighted to heat certain dishes (and also to warm the children when they emerged from the freezing water), and a large cotton rug was spread on the ground. Arrayed on the rug were meatballs stuffed with raisins and mint leaves; potatoes cooked with whole fennel and cumin and fenugreek seeds; chopped goat meat cooked with peas; chick-peas tossed with raw onions, ginger, and green chilies; green beans seasoned with cumin seed, garlic, and lemon; chicken with almonds and yogurt; cauliflower flavored with ginger and Chinese parsley; spiced *pooris* (puffy, deep-fried breads); sour carrot pickles; hot green mango pickles; and spiced cucumbers. The meal was eaten to the accompaniment of tales of adventure and hilarious stories about our ancestors.

After lunch, the older folk would rest, napping on the rug or leaning against rocks and gossiping, and the children would disappear in various directions, fishing, hunting wild berries, or sliding on beds of pine needles. At about four o'clock we would all reassemble for tea. Served in disposable earthenware cups it was accompanied by *mutthris* (biscuits) and my grandmother's thick, sweet tomato chutney. Then the fires were put out, the rugs and utensils were packed, and the whole party would begin the long trek home.

REMEMBERED PICNICS
SIMONE BECK

On Sundays after the hunting season ends in January, my husband and I often go with some close friends, perhaps three other couples, for walks in the forests around Paris; southwest to the Fontainebleau, or to Rambouillet, St. Germain, Marly, or Senlis. We walk for two or three hours, then eat a picnic lunch and return to our cars by another route. There are places, especially in the Fontainebleau, where you can sit down, out of the wind, out of the snow, under a tree, and have a drink and a picnic, and often we picnic on sandwiches that each of us has made and brought with us. There is a certain spirit of competition among us to outdo one another; each is always jealous of what the other has brought, and there are frequent exchanges. You might be interested in the sandwiches that I remember from a recent walk: Strasbourg sausage on *pain de mie,* our fine-textured bread, garnished with mustard butter; *canapés basques,* puréed sardines on toast with lemon and butter; sandwiches of Chester cheese on well-buttered bread with crushed nuts; roast beef sandwiches and bread spread with mustard butter. . . .

I remember many picnics in my life, and they changed a great deal as the years went by. Before World War I, when I was a tiny little girl, there were very, very elegant picnics, which I can just barely remember. After the war life seemed more informal, though still very elegant. I remember especially a picnic that my father arranged in 1922 for some English people whom he had met during the war. We picnicked on the grass above the Falaise at Varengeville. I don't remember everything that was served, but I remember a wonderful *poulet en gelée,* chicken in aspic; each piece wrapped in a large leaf of romaine so that you could eat it without a knife or fork. There were also some "bouquets," little pink shrimps, with buttered bread. And I remember the cheese, Pont l'Evêque, and some sweet pears and a chocolate cake. My father and mother had special low folding chairs, the chauffeur-butler was there to serve everyone, and we drank only champagne.

Then World War II came, and after that life changed again and became more informal still. Today my brother and I take picnics with his children, my nieces and nephews, in the woods down the little River Saane, which flows by our family house in Normandy, where he still lives. Another kind of picnic is the kind my husband and I pack when we go from Provence to Paris. We usually drive, and we never stop in a restaurant but instead in various places along the way that we call our "dining rooms out of doors." We have "dining rooms" in Bourgogne, some with a long view, some in the woods, very pretty places that no one else knows.

Simca's Cuisine

PICNICKING WITH W. C. FIELDS
ROBERT LEWIS TAYLOR

Within minutes he had his colored cook, Dell, laying out big wicker picnic hampers, making sandwiches, hard-boiling eggs, and stuffing celery with Roquefort cheese. He himself got out his ice buckets . . . and filled them. He had a built-in refrigerator in his silver-plated Lincoln, but he wanted to take no chances on running short.

When the ice buckets were in shape, he unlocked his liquor room (which was then secured by two iron bars and four padlocks) and carried down a case of Lanson '28. He added to the champagne several bottles of gin, half a dozen bottles of imported burgundy, and half a dozen bottles of a fine, dry sauterne. . . . He put a case of beer in the Lincoln's refrigerator, then had his chauffeur drive him and the three girls to the Vendome, a fancy catering establishment.

He bought about a hundred dollars' worth of black caviar,

pâté de foie gras, anchovies, smoked oysters, baby shrimps, crab meat, tinned lobster, potted chicken and turkey, several cheeses, including a soft yellow Swiss cheese he was especially fond of, and some strong cheeses like Liederkranz and Camembert, a big bottle of Grecian olives, and three or four jars of glazed fruit. Back home, his cook had made sandwiches out of watercress, chopped olives and nuts, tongue, peanut butter and strawberry preserves, and deviled egg and spiced ham. She had also baked both an angel-food and a devil's-food cake. "What we've missed we'll pick up on the road," Fields said, as he ushered the three girls into the car.

W. C. Fields, His Follies and Fortunes

Feeding on the Train
MAURICE HEALY

You can't get it now, I fear; but if you ever had the luck to break your fast on the eight-thirty A.M. from St. Pancras to Manchester, you must have enjoyed the best breakfast that this world has ever known. First, the welcome; a delightful staff that made you feel that they had been waiting for you, and that this was the red-letter day of their lives. A comfortable car; and the chance of sitting in a non-smoking portion—a rare blessing in an age where everybody enters a dining-room with a lighted cigarette, if not a cigar or pipe. Then the pleasant napery and crockery; and the immediate visit of the argus-eyed attendant who from start to finish never left you without a piece of really hot toast on your plate—and good toast at that: neither too hard nor yet undercrisped: Oh, an artist in toast! And no prunes-or-porridge business here; the porridge, which always looked and smelt excellent, was an alternative to other breakfast cereals, or, what I always took, grapefruit. Out of a tin, no doubt; but grapefruit is one of those things that really is better out of a tin than in its skin. For it did not go into its tin until it was ripe; the wretched things served in their skins have been trying to ripen themselves *en voyage,* when no sap could feed them.

Fish? Have you ever eaten a kipper? Not unless you breakfasted on that train; for there is no place in the world, I swear, where kippers are served in such perfection. A kipper should be moist without being oily; most people succeed in abolishing the oil by a process of drying the kipper. But I must not dwell on this subject; the kipper is the most delicious fish that has ever come out of the sea, and not more than a few thousand people (I do not know how many travel by that train in a year) have ever eaten it at its best —a melancholy thought.

But now the great moment has arrived; Argus has replenished your plate of toast and brought more butter; and behold! the chief attendant comes, bearing a platter spread with every morning delight. In the center are deliciously cooked fried eggs; around them, competing for their shelter, are lovely little kidneys, choice gobbets of liver, tomatoes, and strips of bacon, the edges of which have been crisped while the centres are still soft and juicy. How it is done I cannot guess; a Chinese secret, I imagine. With a plate duly garnished with a selection from this cornucopia, one can only hush and bless one's self in silence, a silence broken by the pleasant noises of mastication, but otherwise untroubled. And the entire tale is not yet told; here is Argus once again, this time with a tray containing two kinds of marmalade, two kinds of honey, several jams and I know not what other good things. Excuse me, sir; that was one of my waistcoat buttons that caught you in the eye; if you had not also enjoyed a royal breakfast you might have been annoyed with me.

A FULL-COURSE MEAL BETWEEN LONDON AND BRIGHTON
JOSEPH WECHSBERG

Each five-car unit has a chief steward, five other stewards, and the chef in the kitchen. Mr. Ronald Simpson, the chef on our train, a competent man of sixty, said he could serve 192 passengers in five cars breakfast, lunch, dinner, or supper, which takes some doing since the journey lasts less than an hour. If the train is sold out there are 384 people on it, but the staff of fourteen (plus conductor and engineer) is able to manage. The kitchen is a model of compactness and organization, no larger than a comfortable clothes closet. There is a small range, an electric grill, a small table, the sink. Mr. Simpson keeps fish (kippers and halibut), sirloin steak, ham, cheeses, butter, salad, and other staples in a small refrigerator. The *Brighton Belle*'s menu features a soup of the day, eggs styled to choice, Welsh rabbit, grilled kippers . . . fried halibut, and grilled sirloin at very moderate prices. If the chef isn't too busy he makes an omelet for a habitué, or other dishes that are not on the menu. Many cold things, too, such as ham sandwiches.

The wine list, "no longer what it used to be, sir," is still amazing. A half bottle of Mumm, Cordon Rouge, is about $2.80 [1971]. (I can hear New York commuters sigh wistfully.) Two clarets, a white Bordeaux, two red Burgundies, two rosés, a Pouilly-Fuissé, a Liebfraumilch, a Zeltinger Riesling, an Alsatian wine, four sherries, a dozen spirits and liqueurs, half a dozen beers, cider, mineral waters, fruit juices, and Pepsi Cola.

WHO DOES NOT ENJOY LUNCHING IN THE TRAIN?

A bell tinkles in the corridor of the Orient Express. Lunch! We get up, with hunger gnawing at our inside, filled with delight at the prospect of eating crisp rolls, and potato mayonnaise, and veal and *petits pois* and slabs of *fromage du pays,* washed down by white wine, drunk *from a tumbler* (which is the only way to drink white wine). And not only does the prospect of food allure us, but the fact that we shall be devouring it in a fantastic chariot of steel and glass, hurtling through a foreign country. There must be something seriously wrong with the man who does not enjoy lunching in the train.

—BEVERLEY NICHOLS
No Place Like Home

LAMENT FOR THE DINING CAR

Molesworth said, "These chaps could use a few lessons in how to run a railroad."

The meal that followed . . . only made the point plainer. It was a picnic in Molesworth's compartment; we were joined by the Belgian girl, Monique, who brought her own cheese. . . . We sat shoulder to shoulder on Molesworth's bed, gloomily picking through our lunch bags.

"I wasn't prepared for this," said Molesworth. "I think each country should have its own dining car. Shunt it on at the frontier and serve slap-up meals." He nibbled a hard-boiled egg and said, "Perhaps we should get together and write a letter to Cook's."

The Orient Express, once unique for its service, is now unique among trains for its lack of it. The Indian Rajdhani Express serves curries in its dining car, and so does the Pakistani Khyber Mail; the Meshed Express serves Iranian chicken kebab, and the train to Sapporo in Northern Japan smoked fish and glutinous rice. Box lunches are sold at the station in Rangoon, and Malaysian Railways always include a dining car that resembles a noodle stall, where you can buy *meehoon* soup; and Amtrak, which I had always thought to be the worst railway in the world, serves hamburgers on the James Whitcomb Riley (Washington–Chicago). Starvation takes the fun out of travel, and from this point of view the Orient Express is more inadequate than the poorest Madrasi train, where you exchange stained lunch coupons for a tin tray of vegetables and a quart of rice.

—PAUL THEROUX
The Great Railway Bazaar

3

Wolf at the Door

Among many things induced by poverty there are two cheerful qualities: gratitude for even the slightest gift of sustenance, and the kind of inventiveness that results in new combinations of food, the culinary creativity that gives every national cuisine some of its finest dishes. A meager dish served to someone who is famished may seem as subtly wrought as an Escoffier masterpiece—indeed, a meal on Skid Row is often more deeply appreciated than a multi-course dinner at La Tour d'Argent bathed in the diffusion of light that burnishes Notre Dame. And in so-called peasant kitchens, since hearthsides became the family center, necessity has been the comfortable mother of invention—who was the first to make a cassoulet? Most of us have met the wolf at the door at one time or another, including Ernest Hemingway, Arthur Rubinstein—and others, great and small.

Hunger Was Good Discipline
ERNEST HEMINGWAY

You got very hungry when you did not eat enough in Paris because all the bakery shops had such good things in the windows and people ate outside at tables on the sidewalk so that you saw and smelled the food. When you had given up journalism and were writing nothing that anyone in America would buy, explaining at home that you were lunching out with someone, the best place to go was the Luxembourg Gardens where you saw and smelled nothing to eat all the way from the Place de L'Observatoire to the rue de Vaugirard. There you could always go into the Luxembourg museum and all the paintings were sharpened and clearer and more beautiful if you were belly-empty, hollow-hungry. I learned to understand Cézanne much better and to see truly how he made landscapes when I was hungry. I used to wonder if he were hungry too when he painted; but I thought possibly it was only that he had forgotten to eat. It was one of those unsound but illuminating thoughts you have when you have been sleepless or hungry. Later I thought Cézanne was probably hungry in a different way.

After you come out if the Luxembourg you could walk down the narrow rue Ferou to the Place St.-Sulpice and there were still no restaurants, only the quiet square with its benches and trees. There was a fountain with lions, and pigeons walked on the pavement and perched on the statues of the bishops. There was the church and there were shops selling religious objects and vestments on the north side of the square.

From this square you could not go further toward the river without passing shops selling fruits, vegetables, wines, or bakery and pastry shops. But by choosing your way carefully you could work to your right around the grey and white stone church and reach the rue de l'Odéon and turn up to your right toward Sylvia Beach's bookshop and on your way you did not pass too many places where things to eat were sold. The rue de l'Odéon was bare of eating places until you reached the square where there were three restaurants.

By the time you reached 12 rue de l'Odéon your hunger was contained but all of your perceptions were heightened again. The photographs looked different and you saw books that you had never seen before.

"You're too thin, Hemingway," Sylvia would say. "Are you eating enough?"

"Sure."

"What did you eat for lunch?"

My stomach would turn over and I would say, "I'm going home for lunch now."

"At three o'clock?"

"I didn't know it was that late."

"Adrienne said the other night she wanted to have you and

Hadley for dinner. We'd ask Fargue. You like Fargue, don't you? Or Larbaud. You like him. I know you like him. Or anyone you really like. Will you speak to Hadley?"

"I know she'd love to come."

"I'll send her a *pneu.* Don't work so hard that you don't eat properly."

"I won't."

"Get home now before it's too late for lunch."

"They'll save it."

"Don't eat cold food either. Eat a good hot lunch."

"Did I have any mail?"

"I don't think so. But let me look."

She looked and found a note and looked up happily and then opened a closed door in her desk.

"This came while I was out," she said. It was a letter and it felt as though it had money in it. "Wedderkop," Sylvia said.

"It must be from *Der Querschnitt.* Did you see Wedderkop?"

"No. But he was here with George. He'll see you. Don't worry. Perhaps he wanted to pay you first."

"It's six hundred francs. He says there will be more."

"I'm awfully glad you reminded me to look. Dear Mr. Awfully Nice."

"It's damned funny that Germany is the only place I can sell anything. To him and the *Frankfurter Zeitung.*"

"Isn't it? But don't you worry ever. You can sell stories to Ford," she teased me.

"Thirty francs a page. Say one story every three months in *The Transatlantic.* Story five pages long make one hundred and fifty francs a quarter. Six hundred francs a year."

"But, Hemingway, don't worry about what they bring now. The point is that you can write them."

"I know. I know I can write them. But nobody will buy them. There is no money coming in since I quit journalism."

"They will sell. Look. You have the money for one right there."

"I'm sorry, Sylvia. Forgive me for speaking about it."

"Forgive you for what? Always talk about anything. Don't you know all writers ever talk about is their troubles? But promise me you won't worry and that you'll eat enough."

"I promise."

"Then get home now and have some lunch."

A Movable Feast

A WORLD WAR I SOUP LINE
ARTHUR RUBINSTEIN

My small money reserve became dreadfully low. The fine golden pounds had already been spent, but I clung tenaciously to the sum I needed for two more weeks of hotel bills. So there was nothing left for real food. For four or five days I ate nothing but the small French grapes which were sold in the street for a few centimes during the season of the wine harvest. I was starving; I was so hungry I couldn't sleep. Those terrible, ravenous days remind me of a tragicomic little interlude: one evening, walking past the Café de la Paix, I noticed in the well-lit restaurant three English officers dining at a table close to the window. One of them was an acquaintance of mine in London. The man, spotting me through the window, made inviting signs and gestures to join them. When I entered the restaurant, he stood up and introduced me to his companions in a flattering way.

"I say, it's good to see you, old chap! Bloody beastly business, this war, ah, what? But, as I say, old boy, we'll beat them, these Jerries!" All this accompanied by loud guffaws.

"Sit down, my dear fellow, and have dinner with us," he said. I answered quickly, without thinking, "No, thank you, I just had my dinner." Something in me couldn't bear the idea of these Englishmen noticing how a ravenously hungry young man devours food. He offered me a cup of coffee, which I accepted, but being nervous, I scorched my tongue with the first sip.

A sleepless night with visions of big chunks of beef with *pommes soufflées* and sauce béarnaise was the result of this frustrating experience.

The next afternoon, I walked all the way to the Café de la

Rotonde, where my friend, the intern, generously offered me a cup of tea. At a neighboring table a man spoke loudly of a *soupe populaire* for artists. I asked about it and learned there was a place on the Champs-Elysées where bowls of soup and bread were served twice a day by some charitable institution to stranded artists. This time I took a bus and found the place without difficulty, but I was told, "You have to wait an hour before they dish out the precious meal." To kill time, I bought another bunch of grapes and ate them, sitting on a bench. By and by, my colleagues in art and hunger began to assemble, about fifty of them. Some of them looked familiar, but they were reserved and uncommunicative, something I understood perfectly.

A few ladies (the charitable ones) appeared behind a large table and busied themselves piling bowls, cutting up bread, and doing other chores. At last, a man put on the table a large terrine of hot soup with a long ladle. We lined up in front of the table and received our portions from two of the ladies. It was a good vegetable soup with pieces of bread in it, and it tasted to me like just about the best meal I had ever eaten. As I was eating it slowly, with a deep respect for every gulp, I heard a voice calling my first name. Gabriel Astruc in person looked at me in amazement. "Arthur, what are you doing in Paris at a time like this?" I blushed, ashamed of being seen by him at a *soupe populaire*.

My Young Years

"As Hungry After as Before Meals"
JOHN MUIR

Breakfast in those auld-lang-syne days was simple oatmeal porridge, usually with a little milk or treacle, served in wooden dishes called "luggies," formed of staves hooped together like miniature tubs about four or five inches in diameter. One of the staves, the lug or ear, a few inches longer than the others, served as a handle, while the number of luggies ranged in a row on a dresser indicated the size of the family. We never dreamed of anything to come after the porridge, or of asking for more. Our portions were consumed in about a couple of minutes; then off to school. At noon we came racing home ravenously hungry. The midday meal, called dinner, was usually vegetable broth, a small piece of boiled mutton, and a barley-meal scone. None of us liked the barley scone bread, therefore we got all we wanted of it, and in desperation had to eat it, for we were always hungry, about as hungry after as before meals. The evening meal was called "tea" and was served on our return from school. It consisted, as far as we children were concerned, of half a slice of white bread without butter, barley scone, and warm water with a little milk and sugar in it, a beverage called "content," which warmed but neither cheered nor inebriated. Immediately after tea we ran across the streets with our books to Grandfather Gilrye, who took pleasure in seeing us and hearing us recite our next day's lessons. Then back home to supper, usually a boiled potato and piece of barley scone. Then family worship, and to bed.

The Story of My Boyhood and Youth

BREAKFAST ON FOOT

I watched the hot dog being built. First the bun was taken out of a large tin pot, mustard was splashed across it from stem to stern, then came the frankfurter itself, shining from the hot, greasy water. The man must have asbestos fingers, I thought, watching as he dipped his bare hands into the steaming sauerkraut.

"Let it drain a little, please," I directed and tried not to look at the dirty fingernails.

He shook the sauerkraut before laying it lovingly over the shiny tube of meat. "Onions?"

"The works," I replied. I gave him my nickel and wandered up the street slowly. I like to relax as I eat breakfast. Besides, it was hot—sluggish hot. Underfoot the macadam had already softened even though the sun had only begun to go to work.

I licked my fingers and wiped away the sauerkraut juice that had run up my arm. I was thirsty. Breakfast just wasn't breakfast without root beer to wash down my hot dog. However, finances were exactly what came after nothing, and yearning only brought the stinging pavement into sharper focus.

—June Havoc
Early Havoc

On the Oregon Trail

They fried doughnuts in bear's grease when there was no shortening, used deer's rennet for cheese-making when there was no calf's rennet, stuffed bear cub for Thanksgiving dinner when there was no pig.

—Nancy Wilson Ross
Westward the Women

"When We Have Nothing Else"

To supply our men and visitors we have killed and eaten ten wild horses bought from the Indians. This will make you pity us, but you had better save your pity for more worthy subjects. I do not prefer it to other meat, but can eat it very well when we have nothing else.

—Narcissa Whitman, 1832

Short Rations After the Mutiny on the Bounty
CAPTAIN WILLIAM BLIGH

Monday, May 18th, 1789. The customary allowance of one twenty-fifth of a pound of bread and one quarter of a pint of water was served out at breakfast, dinner and supper. . . .

Tuesday, May 26th, 1789. To make the bread a little savoury, most of the people frequently dipped it in salt water; but I generally broke mine into small pieces, and eat it in my allowance of water, out of a coco-nut shell, with a spoon, economically avoiding to take too large a piece at a time, so that I was as long at dinner as if it had been a much more plentiful meal.

"Beating the System"

I returned to New York to live in a cold-water flat in Hell's Kitchen on the West Side. This time I had to wait almost a year before I was able to afford a small second-hand gas stove and a wheezy old refrigerator. . . . My emphasis was on survival, though I learned to be a pretty good cook and cooking became a source of great pleasure to me. I had learned where to buy food very cheaply in New York. I used to buy my fruit and vegetables late Saturday evenings just before the stores closed and I would bargain for the produce that was still good but beginning to "turn." I would buy mussels or whiting for fifteen cents a pound and chickens for eighteen cents a pound. I could cook a three-course dinner for six for a dollar and twenty-five cents and, even today, by shopping in the same area, I can buy the ingredients and prepare the same meal for a dollar seventy-five to two dollars.

I would often ask the butcher, in those days, for a few bones "for my dog." Then I would make the most exquisite soup of those bones, and I always had a pot steaming on the stove. It was several years before my butcher realized that I didn't have a dog. I would buy a beef kidney for fifteen cents and make it last for three meals, adding fresh peas one time, asparagus another, pasta still another time.

I enjoyed then—and still do—beating the system.

—Edward Giobbi
Italian Family Cooking

"O dear! How can I tell it. Squash again for breakfast."
Diary of a Pioneer Woman

"Everything Contains Beans"
ANNE FRANK

Dear Kitty,

Contrary to my usual custom, I will for once write more fully about food because it has become a very difficult and important matter, not only here in the "Secret Annexe" but in the whole of Holland, all Europe and even beyond.

In the twenty-one months that we've spent here we have been through a good many "food cycles"—you'll understand what that means in a minute. When I talk of "food cycles" I mean periods in which one has nothing else to eat but one particular dish or kind of vegetable. We had nothing but endive for a long time, day in, day out, endive with sand, endive without sand, stew with endive, boiled or *en casserole;* then it was spinach, and after that followed kohlrabi, salsify, cucumbers, tomatoes, sauerkraut, etc., etc.

For instance, it's really disagreeable to eat a lot of sauerkraut for lunch and supper every day, but you do it if you're hungry. However, we have the most delightful period of all now, because we don't get any fresh vegetables at all. Our weekly menu for supper consists of kidney beans, pea soup, potatoes with dumplings, potato-chalet and, by the grace of God, occasionally turnip tops or rotten carrots, and then the kidney beans once again. We eat potatoes at every meal, beginning with breakfast, because of the bread shortage. We make our soup from kidney or haricot beans, potatoes, Julienne soup in packets, French beans in packets, kidney beans in packets. Everything contains beans, not to mention the bread!

In the evening we always have potatoes with gravy substitute and—thank goodness we've still got it—beetroot salad. I must still tell you about the dumplings, which we make out of government flour, water, and yeast. They are so sticky and tough, they are like stones in one's stomach— ah, well!

The great attraction each week is a slice of liver sausage, and jam on dry bread. But we're still alive, and quite often we even enjoy our poor meals.

Yours, Anne

WEDNESDAY, 3 MAY, 1944

Since Saturday we're changed over, and have lunch at half past eleven in the mornings, so we have to last out with one cupful of porridge; this saves us a meal. Vegetables are still difficult to obtain: we had rotten boiled lettuce this afternoon. Ordinary lettuce, spinach and boiled lettuce, there's nothing else. With these we eat rotten potatoes, so it's a delicious combination! . . .

MONDAY, 8 MAY, 1944

. . . Miep told us this morning about a party she went to, to celebrate an engagement. Both the future bride and bridegroom came from rich families and everything was very grand. Miep made our mouths water telling us about the food they had: vegetable soup with minced meatballs in it, cheese, rolls, hors d'oeuvre with eggs and roast beef, fancy cakes, wine and cigarettes, as much as you wanted of everything (black market). . . .

She made our mouths water. We, who get nothing but two spoonfuls of porridge for our breakfast and whose tummies were so empty that they were positively rattling, we, who get nothing but half-cooked spinach (to preserve the vitamins) and rotten potatoes day after day, we, who get nothing but lettuce, cooked or raw, spinach and yet again spinach in our hollow stomachs. Perhaps we may yet grow to be as strong as Popeye, although I don't see much sign of it at present! . . .

Anne Frank: The Diary of a Young Girl

PRISON DIET

The food supplied to prisoners is entirely inadequate. Most of it is revolting in character. All of it is insufficient. Every prisoner suffers day and night from hunger. A certain amount of food is carefully weighed out ounce by ounce for each prisoner. It is just enough to sustain, not life exactly, but existence. But one is always racked by the pain and the sickness of hunger.

The result of the food—which in most cases consists of weak gruel, badly-baked bread, suet, and water—is disease in the form of incessant diarrhea.

—OSCAR WILDE
Letters

OYSTERS

ANTON CHEKHOV

I can easily recall the rainy twilight autumn evening when I stood with my father in a crowded Moscow street and fell ill, strangely. I suffered no pain, but my legs gave way, my head hung on one side, and mys speech failed. I felt that I should soon fall.

Had I been taken to a hospital at the moment, the doctor would have written: "Fames"—a complaint common in medical textbooks.

Beside me on the pavement stood my father in a ragged summer overcoat and a check cap. On his feet were big, clumsy galoshes. Fearing that people might see he had neither boots nor stockings, he wrapped his legs in old gaiters.

The more tattered and dirty became that once smart summer overcoat, the greater became my love. He had come to the capital five months before to seek work as a clerk. Five months he had tramped the city, seeking employment; only today for the first time he had screwed up his courage to beg for alms in the street.

In front of us rose a big, three-storied house with a blue sign-board "Restaurant." My head hung helplessly back, and on one side. Involuntarily I looked upward at the bright restaurant windows. Behind them glimmered human figures. To the right were an orchestrion, two oleographs, and hanging lamps. While trying to pierce the obscurity my eyes fell on a white patch. The patch was motionless; its rectangular contour stood out sharply against the universal background of dark brown. When I strained my eyes could see that the patch was a notice on the wall, and it was plain that something was printed upon it, but what that something was I could not see.

I must have kept my eyes on the notice at least half an hour. Its whiteness beckoned to me, and, it seemed, almost hypnotised my brain. I tried to read it, and my attempts were fruitless.

But at last the strange sickness entered into its rights.

The roar of the traffic rose to thunder; in the smell of the street I could distinguish a thousand smells; and the restaurant lights and street lamps seemed to flash like lightning. And I began to make out things that I could not make out before.

"Oysters," I read on the notice.

A strange word. I had lived in the world already eight years and three months, and had never heard this word. What did it mean? Was it the proprietor's surname? No, for signboards with innkeepers' names hang outside the doors, and not on walls inside.

"Father, what are oysters?" I asked hoarsely, trying to turn my face towards his.

My father did not hear me. He was looking at the flow of the crowd, and following every passerby with his eyes. From his face I judged that he dearly longed to speak to the passers, but the fatal, leaden words hung on his trembling lips, and would not tear themselves off. One passerby he even stopped and touched on the sleeve, but when the man turned to him my father stammered, "I beg your pardon," and fell back in confusion.

"Papa, what does 'oysters' mean?" I repeated.

"It is a kind of animal. . . . It lives in the sea. . . ."

And in a wink I visualized this mysterious animal. Something between a fish and a crab, it must be, I concluded; and as it came from the sea, of course it made up into delightful dishes, hot *bouillabaisse* with fragrant peppercorns and bay leaves, or *solianka* with gristle, crab sauce, or cold with horseradish. . . . I vividly pictured to myself how this fish is brought from the market, cleaned, and thrust quickly into a pot . . . quickly, quickly, because one is very hungry . . . frightfully hungry. From the restaurant kitchen came the smell of boiled fish and crab soup.

The smell began to tickle my palate and nostrils; I felt it permeating my whole body. The restaurant, my father, the white notice, my sleeve, all exhaled it so strongly that I began to chew. I chewed and swallowed as if my mouth were really full of the strange animal that lives in the sea. . . .

The pleasure was too much for my strength, and to prevent myself falling I caught my father's cuff, and leaned against his wet summer overcoat. My father shuddered. He was cold. . . .

"Father, can you eat oysters on fast days?" I asked.

"You eat them alive. . . ." he answered. "They are in shells . . . like tortoises, only in double shells."

The seductive smell suddenly ceased to tickle my nostrils, and the illusion faded. Now I understood!

"How horrible!" I exclaimed. "How hideous!"

So that was the meaning of oysters! However, hideous as they were, my imagination could paint them. I imagined an animal like a frog. The frog sat in the shell, looked out with big, bright eyes, and moved its disgusting jaws. What on earth could be more horrible to a boy who had lived in the world just eight years and three months? Frenchmen, they said, ate frogs. But children— never! And I saw this fish being carried from market in its shell, with claws, bright eyes, and shiny tail. . . . The children all hide themselves, and the cook, blinking squeamishly, takes the animal by its claws, puts it on a dish, and carries it to the dining room. The grown-ups take it, and eat . . . eat it alive, eyes, teeth, claws. And it hisses, and tries to bite their lips.

I frowned disgustedly. But why did my teeth begin to chew? An animal, disgusting, detestable, frightful, but still I ate it, ate it greedily, fearing to notice its taste and smell. I ate in imagination, and my nerves seemed braced, and my heart beat stronger. . . . One animal was finished, already I saw the bright eyes of a second, a third. . . . I ate these also. At last I ate the table napkin, the plate, my father's galoshes, the white notice. . . . I ate everything before me, because I felt that only eating would cure my complaint. The oysters glared frightfully from their bright eyes, they made me sick, I shuddered at the thought of them, but I wanted to eat, to eat!

"Give me some oysters! Give me some oysters." The cry burst from my lips, and I stretched out my hands.

"Give me a kopeck, gentlemen!" I heard suddenly my father's dulled, choked voice. "I am ashamed to ask, but, my God, I can bear it no longer!"

"Give me some oysters!" I cried, seizing my father's coat tails.

"And so you eat oysters! Such a little whippersnapper!" I heard a voice beside me.

Before me stood two men in silk hats, and looked at me with a laugh.

"Do you mean to say that this little manikin eats oysters? Really! This is too delightful! How does he eat them?"

I remember a strong hand dragged me into the glaring restaurant. In a minute a crowd had gathered, and looked at me with curiosity and amusement. I sat at a table, and ate something slippy, damp, and mouldy. I ate greedily, not chewing, not daring to look, not even knowing what I ate. It seemed to me that if I opened my eyes, I should see at once the bright eyes, the claws, the sharp teeth.

I began to chew something hard. There was a crunching sound.

"Good heavens, he's eating the shells!" laughed the crowd. "Donkey, who ever heard of eating oyster shells?"

After this, I remember only my terrible thirst. I lay on my bed, kept awake by repletion, and by a strange taste in my hot mouth. My father walked up and down the room and gesticulated.

"I have caught cold, I think!" he said. "I feel something queer in my head. . . . As if there is something inside it. . . . But perhaps it is only . . . because I had no food today. I have been strange altogether . . . stupid. I saw those gentlemen paying ten rubles for oysters; why didn't I go and ask them for something . . . in loan? I am sure they would have given it."

Towards morning I fell asleep, and dreamed of a frog sitting in a shell and twitching its eyes. At midday thirst awoke me. I sought my father; he still walked up and down the room and gesticulated.

The Best Known Works of Anton Chekhov

"To Get Money Easily One Must Be a Woman"
GEORGE ORWELL

Charlie told us a good story one Saturday night in the *bistro*. Try and picture him—drunk, but sober enough to talk consecutively. He bangs on the zinc bar and yells for silence:

"Silence, *messieurs et dames*—silence, I implore you! Listen to this story that I am about to tell you. A memorable story, an instructive story, one of the souvenirs of a refined and civilised life. Silence, *messieurs et dames!*

"It happened at a time when I was hard up. You know what that is like—how damnable, that a man of refinement should ever be in such a condition. My money had not come from home; I had pawned everything, and there was nothing open to me except to work, which is a thing I will not do. I was living with a girl at the time—Yvonne her name was—a great half-witted peasant girl like Azaya there, with yellow hair and fat legs. The two of us had eaten nothing in three days. *Mon Dieu,* what sufferings! The girl used to walk up and down the room with her hands on her belly, howling like a dog that she was dying of starvation. It was terrible.

"But to a man of intelligence nothing is impossible. I propounded to myself the question, 'What is the easiest way to get money without working?' And immediately the answer came: 'To get money easily one must be a woman. Has not every woman something to sell?' And then, as I lay reflecting upon the things I should do if I were a woman, an idea came into my head. I remembered the Government maternity hospitals—you know the Government maternity hospitals? They are places where women who are *enceinte* are given meals free and no questions are asked. It is done to encourage childbearing. Any woman can go there and demand a meal, and she is given it immediately.

" *'Mon Dieu!'* I thought, 'if only I were a woman! I would eat at one of those places every day. Who can tell whether a woman is *enceinte* or not, without an examination?'

"I turned to Yvonne. 'Stop that insufferable bawling.' I said, 'I have thought of a way to get food.'

" 'How?' said she.

" 'It is simple,' I said. 'Go to the Government maternity hospital. Tell them you are *enceinte* and ask for food. They will give you a good meal and ask no question.'

"Yvonne was appalled. *'Mais, mon Dieu,'* she cried, 'I am not *enceinte!'*

" 'Who cares?' I said. 'That is easily remedied. What do you need except a cushion—two cushions if necessary? It is an inspiration from heaven, *ma chère.* Don't waste it.'

"Well, in the end I persuaded her, and then we borrowed a cushion and I got her ready and took her to the maternity hospital. They received her with open arms. They gave her cabbage soup, a ragoût of beef, a purée of potatoes, bread and cheese and beer, and all kinds of advice about her baby. Yvonne gorged till she almost burst her skin, and managed to slip some of the bread and cheese into her pocket for me. I took her there every day until I had money again. My intelligence had saved us. . . ."

Down and Out in Paris and London

One Fish Ball
ANONYMOUS

A wretched man walked up and down
To buy his dinner in the town.
At last he found a wretched place
And entered it with modest grace,
Took off his coat, took off his hat,
And wiped his feet upon the mat,
Took out his purse to count his pence,
And found he had but two half-cents.
The bill of fare, he scanned it through
To see what two half-cents would do.
The only item of them all
For two half-cents was one fish ball.
So to the waiter he did call
And gently whispered: "One fish ball."
The waiter bellowed down the hall:
"The gentleman wants one fish ball."
The diners looked both one and all
To see who wanted one fish ball.
The wretched man, all ill at ease,
Said: "A little bread, sir, if you please."

The waiter bellowed down the hall:
"We don't serve bread with one fish ball."
The wretched man, he felt so small,
He quickly left the dining hall.
The wretched man, he went outside
And shot himself until he died.
This is the moral of it all,
Don't ask for bread with one fish ball.

EATING WHEN PENNILESS

One day Goha went to the market. He stopped to gaze into the window of a restaurant where pilavs, stews, chickens, fish, and other appetizing dishes were displayed. As he stood there enjoying the delicious aromas which reached him through the open door, the head cook hailed him: "Come in, sir, and make yourself at home!"

Believing that he was being invited as a guest, Goha accepted. He sat down and ate as much as he could of all the dishes, filling his pockets with pilav to take home to his son. But as he got up to leave, the head cook called out: "Pay me! You have eaten ten piasters worth of food."

"But I haven't any money," Goha replied. "I thought I was your guest."

The head cook dragged Goha before the Emir, who ordered him to be driven through the streets sitting backwards on a donkey as punishment. As he proceeded through the town in this manner, followed by a train of jeering onlookers, some of them even playing music on pipes and drums, a friend saw him and exclaimed: "What are you doing, Goha? Why are they treating you in this manner?"

"I was served good pilav for nothing, with extra thrown in for my son," replied Goha. "And now I am having a free donkey ride with free music as well."

—CLAUDIA RODEN
A Book of Middle Eastern Food

4

Worth a Special Journey

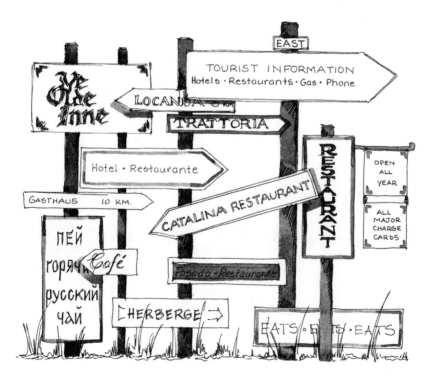

Table excellente, mérite un détour, says the Michelin guide; *tables merveilleuses, gloire de la cuisine française.* No need to translate such words —long before the turn of the century, when Frenchmen began getting annual assessments of tables excellent and marvelous, discriminating travelers as diverse as Jefferson and Stendhal sought out *auberges,* often obscurely located, in order to eat as well as possible and learn a little more about a region and its people. In the 1970s, gallivanting for what once were almost noble purposes has become a game for relatively everyone who has sufficient money or credit. Yet though affluence is often a help, it is not the key factor in a memorable experience—a good palate is of service on a gastronomic junket, and on a Grand Tour of the imagination the thing to possess is an appetite that can be satisfied vicariously.

PETIT TOUR DE FRANCE
E. S. TURNER

O Michelin, cherish
  Me, chasten and guide me!
And let me not perish
  With songbirds inside me
On the beaches of D-Day,
Sans bain and *sans bidet.*

The Chiribim
Is *fermé dim.,*
  And cannot mend a *pneu.*
The Oriflamme

Is *fermé sam.,*
    But offers *truite au bleu.*

The brasserie
Of Tante Julie
Is *interdit*
    Aux chiens.
Le Chat Qui Chante
Lacks *eau courante—*
    Tiens!

The Auberge Bon Accueil
Has *volaille demi deuil,*
    Whatever that is,
    With *parking* gratis.

The Chez Dumas (good Chez Dumas!)
Sans TV *pendant les repas.*
The Chez Ron-ron (petit pat-apon)
Is *fermé jeudi, hors saison.*
It's *convenable,* with *douche publique,*
But scarcely, it would seem, unique.

The Château Cavour
    On its elegant *plage*
Is worth *le détour,*
    But not worth *le voyage.*

Behold, *enfin,*
The Vieux Moulin
Has *matelote de Rhin*
Au vin,
And furthermore, *un beau jardin*
To rest in after such *délices*
As *gratin de queues d'écrevisses,*
Or *langouste grillé cardinal,*
Which sounds a long way from banal.

O scene
Of high-class nutriment!
My pulse beats plus fifteen
Per cent.

What of the Cochon Noir?
It's *fermé trois prem, sem.*
d'août et lundi soir.

The Lion d'Or is *isolé,*
With *nombre de couverts limité;*
It boasts *terrine de caneton*
Au foie gras truffé . . . Zut, mais non!

I suddenly feel queasy.
Let's take it easy.

Right here I say
Farewell, *mon cher,*
To *fricassée*
de fruits de mer.
Farewell to *lamproie bordelaise*
(Or *lyonnaise* or *béarnaise*),
Goodbye to *gratin dauphinois*
And all *grillades au feu de bois;*
I'd HATE
A plate
of *petit pois.*

I think I'd like—the way things are—
A sandwich at the Buffet Gare
De St. Lazare.

"What She Says About Cayman Fish Stew"
ARCHIE CARR

Start the seven-mile drive to windward, but keep your pace down, and when you hear the hoot of a blown conch, stop for an image to take away, when a bicycle crunches by on the white rock road, pedaled by a gangling tan man with long bare feet and a wide straw hat, who raises the shell twice a minute and blows one long note to cry the conchs and goatfish in his saddle basket. It is that sort of thing you will see if you are willing; and the little store beside the incandescent road out where the town wanes, with the chalked sign in big letters like train-times at the depot, and the sign says:

Just arrive
Sweet potatoes
Skellion
Fresh bullas
Chochoes
Cocoes

When you get there, don't just go by—make the Potters stop and tell you what just arrived. They will enjoy the trip a lot more for it.

Then when you are still hardly under way, ask George which house belongs to Rosabelle Byrd, whom they call the best cook in Georgetown, which is saying a great deal. When he points out the gnome-hut, the only one nearby with a thatch roof, go in and tell Rosabelle you always liked to eat, and hide the wince when she pokes you in the ribs for love of you, and listen to what she says about Cayman fish stew, which is what happens to bouillabaisse in the islands, or about codfish-and-akees or black crab stuffed, or the things they do with green turtles to make Caymanians strong and unafraid of the sea. Get a firm commitment for her to cook you a meal. . . .

The Windward Road

"THIS WAS NO ORDINARY CAFÉ ROUTIER"
ELIZABETH DAVID

I vividly remember . . . the occasion when, having stopped for petrol at a filling station at Remoulins near the Pont du Gard, we decided to go into the café attached to it, and have a glass of wine. It was only eleven o'clock in the morning but for some reason we were very hungry. The place was empty, but we asked if we could have some bread, butter and sausage. Seeing that we were English, the old lady in charge tried to give us a ham sandwich, and when we politely but firmly declined this treat she went in search of the *patron* to ask what she should give us.

He was an intelligent and alert young man who understood at once what we wanted. In a few minutes he reappeared and set before us a big rectangular platter in the centre of which were thick slices of home-made pork and liver pâté, and on either side fine slices of the local raw ham and sausage; these were flanked with black olives, green olives, freshly washed radishes still retaining some of their green leaves, and butter.

By the time we had consumed these things, with wine and good fresh bread, we realised that this was no ordinary *café routier.* The patron was pleased when we complimented him on his pâté and told us that many of his customers came to him specially for it. It was now nearly midday and the place was fast filling up with these customers. They were lorry drivers, on their way from Sète, on the coast, up through France with their immense tanker lorries loaded with Algerian wine. The noise and bustle and friendly atmosphere soon made us realise that this must be the most popular place in the neighbourhood. We stayed, of course, for lunch. Chance having brought us there it would have been absurd to stick to our original plans of driving on to some star restaurant or other where we probably wouldn't have eaten so well (my travels in France are studded with memories of the places to which I have taken a fancy but where I could not stop—the café at Silery where the still champagne was so good, the restaurant at Bray-sur-Seine where we had a late breakfast of raw country ham, beautiful butter and fresh thin *baguettes* of bread, and longed to stay for lunch—inflexible planning is the enemy of good eating.) But here at Remoulins we stayed, and enjoyed a good sound lunch, unusually well-presented for a *café routier*.

We came back the next night for a specially ordered dinner of Provençal dishes, for the proprietor was a Marseillais and his wife the daughter of the owners of the house, which had been converted from a farm to a restaurant–filling station. The young man was a cook of rare quality and the dinner he prepared to order put to shame the world-famous Provençal three-star establishment where we had dined a day or two previously. But had it not been for the appearance of the delicious hors-d'oeuvre, which was so exactly the right food at the right moment, we should have had our drink and paid our bill and gone on our way not knowing. . . .

French Provincial Cooking

Luncheon in Provence
WILLIAM SANSOM

And so Mme. Baudoin raises her arm to beckon Pasqualine, the chef of the hors d'oeuvre: and plate after plate is presented to us by a swirling skirted posse of billow-bloused waitresses—whom one had better call *"serveuses,"* for they are more than waitresses, they have the dedicated look of priestesses ministering at a most holy, dedicated rite. This hors d'oeuvre, comprising up to forty or so separate dishes, is a specialty of the restaurant. A list would sound tendentious—it varies from Greek-pickled mushrooms to a fenneled artichoke, from stuffed fresh sardines to saffroned cuttlefish—and it is all a paradox, for this extraordinary richness has its root in poverty. The Provençal coast has always been poor, dry, hot country compared with the fertile interior. Thus the basis of its kitchen is to make much out of little, to make liberal use of herbs, garlic and other appetizers—simply to make the bread or the rice or pasta go further. But taken to the rich degree of this *auberge,* distilled into tasty little bits of everything under the southern sun—the result turns the palate into an engagingly complex kaleidoscope. So we wrap our tongues around a pellet of green omelette, eggs tasting vaguely of summer trees; and dig our teeth into a soft cylinder of celeriac stuffed with tender veal and spiced rice; and let swim across our palates a sardine, a mussel, a small octopus and the best cut of a mackerel soused in white wine. And on and on come the plates, the diverse tastes, the eggplants, the baby marrows, the pimentos all exquisitely stuffed—until the dizzied palate-brain cries halt. For we are in for a lobster-and-truffle pie, and after that an entrecote doused in a butter-and-claret sauce. You can make a meal of just the hors d'oeuvre here; and a pleasant and leisurely fulfilment this can be. But today we are bound for sterner stuff. And as the raingold, chilled white wine from Baudoin's own St. Blaise vineyard irradiates the last of our choice—a fresh artichoke touched with a special anchovy sauce—we sit back prepared to wait.

But waiting is an art as well as cooking, and wait we do not, for the waitress is already upon us. Or to be more exact, a wait of perhaps two minutes seems to be specifically ordained—as if the patron is watching and counting a pause, just the right pause—before the lobster pie arrives. Lobster is also not exact—the meat of those pies is made of the best cuts from an indigenous *langouste.*

So on our plates arrive oval pies as big as a big hand, and four fat fingers high, and stuffed with cream and *langouste* and truffles and mushrooms. The pastry is golden-brown, and its crown decorated with truffles cut into thin black bootlace slivers, a Steinberg drawing in black truffle-lace.

Me or You: "Another glass of St. Blaise? Or something a little differ—"

Mme. Baudoin (from above): "Eat! Eat while it is just exactly hot! The wine will wait. Anyhow the wine you have is still the right one. But *eat!*"

And our silver forks break the pastry. Mme. Baudoin has spoken in no intrusive school-mistressly manner: she knows the food and wishes it well, and she knows that one of the supremacies of La Bonne Auberge is Pascal, the pastry cook, who forges the light flakes of his airborne pastry in a special kitchen of his own. The *croustade* is very good—how cleverly the light crispness of the pastry mixes in the mouth with the creamed softness of the sauce, and how expertly the sea-sharp savour of the *langouste* is balanced by the cloudy, subtler ambience of mushrooms and, occasionally, suddenly, by the sweet bitterness of an instantly all-pervasive truffle.

Meanwhile the shaded Mediterranean sunlight makes blue shadows among the flowers, draws a mauve ellipse from a silver pepper-pot across the fine white cloth . . . and M. Baudoin, noting that we seem to have some special interest in his food, invites us to see how the steak and its wine sauce is cooked. But first— consult the *sommelier* on the question of a red wine. So much is on offer here: when we ask Baudoin what he feels are the best Bordeaux years presently usable, the answer comes like a single word gabbled on an over-speed recording machine tape: "34-37-45-49-53." Being a claret man myself, and you being immaculately selfless, a Margaux is commanded. And we move across the room, past that vast table of fresh vegetables and fruits and fish, to where through its glass screen the kitchen can be seen.

Once inside—no smell at all! At least, unless you bend right over the huge central steel charcoal-driven stove. Cool turquoise blue tiles and air-conditioning make this kitchen, with its wood-fire spits and its copper pans lined with real silver, the antithesis of the familiar sweat-house.

At this point, while we stand with Robert the head chef and watch him select the entrecote and arrange his ingredients for the exact timing of the cooking, it is necessary to mention one of the principles upon which this restaurant is run. A measure of *simplicity* is axiomatic at the *auberge.* Baudoin insists that the enormously complicated dishes and menus of the past are a thing of the past. People cannot allow the same time for eating, nor women the same expansion of their figures: everyone wants to live longer, and there is no longer the leisure for such counter-irritants as horse-riding and spas. So the menu, though rich and varied, is confined to dishes which can be prepared fairly quickly without the day-long confection of a meal like an opera. Of course, you can have anything on command—frosted pineapple veiled in sugar gauze *(ananas givré et voilé à l'orientale)* or a sucking pig. But normally Robert (only thirty-seven years old) prefers to attack the fairly simple, which is in any case complicated enough, with the triple energies of a chemist, physician and painter. Chemist, for he deals with heat and exact quantities (*most* important, and one reason why most circulated recipes are useless), and qualities—for instance he cooks only on absolutely tasteless *silver:* physician, because the food must be digestible and good: painter because he is concerned with textures, the crisp against the smooth and the exact viscosities of sauces, and with colour, for the eye as well as the nose stimulates the gastric juices (note how few dishes are blue, the mark of poison: purples are always red purples). One might also add philosopher to these accomplishments, for much of the time he must play the bitter against the sweet, and always include both.

And now the steak—the *marchand de vin.* The red meat was first tossed about in butter over the immense stove, then removed in a porcelain dish to the hot plate. Then the sauce was begun—two previously prepared wine-and-butter sauces were waiting, and these now went into the *sauté* pan, with an extra slab of butter, which the cook whisked with one hand—the pan was heavy and thus truly filled with heat— holding his other arm urgently aside, like a man viciously prodding at the button of a pintable. Then a spoon to taste it. Impatience across the face, more butter, more from the wine-boat. More whisking—assiduous, muscular whisking. Another taste. More butter. More whisking. Taste. And so on —always *regulating quantities.* He was building with the eye, which noted the sauce's texture, and with the tongue. At last done, the sauce was poured over the entrecote and served. As simple, as complicated as that. Why an entrecote? Much more taste than a fillet, the sharp teeth of Mme. Baudoin informed me.

To table again—and just before the food arrives, the approach of the wine-waiter. An interesting man to watch. He serves his wines with the silent grace of a cat or an Arab. Dressed in a dark blue blouse and apron, his cutting and dusting and sniffing of the cork are both graceful and gracious but never sacerdotal, for wine is for pleasure, not worship. I happened to lunch a few days later in one of Paris's three-star restaurants, and the venerable *sommelier* there, with his thumping honest expertise, had nothing on the considerate stealth of this cool magician from the south.

And so we cross over from the light pink-and-white world of fish to the red velvet darkness of meat and night-shade wine. The entrecote of its nature has more fibre than fillet—but our patronne is right, a much juicier and thicker taste. The sauce—how can one describe a sauce? Rich, reflecting the meat, adding to the meat—it seems to make each mouthful into a hall of reflecting mirrors: taste does not end with a bite, but repeats itself round the palate a hundred times. Yet it feels fresh; and it is fresh. Like the side plates of vegetables—green peas, French beans, small steamed potatoes, each freshly picked from the garden within a few hours, so that nothing whatsoever is lost of the vitamin and mineral goodness which otherwise, overnight in the market, would have disappeared.

To finish the red wine, cheeses are brought. A little city of towers and domes clustered together on their board, cheeses from everywhere, St. Duc, Roquefort, Gruyère, cow's and goat's and mare's milk moulded into castles of biscuit colour and green-flecked white.

Me: "Heavens, how can one do this every day?"

You (who know a thing or two): "Do in Rome as the Romans —don't. No one here eats heavily twice a day. Appetites must be healthy appetites—the French here would take a simple salami sandwich or a slice of pissaladiera, which you will know is olive and onion and anchovy tart, for a light after-bathe luncheon before dining properly in the evening. It is the curse of the tourist that he must try to pack in too much during his short escapade. It is no life."

Me: "Fattening for an early death?"

A Waitress: "Le Sorbet au Citron!"

And there for each of us has arrived a whole lemon hatted with a cockade of its own green leaves. An important moment. The top of the lemon is removable, the inside of the rind is filled with the coldest of cold lemon-juiced water-ice, much more refreshing than any ice cream. This is an old aid to digestion, well known as an interval-marker, together with a Russian cigarette, to the great twelve-course banquets of yesterday.

Refreshed, it is now the purpose of the *pâtissier* to please us. And from Pascal's kitchen comes the *Désir du Roy*, a pastry pagoda whose tiers are filled alternately with sweet whipped cream and ice-cream, and over which is now poured a hot chocolate sauce. Even then—so well are the details contrived—it is the last mouthful, the thicker biscuity base, which tastes best. All accompanied by a sweetish still champagne, a *blanc de blancs*. (Overcoming the temptation to try the first Mumm Rosé '52 with its curious Japanese designed label; or what is perhaps the best of lively champagnes, a Moët et Chandon Dom Pérignon, whose elegant antique bottle, thin-necked and ungilded and crowned with good black wax, adds a reticent pleasure to the eye.

Fruit now? A properly Gallic choice here. Mine is a fig whose long pale shape earns the soubriquet *"col de dame"*; and you have chosen a comice pear called *"cuisse de dame."*

And coffee, with *pâtissier* Pascal intruding again with a plate of *friandises*, fresh-cooked biscuits and cakelets of all kinds, an elegant sop to the Turkish brew. And overheard at the next table—only just within earshot—the sigh of a man as he dips one of these, a *sablé à la confiture*, a jammy sugar-dusted pastry, into his coffee....

Blue Skies, Brown Studies

"THE TOUR D'ARGENT LIVES ON"
ROBERT COURTINE

From 1582 to 1890, the bank of the Seine opposite Notre Dame was both the stage and the wings of history.

From the Tour d'Argent itself—built in 1582 of stone brought down by barge from the chalky quarries of the Champagne, stone so pale that the sunlight playing on it seemed to turn it to silver —to the original and humble Tour d'Argent restaurant with its wooden frame—outside the door of which, in 1887, the new owner Frédéric had himself photographed in his intellectual's pince-nez and his heavy Victorian-father style mane and beard— history with a capital H was consistently paralleled by the history of the table.

It was hereabouts, for a start, that the fork first entered our daily lives, in the time of Henry III, of the Italian ballets at the Louvre, of doublets with slashed and ballooning sleeves.

And from then on, figure after figure springs to brief life: La Grande Mademoiselle, Anne Marie Louise d'Orléans, ordering the cannons of the Bastille fired to the greater glory of *le Grand Siècle,* in the reign of Louis XIV, and the *canard au sang* that was to oust the favorite *poule au pot* of Henri IV's reign. Then the court gossip, Mme. de Sévigné, discovering hot chocolate for the first time, served in tiny cups that she was to look back on in later life with such nostalgia. Then the Regency, then the Court abbés and enlightened philosophers speeding toward the brink of '89. The Romantic movement explodes. Balzac comes probing and noting. Dumas brings his camelia-wearing daughter-in-law here on his arm. No, no, the man with the goatee isn't a bank clerk on the spree; it's M. France, you must know that! Anatole! That terrifying roar? The actor Mounet-Sully. That tempest? Sarah Bernhardt. And meanwhile, Frédéric, looking rather like a moral tutor, is trussing his ducklings and rising to the realm of fame, with three centuries of memories in tow.

Daudet describes him in his memoirs "with his pince-nez, his graying side-whiskers, and his unshakable gravity, cutting up his plump, already trussed and singed quack-quack, dropping the pieces into a pan, making his sauce, salting and peppering the way Claude Monet painted, with the objectivity of perfect instinct and a mathematician's precision, opening up for one in advance with that infallible hand all the vistas of the palate."

For Frédéric had made over that perennial recipe for *canard au sang* and found a new way of cooking and serving it: "He has made it into a double dish, the *canard au sang* first, followed by an equally exquisite grill."

When did he first get the idea of numbering his ducklings? In 1890, very probably. And it is also probable that he entered his own name in the original Log Book—which has since vanished, alas!—as the consumer of number *one.*

Several months after that, the Prince of Wales, the future Edward VII, was devouring duckling number 328.

A quarter century later, in 1914, Alphonse XIII was having duckling number 40,362 dismembered for him.

I can imagine a statistician enthusiastically plotting the future probabilities of this progression of ducklings at the Tour d'Argent. But first let us skip another quarter of a century. We are in 1938, and duckling number 147,888 is being served up to the Duke of Windsor.

Which means that whereas the first twenty-five years spelt doom to a mere 40,000 ducklings, the next twenty-five involved the massacre of 100,000. Let us jump another twenty-five years, and we have reached 1963 and duckling number 324,047, which means 175,000 suffocated ducklings in that one quarter of a century. And in between, I note, the young Princess Elizabeth and the Duke of Edinburgh (in 1948) had devoured numbers 185,397 and 185,398. A royal appetite! And your humble servant, not very long ago, ate number 388,065.

At the present rate, an expert has calculated, the first year of the next century may well see the breathless death, on the Quai de la Tournelle, of duckling number 750,000.

Last century, the Marquis Lauzières de Thémines, a frequenter of the muses as well as of the great Frédéric's restaurant, put this recipe into verse of a kind. The result could be sung, he affirmed, to the tune of the popular song "La Corde sensible." The tune has been forgotten, and M. le Marquis as well, but the Tour d'Argent lives on, and . . ."

> There, of a duckling the carcass remaining
> By visible means they crush and reduce;
> An engine descends, and then, by straining,
> They extract a rich and delectable juice.
> And many plump slices once carved from the breast,
> They strip off the skin, serve the legs on their own
> Then far from discarding the ribs and the rest,
> The carcass is used to the very last bone. . . ."

So now you can even *recite* the *canard à la presse.* Which is as it should be, since it is a very theatrical dish. So much so that a theater has now been placed in the upstairs room of the present

Tour d'Argent, overlooking the Seine and Notre-Dame. Or, to be more exact, a scale model of the Paris Opéra, in which, in the backdrop, you can see the "duck-pressers" at work in a Jordaens lighting. And this spectacle, "opening up in advance all the vistas of the palate," can even make you forget Notre-Dame outside, silhouetted against the gray sky.

The Hundred Glories of French Cooking

The Pressed Duck's Beginnings

Most of the Paris restaurants, now that Frédéric is no more, have their silver turnscrew, and they do not feel guilty of plagiarism, for Frédéric did not really originate this trick but adapted it from the practice of French peasants who tried to get as much juice as possible out of their tough skinny ducks by smashing the carcasses with stones.

—Henry T. Finck
Food and Flavor

"Not a Place That Would Have Good Restaurants"
JAMES A. MICHENER

We came to a hill from which we could see the modest but very old city of Astorga, and if Don Luis had at that moment told me that down there I would have the best meal I was to encounter in Spain, I would have derided the suggestion, because Astorga did not look like a place that would have good restaurants. Nor did it. Don Luis said, "There is, however, this little place owned by a woman whose husband helps her, and it will have something acceptable." He led us to the Restaurante La Peseta in one of Astorga's little streets, and as I entered and saw one small room and a crowded old-fashioned kitchen, I had only modest expectations. But before we sat down to eat we happened to look into the kitchen and there we found some six or seven elderly women tending a collection of pots which bubbled in a very businesslike way.

"You looking for some real Spanish food?" one of the old women asked me.

"Yes," I said tentatively, and she took me into her part of the kitchen where she worked at a table positively cluttered with slabs of raw meat, herbs, vegetables and shellfish.

"What would you like?" she asked. It was a hot day and I doubted that I wanted heavy food, but she whispered in confidence, "Take the lomo de cerdo adobado." I signified my ignorance and she pointed to a long square chunk of dark meat and to myself I translated the name she repeated: "Loin of pork adobado." But what was adobado?

"Is it good?" I asked, for it certainly did not look so, and loin of pork was scarcely something that I would normally order from a menu, especially in midsummer.

"When I finish cooking it," she began, abruptly stopping and sort of shouting at me, "Garbanzos, too."

"Garbanzos?" These are heavy, tasteless chickpeas which spoil so much Spanish cooking. Garbanzos I did not want, but she took me firmly by the arm and led me to the pot for which she seemed to be specially responsible.

"You have never tasted garbanzos," she said sternly. "Now sit down and order some Rioja wine."

Don Luis asked what I had ordered, and when I said, "Lomo de cerdo adobado," his face brightened, and while we waited, tasting the Rioja, he said, "In the old days when I was a boy many families butchered one or two hogs, and when the loins were cut out, long slabs of meat squared on the sides, they were marinated for five or six months in a mixture of parsley, garlic, onion, oregano, salt, pepper, oil and vinegar. Then they were smoked until they became one of the best tasting meats on earth. Michener, you've stumbled into a gastronomic gold mine."

"But it's being served with garbanzos," I said, and his face fell. "With garbanzos you can't do much," he said.

Finally the dishes arrived. The regular waiter brought the ordinary one for Don Luis and the rest of the party, but the old woman brought mine, a huge country plate with five slices of pork neatly arranged on one side, plus a heap of garbanzos on the other. As I took my fork, the woman grabbed my wrist and whispered benevolently, "What you're about to do you won't forget."

It was not hyperbole. The meat was something unique into which all of rural life had somehow been compressed, for it was both savory and smoky; it was firm to the knife but succulent to the tooth; it had no trace of fat, but the forests of northern Spain seemed to have crept into it, and I have never tasted better smoked meat. It was, however, the garbanzos that astonished me, and the others too, for when I said how good they were, everyone nibbled from my plate and we called the old cook to bring us additional dishes. She put them on the table and smiled approvingly as we dug in. Softly she said, "My garbanzos are soaked for two days in cold salt water. They are cooked slowly, and when they are sure of themselves I throw in some salty ham, three different kinds of hot sausages, some potatoes and cabbage, and they stew for eight hours. If you're a workman with little money, you eat garbanzos as your only dish, with meat and vegetables thrown in. But if you're wealthy like a norteamericano, you can afford the garbanzos plain. Because I charge you as much as if you'd taken the meat too."

Iberia

"A Favorite Way to Get Over Here"
JOHN McNULTY

In a talk with Thomas Dewey I learned that there is no *chef de cuisine* at Gage & Tollner's. "We have cooks, but nobody is *called* chef," he said. "If we had a fancy chef, then his ideas would prevail, and our food would lose its individuality."

That seemed a profitable idea, for the restaurant, which seats 144 persons, was full and people were waiting. I asked Leon Gaskill about notables who have been customers.

"Most every old restaurant claims Diamond Jim Brady as a customer," he said, "but this is one place he really came, and he could eat prodigious meals. I remember one time he played hookey from a Baltimore hospital, came straight here for dinner, then went back to Baltimore. . . ."

Leon's memory is long and filled with lore. "When I was first here as a bus boy, a favorite way to get over here from Manhattan was the Fulton Street ferry; the fare was three cents. The Long Island Railroad ran clear down to the river—with steam engines, of course; electric trolleys ran on Fulton Street, but they still had horsecars on Smith Street. People arrived at our door in carriages and hansom cabs, and later they came in Fords and Packards."

I wanted to know some of Gage & Tollner's more famous dishes. "Green turtle soup is one," Mr. Ed said. "We use a recipe my great-grandfather used in the Fulton Street, Manhattan, restaurant, where he also served venison and bear steaks. We buy whole turtles, about 100 pounds apiece, from Moore and Co.; they come from the Gulf of Mexico. After they're cleaned we simmer them two days and nights as the first step in making the soup. It is heavily laced with sherry, and of course we add spices and herbs. I can't tell you much more than that—it's been a family secret for years.

"Mackerel used to be a popular fish," Mr. Ed said, "but for some reason it's lost favor and we're about ready to drop it. On the other hand, red snapper is becoming more and more popular. We're proud of our boned shad because this is a dish I believe my father was one of the first to serve. Shad is one of the boniest fish and the flesh is delicate—an amateur would tear it to pieces. So we have a shad boner who does it like a surgeon with scalpel and tweezers. Our fish is cooked simply, and I prefer broiling. We broil fish skin-side up so that the heat will sear it and hold the juices."

Lobster Maryland—fried lobster served with white sauce, corn fritters, and bacon, in a sort of Southern style—is another specialty. So are Dewey Pan-Roast Clams, garnished with green peppers and pimento; Crabmeat Dewey, which is crab meat *au gratin,* with peppers and pimento garnish; and Duxbury Stew, which is diced soft clams with sherry.

The meals our threesome ordered that evening were difficult to choose. We agreed not to have the same thing. I ordered first and perhaps least adventurously: large oysters, filet mignon, potatoes *au gratin,* a salad of lettuce, tomato and cucumber with French dressing, and Nesselrode pie. My wife chose a seafood cocktail of shrimp, lobster and crab; broiled shad roe with bacon, asparagus hollandaise, green salad and a raspberry ice. The physicist had green turtle soup, a broiled English mutton chop (which turned out to be four inches thick and the size of a tenderloin steak), grilled tomatoes, hashed-browned potatoes and a "Georgia" salad of finely chopped cabbage with a spicy French dressing. He finished off with apple pie and cheddar cheese. Mr. Ed recommended an imported Graves, Château de la Bred, to go with my wife's shad roe, and a sparkling Burgundy, Champy Pére, for our meat dishes....

The dinner was superb. Each of us was too pleased to envy more than passingly the other's choice. There was nothing fancy about any of our dishes. Filet mignon and *au gratin* potatoes don't sound exotic. Even a mutton chop, though rarer, is not elegantly unusual. Gourmets might even call such food unimaginative. We called the whole thing wonderful.

"Where simplicity is paramount," said the physicist, "there stands a treasure house.... When dinner is over at other places, say in Manhattan, you feel like going to a night club or a show. Dinner here makes you think of the old-fashioned pleasures, like sitting around talking with good friends, enjoying the delights of home."

Holiday Magazine

THE CATALINA RESTAURANT IN THE BAYOUS
CASKIE STINNETT

Hurrying back to Mobile through the marshland, I saw a sign pointing down an unpaved road to a place called Bayou La Batre. It didn't look promising; even the sign seemed to possess an apologetic air. But I had breakfasted in Mobile, and I wasn't overly anxious to return there for lunch. I turned down the road to Bayou La Batre.

The country was bleak and flat, and there were few houses. In fields of weeds, ancient automobiles resting on Nehi and Dr. Pepper crates rusted silently and forlorn. Most of the dwellings were summer fishing shacks, surrounded by pines and scrub growth, and all were touched with the decay of abandonment. Advertisements for snuff adorned the outbuildings. I gathered that Society Brand was the favorite, but Banjo was a comer. Pecan trees shaded a few of the shacks, and there was an occasional crepe myrtle, but mostly the landscape was relieved only by pines. It was incomparably ugly, and as I pushed farther along the road the sky became heavily overcast and a light rain started to fall. My hunger grew, and there was nothing to indicate whether Bayou La Batre was ten miles away or a hundred.

Some distance down the road I saw a man walking toward me. I flipped on the windshield wiper to make sure my imagination was not getting the upper hand. When I came abreast of him, I stopped and rolled down the window. He was wearing a baseball cap and a grin wide enough to expose two front teeth which, so far as I could see, were all that he possessed. I asked if I was anywhere near a place to eat. His grin widened to confirm my estimate. "You're mighty lucky," he replied. I waited, but he stood there as though the next move were up to me. The pause became awkward; sooner or later one of us would have to speak. "Why am I lucky? " I asked, breaking the strange silence. "Because," he said, "you're no more than half a mile from the best restaurant in Alabama *and* Louisiana. Anything you eat after that gonna make you think you camping out." He paused again and stared at me in silence. I asked if the restaurant had a name. "Catalina," he said. I thanked him and started to drive off. He held up his hand, and I stopped. "Don't look so good on the outside," he warned.

The Catalina appeared a few minutes later, and it looked dismal. Almost covered by an enormous live oak tree, it was a sprawling one-story brick building set back only a few feet from the shoulder of the road. A letter had long ago fallen from its sign, and it now read ESTAURANT. I parked my car, and went through the screen door, letting it bang behind me.

Drawing a picture of the Catalina Restaurant isn't easy, but I'll try. A cavernous dining room opened from a small entrance hall, which seemed to serve as an estuary leading to other rooms. The dining room contained possibly forty or fifty tables, and all were unadorned, rough, and accommodated four people. On top of each table was a huge bottle of catsup, several different brands of steak sauce, a bottle of Tabasco, and a large jar of salad dressing from a supermarket. I got the impression that the proprietor had found out what the customers wanted, and had supplied it in quantity. Bright overhead lights did away with any foolish thoughts of a romantic atmosphere. Apparently the customers were not to be pampered; one found an empty table and sat there. A middle-aged woman, carrying an empty tray, came to my table and, smiling affably, asked, "What'll it be?"

I said I'd start with a bloody mary. "Not here, you won't," she said. "No booze." Her gaze roamed the room, and my eyes followed hers. About half the tables were filled, and I suddenly realized that all the customers were men. "What do you want to eat?" she asked, turning back to me.

I said I didn't know. "Have you a menu?" I asked.

"I can get you a menu," she said, "but there isn't all that much on it. I can tell you what we got."

I tried a new tack. "What do you recommend?" I asked.

"You like shrimp?" she inquired. I said that I did. "Okay," she said. "The shrimp's good. Buy them every day down the road at Bayou La Batre. Strictly fresh. How about a side of shrimp for starters?"

I asked how they were cooked, and she looked at me curiously. Obviously, she had drawn a problem eater. An out-of-stater most likely. "Boiled," she said, "with a little Tabasco in the water to spice them up. I eat them myself, every day." The latter, I realized, was her ultimate reassurance. If that didn't clinch the deal, nothing would.

I settled for shrimp to begin with. "What after that?" I inquired. "I'm hungry."

She thought a moment. "How about the West Indies salad?"

I was back being a problem eater again. "What's that?" I wanted to know.

"You not from around here, are you?" she asked. Her worst suspicions were proving true. I said I was from New York, and she permitted her eyes to roll ceilingward. "West Indies salad is our specialty," she explained, keeping a steady grip on her patience. "Most all of these folks are eating it." She waved vaguely about the room. "It's fresh crabmeat marinated for fourteen hours."

"Marinated in what?" I asked.

"That's for me to know and you to find out," she replied tartly. There was a brief silence as we gazed at each other. "It's a secret," she said.

"Okay," I said. "I'll try it."

She started away, then turned back to me. "And to drink?" she inquired.

I said I'd settle for a beer.

"Not here you won't," she said. "No booze." Again we were at a standoff. I asked what she recommended, following a now-familiar path.

"Mr. Pibb," she said flatly. "I like Mr. Pibb. Or you can have ice tea."

I said I'd have a Mr. Pibb, but I couldn't put the force of much enthusiasm behind it.

"It goes good with West Indies salad," she reassured me. "You did the right thing." Then she was gone.

Service was fast. She was back almost instantly with a plate containing a mound of steaming shrimp that I could see at a glance was enough for not one but several people. She placed the plate in front of me, handed me several paper napkins, pointed to the various bottles on the table, and said: "If you don't see what you want, ask for it."

I peeled a shrimp and ate it, and I am prepared to depose under oath it was the finest shrimp I had ever tasted. It was fresh, tender, cooked just enough, and the Tabasco lent it a spicy taste that made shrimp sauce superfluous. I ate possibly half of them, and then pushed the plate aside. I had to give the West Indies salad a fair shake. The waitress passed and I stopped her. "What's the matter?" she asked, eyeing the plate. "Didn't you like them?" I liked them fine, I said, but I was saving room for the main course. She nodded sagely and took the plate away.

The West Indies salad, when it was placed in front of me, left me with the suspicion that I should have quit with the shrimps when I was ahead. The chunks of crabmeat were gray, not white, and they floated in what appeared to be a sea of oil. "You can eat it out the bowl," the waitress said, "or spoon it out on your plate. Some like it one way, some the other. That's why I brought you a plate. Now I'll get you your Mr. Pibb."

I decided to get the crabmeat out of the oil with all possible speed; fourteen hours was enough. I scooped up a spoonful, let it drain against the edge of the bowl, and deposited it on my plate, where it looked no more appealing than it had afloat. I tasted it tentatively. Wonderful is a tricky and imprecise word to employ describing food, but before I get into specifics I want to put the word wonderful on the record. The crabmeat, despite its appearance, was firm and fresh, lime juice or lemon juice imparted a tart taste, and some unidentified spices gave it a flavor unlike anything I had known before. I settled down to it happily.

The waitress looked at me approvingly when she brought the Mr. Pibb. Out-of-staters were often crazy, God knows, but they recognized good food when they found it. She obviously enjoyed seeing a man relish what he ate. "Most folks drink Mr. Pibb out of the bottle," she said. "You want a glass I'll get you one." I shook my head; my mouth was full.

I ate all of the West Indies salad. And I drank some of the Mr. Pibb. I sat there, in the Catalina Restaurant, for nearly half an hour after I finished eating, too satisfied to move. Then I paid the check, which was a little less than three dollars, and walked out through the entrance hall to the screen door. "Come again, you hear," the waitress had said when she took my money. It was raining hard now, and I ran from the door to my car. I started the motor and turned on the windshield wiper. The waitress's words rang in my ears. I would come again, I decided, come hell or Hiawatha, as an aunt of mine who read too much used to say.

Grand and Private Pleasures

THE AWARDING OF THE STARS
CYRIL RAY

Not every Michelin man is as roly-poly as the pneumatic M. Bibendum, the firm's trade-mark—not even those who eat and drink for their living in the service of that meticulous work of gastronomic scholarship, the *Guide Michelin*. Pierre, for instance, one of the *Guide's* anonymous inspectors, is a mere twenty-eight —a slim, tanned, eupeptic youngster who has been a better-than-average Rugby footballer.

It was hard to believe, when I first met him, that here was the experience or the seriousness or the attention to detail that, as a student of the *Guide*, I looked for in its inspectors: I delighted in Pierre's charm; but I doubted his scholarship. His next morning's written report on our first London meal dispelled all doubt; if you had never seen or heard of the restaurant, you could almost have built a scale-model of it in colour from the report, correct as to the materials it was built of, the uniform of its doorman, the system of lighting, and the colour and consistency of the pudding.

Much of the credit for this goes to the standard Michelin form on which Pierre wrote his report. Nothing in the firm's tyre factories or laboratories is a more closely guarded trade secret than these elaborate forms—and I was told impressively in Michelin's Paris office that I am the only outsider ever to have been allowed to see, let alone study and take notes from, a set of them completed.

One side of each concerns itself, under thirty-two suggested sub-headings, with *la classe*—from the apparent wealth and social standing of the restaurant's clients to the view from the terrace; from lavatories to car-park; from the pattern of the carpet to the quality and cleanliness of the cutlery; from welcome to fare-you-well. It is this part of the form that decides how many crossed spoons and forks are awarded (see page twenty of your current *Guide*), from the one, that signifies "plain but good," to the five, that mean *de grand luxe*.

What decides the stars, from the three awarded [in 1961] to only ten restaurants in all France *("Tables memorables, gloires de la cuisine française, grands vins, service impeccable, cadre élégant . . .")* by way of the sixty-three two-star ("worth a *détour*") to the 586 one-star ("good of their kind")—and the inclusion of the other 2,313 restaurants that are worth Michelin's mention at all—is on the other side of the form. Here across fourteen columns the inspector describes, defines and classifies the particular dishes and wines (and the coffee); comments on the menus and wine-lists in general; gives the prices and the size of the portions; and sums up and recommends as to stars, if any.

The present head of Michelin in Paris, André Amiel, argues that as every entry in the Guide is a piece of teamwork, every member of the team must speak the same "language," and the form provides a precise common vocabulary. A star is awarded or withdrawn only after a Michelin "council meeting," probably more than one; the notion is nonsense that a restaurant could lose a star because of a row with one inspector, or gain one by bribery.

The "team" is surprisingly small: Pierre is one of eight travelling inspectors, half of them under thirty, and only two over fifty. They cover all France, hotels and restaurants, every other year (many are reported on oftener than that); and France is so divided into inspection zones, and the inspectors so swap about that their incognito remains pretty safe. Usually the team is recruited from other parts of the Michelin organisation: an inspector will have been a salesman or a buyer or a clerk. Pierre had worked in a bank and in an import-export firm before joining Michelin.

Michelin, I gathered, had confidence in him. Not only in his incorruptibility—that would have been taken for granted. But *"pas de piston pas de pot de vin"* ("no bribery") is one of the slogans in the *Guide,* and Michelin is sternly earnest about integrity, though it doesn't do as some firms might, and pay immensely high salaries and perks as an insurance against the other thing. Pierre is paid little more than he would be earning if he had stayed in the bank. His firm allows him only the commonest and cheapest of French cars, and he works something like eight or nine months of the year on the road, with a couple of months at the editorial office in Paris.

There has to be confidence also in Pierre's objectivity and balance: this is a job for pedants rather than for poets. Pierre says of what he calls the "gastronomic chroniclers" that proliferate in the

French newspapers that even if they are competent and honest, they cannot give fair judgment if they are already known to the restaurant.

We visited five English restaurants together: In London, two fashionable and expensive ones and a medium-priced one. At none was I known by sight, and at each the table was booked in another name. All are in Raymond Postgate's admirable *Good Food Guide,* and all but one, I should have said, justly so—English standards being what they are. It is at Michelin's request that I do not name them: it would be unfair, Michelin points out, to attach their inspectors' criticisms to a specified place on the evidence of one visit. But five such criticisms, not directed at any one place by name, can give a fair idea of English standards.

What soon impressed me about Pierre's critical approach was that he considered each course quite separately, and each major component of a course separately from its sauce, never allowing himself to be swayed by a single solecism or a happy chance into praising or condemning a restaurant as a whole. Thus, at the first (and what I hoped would prove the finest) of the five—a luxurious West End hotel noted for its *cuisine*—the *terrine maison* was dismissed in the following morning's report as (I translate literally) "portion ridiculously small, well enough made, taste not pronounced enough, though a little too salty," whereas the sweetbreads in madeira sauce were "sweetbreads of the finest quality but the sauce too light and airy."

At the other expensive London restaurant, currently very fashionable, his *coquilles St. Jacques* were praised in his subsequent report as "preparation quite classic, although on the menu under a fancy name—the materials perfectly fresh, and the dish therefore good and pleasing," but he said of his neighbour's dish, "they shouldn't call that a *poussin:* it's a broiler."

That restaurant had two dishes in the one-star class—the scallops and the *terrine* which, unlike the first restaurant's, was "good-sized, creamy, fine and delicate, savoury-smelling, strong enough taste . . . good"—and two of which were disastrous (as were the service and, alone among the five, the wines). Pierre wrote of the cheese-board that there was "only a small choice. Took the

Camembert which was too 'advanced' and had been kept in the 'fridge, and a goat's cheese which was commonplace, and the wild strawberries had gone off." His verdict: Three crossed spoons and forks out of five ("very comfortable"); a star not even considered.

To an English eye, these quotations suggest that Pierre is more of a gourmet or a gastronome than modesty will let him admit. But he isn't: he regards himself objectively as a pretty ordinary man working hard at a skilled but by no means esoteric job. In France, its is no more unusual or absurd for a young Rugby footballer to know and to care about food than it is in Russia for a private soldier to be a folk-dancer, or in England to know about motor-bicycles.

Pierre is from Burgundy, where his father is in the wine trade; not only is the root of the matter in him, as in most Frenchmen, but it goes pretty deep. He had a couple of years under instruction on the road once he had been picked for the *Guide;* he was taught to test where possible by the classic dishes, and it makes it easier for a gastronomic guide and inspectors that there *are* classic dishes in France and that every Frenchman knows how they should be made, and what they should taste and look like. He was taught to remember tastes as others remember sights and sounds.

What *I* remembered was that every time a waiter passed behind my chair he jogged the back and his sleeve brushed my hair: and that a squeeze of lemon from the next table splashed me and my next-door neighbour. The difference between the gastronomic chronicler and the Michelin man was that Pierre, while he didn't let this go unnoticed, was still sufficiently unruffled to distinguish between the sweetbreads and the sauce. The *Observer* man was a little bloody-minded all evening.

The more so because this old-established restaurant is one that I have often held to be the best in London, and André Simon has agreed with me. But would it earn even a single star in Michelin? No.

Pierre praised its wines and observed how badly one of them was served and how well the others; he was surprised at what he called the *dissonance* in quality between courses—the *terrine* poor, the *entrée* goodish, though not quite one-star; the cheeses excellent;

the strawberry mousse mawkish. He liked the comfort, the quality of the room and the table furniture, the service of the food (though not altogether the wines), and was surprised that in a restaurant of this class the tables were so close together and the atmosphere so stuffy. He summed it up as being worth five spoons and forks but never a star.

His standard of comparison was the one-star Hôtel Splendide at Bordeaux—presumably because it would have been unkind to apply Paris standards. Not, of course, that a star in Michelin would be given or denied on the strength of one visit: this was a sort of dummy run—to show me how the *Guide* works, and to show Michelin something of London's restaurants.

Far more than I expected, it was poor service or general lack of courtesy that let England down as much as the food. There was some such failure in every one of the five restaurants. At the more modest of the two country hotels (an old-fashioned pub that now goes in for above-average plain cooking) it did not come until the very end, and this is how Pierre told the story in his report: ". . . after lunch, after a walk in the garden, when we went to sit down again in the lounge, the *patron* told us it was closed and almost pushed us through the door! It was three o'clock."

His summing-up, after goodish marks for food, wine, service and a pleasant atmosphere was simply, *"le patron est un mufle,"* and when I looked up *mufle* I found it to mean, "cad, rotter, skunk, boor, dirty dog, bounder." Pierre would have been surprised how many of the same sort I could have shown him: the five restaurants of our choice had been picked to please.

What *did* please Pierre was, in every restaurant but one—and that the fashionable and expensive London one—the selection and the condition (but not the service) of the wines. This I had expected: it is easier to get good wine in England than good food. He liked the quality of the meat: in the medium-priced London restaurant, noted for its roasts, he asked for a second helping of the pork crackling, but was shocked that all the vegetables were tinned or frozen.

Usually, Pierre chose dishes he knew, so that he could judge them by standards he understood. But he met soused herring for the first time, and was delighted *("mariné dans un vinaigre de vin—aromate, très anglais, très bon")*—though it was here that I think he detected cloves in the marinade, where I would swear there were only peppercorns and bay leaves. He was introduced, at the summer country hotel (modish, fairly expensive, with a high current reputation for its food) to *crème brûlée* which, in spite of its name, is a purely English (more precisely, indeed, a Cambridge) dish, and he knew, without my telling him, that it had been badly made (overcooked, I think): he reported it as "a kind of *crème caramel flambée*, good flavour, but the cream doughy and lumpy."

Pierre found everything cheap, but he comes from a country where a lorry driver will spend fifteen shillings on a meal as a matter of daily course. It surprised him in London to see well-dressed business men eating for a mere pound.

Apart from the service (at the smart and fashionable place in London he noted "wine waiter tactless and too familiar"; at the ambitious country place, "service ill-mannered and incompetent") what most disappointed him was the unevenness of even the best of the menus: a *coq au vin* in the smart country hotel that as an individual dish was up to one-star standard ("prepared according to the rule, the flesh excellent, tender and rich; the sauce well-blended and savoury-smelling; the mushrooms and cubes of bacon perfect, and the accompanying vegetables very suitable") was followed by that lumpy, doughy *crème brulée* and a Brie "badly made, in spite of a tempting appearance, and too salty." Perhaps his summing up of this particular restaurant could stand for his English experience as a whole: "The meal was disappointing, the wines magnificent. Perhaps being spoiled by success."

The standards applied are those of an observer with a hawk's eye and a palate like litmus paper. When in Paris a few days later we had lunch together at a small one-star restaurant, Pierre had *beignets de langoustines* (which the French are already beginning to call *scampi*). We began early, and half-an-hour or so later, as we drank our coffee, Pierre noticed that they were having the same dish at the next table. Quite casually, in the middle of talk about something else, Pierre observed, "It's time they changed the oil they're frying those *beignets* in: look how dark they're getting."

The *Guide Michelin* has been applying that sort of eye to the French restaurants for sixty years, and who can say with how much benefit to the present standard of French catering? If it started a Guide to Britain, it could do the same service here, I believe—but sixty years wouldn't be a minute too long.

The Observer, July 16, 1961

Editor's note: When the first Michelin *Guide to Great Britain and Ireland* was published fourteen years later, in 1975, only a handful of hostelries were distinguished by a single star; none was awarded a higher rating.

GOURMET'S FRANCE

GREAT CHEFS OF FRANCE

Gardening for Cooks

THE NEW SETTLEMENT COOKBOOK

BREAD

HERBS IN THE KITCHEN

CHEESE

AMERICAN HERITAGE COOKBOOK

JOY OF COOKING

FANNIE MERRITT FARMER

5

"Cookery is Become an Art"

PERFECTION

It takes years of study and experience to produce a perfect dish. I have spent my life perfecting five or six dishes. I will serve only these, but I will be sure of doing them perfectly.
—MME. FILLIOUX, CHEF AT LA MÈRE FILLIOUX, LYONS

Change a recipe? Why, madame, I began cooking at this restaurant when I was twenty years old, in 1929, and I have served three generations of the same families. People come here expecting to find the same grilled kidneys, my special *sole meunière* and pork roasted with bits of garlic, and my *clafouti*. To change recipes would be to disappoint my clientele.
—MME. GERMAINE SAUNIÈRE, CHEF AT AU COCHON D'OR, PARIS

The great sin in cookery is indulgence, sentimentality, flowery rhetoric.
—JOSEPH DELTEIL

He who flatters the cook never goes hungry.
—OLD PROVERB

MURDER IN THE KITCHEN
ALICE B. TOKLAS

When we first began reading Dashiell Hammett, Gertrude Stein remarked that it was his modern note to have disposed of his victims before the story commenced. Goodness knows how many were required to follow as the result of the first crime. And so it is in the kitchen. Murder and sudden death seem as unnatural there as they should be anywhere else. They can't, they can never become acceptable facts. Food is far too pleasant to combine with horror. All the same, facts, even distasteful facts, must be accepted and we shall see how, before any story of cooking begins, crime is inevitable. That is why cooking is not an entirely agreeable pastime. There is too much that must happen in advance of the actual cooking. This doesn't of course apply to food that emerges stainless from the deep freeze. But the marketing and cooking I know are French and it was in France, where freezing units are unknown, that in due course I graduated at the stove. . . .

The only way to learn to cook is to cook, and for me, as for so many others, it suddenly and unexpectedly became a disagreeable necessity to have to do it when war came and Occupation followed. It was in those conditions of rationing and shortage that I learned not only to cook seriously but to buy food in a restricted market and not to take too much time in doing it, since there were so many more important and amusing things to do. It was at this time, then, that murder in the kitchen began.

The first victim was a lively carp brought to the kitchen in a covered basket from which nothing could escape. The fish man who sold me the carp said he had no time to kill, scale or clean it, nor would he tell me with which of these horrible necessities one began. It wasn't difficult to know which was the most repellent. So quickly to the murder and have it over with. On the docks of Puget Sound I had seen fishermen grasp the tail of a huge salmon and lifting it high bring it down on the dock with enough force to kill it. Obviously I was not a fisherman nor was the kitchen table a dock. Should I not dispatch my first victim with a blow on the head from a heavy mallet? After an appraising glance at the lively fish it was evident he would escape attempts aimed at his head. A heavy sharp knife came to my mind as the classic, the perfect choice, so grasping, with my left hand covered with a dishcloth, for the teeth might be sharp, the lower jaw of the carp, and the knife in my right, I carefully, deliberately found the base of its vertebral column and plunged the knife in. I let go my grasp and looked to see what had happened. Horror of horrors. The carp was dead, killed, assassinated, murdered in the first, second and third degree. Limp, I fell into a chair, with my hands still unwashed reached for a cigarette, lighted it, and waited for the police to come and take me into custody. After a second cigarette my courage returned and I went to prepare poor Mr. Carp for the table. I scraped off the scales, cut off the fins, cut open the underside and emptied out a great deal of what I did not care to look at. . . .

It was in the market of Palma de Mallorca that our French cook tried to teach me to murder by smothering. There is no reason why this crime should have been committed publicly or that I should have been expected to participate. Jeanne was just showing off. When the crowd of market women who had gathered about her began screaming and gesticulating, I retreated. When we met later to drive back in the carry-all filled with our marketing to Terreno where we had a villa I refused to sympathise with Jeanne. She said the Mallorcans were bloodthirsty, didn't they go to bullfights and pay an advanced price for the meat of the beasts they had seen killed in the ring, didn't they prefer to chop off the heads of the innocent pigeons instead of humanely smothering them which was the way to prevent all fowl from bleeding to death and make them fuller and tastier. Had not she tried to explain this to them, to teach them, to show them how an intelligent humane person went about killing pigeons, but no they didn't want to learn, they preferred their own brutal ways. At lunch when she served the pigeons Jeanne discreetly said nothing. Discussing food which she enjoyed above everything had been discouraged at table. But her fine black eyes were eloquent. If the small-sized pigeons the island produced had not achieved jumbo size, squabs they unquestionably were, and larger and more succulent squabs than those we had eaten at the excellent restaurant at Palma.

Later we went back to Paris and then there was war and after a lifetime there was peace. One day passing the *concierge*'s *loge* he called me and said he had something someone had left for us. He said he would bring it to me, which he did and which I wished he hadn't when I saw what it was, a crate of six white pigeons and a note from a friend saying she had nothing better to offer us from her home in the country, ending with But as Alice is clever she will make something delicious of them. It is certainly a mistake to allow a reputation for cleverness to be born and spread by loving friends.

It is so cheaply acquired and so dearly paid for. Six white pigeons to be smothered, to be plucked, to be cleaned and all this to be accomplished before Gertrude Stein returned for she didn't like to see work being done. If only I had the courage the two hours before her return would easily suffice. A large cup of strong black coffee would help. This was before a lovely Brazilian told me that in her country a large cup of black coffee was always served before going to bed to ensure a good night's rest. Not yet having acquired this knowledge the black coffee made me lively and courageous. I carefully found the spot on poor innocent Dove's throat where I was to press and pressed. The realization had never come to me before that one saw with one's fingertips as well as with one's eyes. It was a most unpleasant experience, though as I laid out one by one the sweet young corpses there was no denying one could become accustomed to murdering. . . .

The Alice B. Toklas Cook Book

THE MOLNAR "CASE"

Everyone in New York literary circles knows about the Molnar "case." Ferenc Molnar, author of *Liliom* and a dozen other plays, lives* in the Plaza Hotel, in one room. If you are fortunate enough to be invited into this retreat, Molnar will take you at once to see his "kitchenette." It is in the clothes closet, in a steamer trunk. . . . The top drawer contains various cheeses; the next all sorts of crackers and condiments; fruit preserves are in the next; coffee and tea and eggs fill up another drawer; and in the bottom one, where ordinary men carry their shoes, Molnar keeps the silver. There is an electric percolator and an electric stewpan on a small table. [As a cook] the famous playwright is famous for his *fondue bonne femme.*

—ILES BRODY
On the Tip of My Tongue

*Molnar died in 1952.

NOEL COWARD AS COOK AND BOTTLE WASHER
COLE LESLEY

Apart from a statuesque lady called Doris who came in the mornings and laguidly vacuumed, we had no domestic help whatever at Spithead Lodge [across the Sound from Hamilton, Bermuda]. A cook was not to be had for love or the large amount of money we offered, and so we did the cooking ourselves. I was by now an efficient all-round cook except that I scrupulously avoided anything to do with flour; the making of pastry, pies, cakes and soufflés to this day remains to me a deep mystery, and all these were the things Noel particularly liked to eat. He, knowing as little as I about the subject, regarded this as a splendid challenge which he of course would overcome, as he did [and as Noel's journal shows]:

> Our kitchen scenes are good sound slapstick comedy and the cursing and swearing and getting in each other's way adds up to some nice clean belly laughs. It seems to me that I do nothing but buy things. I go to the Super Mart for one tin of tomato purée and come out wheeling a barrow piled to the skies with comestibles for which there is No Room at the Inn. But still, while the cooking craze lasts, I had better give it its head. We have electric frying-pans, waffle-irons, egg-beaters, percolators, pressure-saucepans, double-boilers, cake-tins, moulds and a sea of bowls. We also have shelves crowded with canned herbs, canned fruit, canned meat, canned everything. I have so far made, unaided, pancakes, chocolate cake, coffee mousse, crab mousse and a sensational Yorkshire pudding.

He also boasted that he had made a consommé devoutly to be wished. A most unexpected sideline to Noel's culinary activities was that he genuinely loved to do the washing-up. He didn't want to help to dry, he wanted to plunge his arms up to his elbows in the greasy suds, and scoured the pots and pans until they were all shining bright and clinically clean.

The weather in August became grillingly hot with high humidity and so, although the kitchen was large and pleasant, one wore as little as possible while the oven and the gas-rings were on. Noel, alone one morning, was, in fact, wearing nothing at all except Doris's little plastic apron patterned with rosebuds, when a dignified-looking gentleman appeared at the kitchen door and explained that he was the Bishop of Bermuda. Noel said, "How do you do," and would the Bishop give him *one* moment to see how his vol-au-vent cases were getting on. Bending over to see how they were getting on involved exposing his bare bottom (bare except for the rosebudded bow tied above it) and by the time he straightened himself and turned from the oven, the Bishop had fled and never called again.

Remembered Laughter

AN EXPLORER COOKS IN ANTARCTICA
ADM. RICHARD E. BYRD

Breakfast didn't count. I rarely took more than tea and a whole-wheat biscuit. Lunch was habitually an out-of-the-can affair, consisting usually of tomato juice, Eskimo biscuits, and frequently a cold meat or fish—either corned beef, tongue, or sardines. These I prepared in masterly fashion. But supper, by rights the high spot in an explorer's day, the hot meal toward which a cold and hungry man looks with mounting anticipation—this meal for a while was a daily fiasco.

I have only to close my eyes to witness again the succession of culinary disasters. Consider what my diary designated as The Corn Meal Incident. Into a boiler I dumped what seemed a moderate quantity of meal, added a little water, and stood it on the stove to boil. The simple formula gave birth to a Hydra-headed monster. The stuff began to swell and dry up, swell and dry up, with fearful blowing and sucking noises. All innocently I added water, more water and still more water. Whereupon the boiler erupted like Vesuvius. All the pots and pans within reach couldn't begin to contain the corn meal that overflowed. It oozed over the stove. It spattered the ceiling. It covered me from head to foot. If I hadn't acted resolutely, I might have been drowned in corn meal. Seizing the container in my mittened hands, I rushed it to the door and hurled it far into the food tunnel. There it continued to give off deadly golden lava until the cold finally stilled the crater.

There were other disasters of the same order. There was the Dried Lima Beans Incident of April 10th ("It's amazing," the diary reports soberly, "how much water lima beans can absorb, and how long it takes them to cook. At supper time I had enough half-cooked lima beans to feed a ship's company.") My first jelly dessert bounded like a rubber ball under my knife; the flapjacks had to be scraped from the pan with a chisel. "And you, the man who sat at a thousand banquets," goes the accusing entry of April 12th.) I dreaded banquets before I went to Advance Base; and I have come to dread them since. But in April's dark hours I ransacked my memory, trying to remember what they were like. All that I could recall was *filet mignon* spiced and darkened to the color of an old cavalry boot; or lobster thermidor; or squabs perched on triangles of toast, or chicken salad heaped on billowing lettuce. All these were far beyond the simple foods in my larder. When I did experiment the results filled the shack with pungent burning smells and coated the skillets with awful gummy residues. But in spite of the missing cook book, the record was not one of unmitigated failure. Resolved to make a last stand, I took the surviving chicken, hung it for two days from a nail over the stove to thaw, boiled it all one day, seasoned it with salt and pepper, and served. The soup, which was an unexpected by-product, was delicious; that night I broached a bottle of cider and drank a toast to Escoffier.

Alone

VIRGINIA WOOLF TEACHES BREAD-BAKING
LOUIE MAYER

There was one thing in the kitchen that Mrs. Woolf was very good at doing: she could make beautiful bread. The first thing she asked me when I went to Monks House [as cook] was if I knew how to make it. I told her that I had made some for my family, but I was not expert at it. "I will come into the kitchen, Louie," she said, "and show you how to do it. We always have made our own bread." I was surprised how complicated the process was and how accurately Mrs. Woolf carried it out. She showed me how to make the dough with the right quantities of yeast and flour, and then how to knead it. She returned three or four times during the morning to knead it again. Finally, she made the dough into the shape of a cottage loaf and baked it at just the right temperature. I would say that Mrs. Woolf was not a practical person—for instance, she could not sew or knit or drive a car—but this was a job needing practical skill which she was able to do well every time.

Recollections of Virginia Woolf, ed. Joan Russell Nobel

BALLAD OF CULINARY FRUSTRATION
PHYLLIS McGINLEY

The world is full of wistful ones who hoard their souvenirs.
The spinster keeps a faded rose through all the faded years,
A travel folder lures the clerk while he dreams of a foreign sky,
But I preserve the recipes I'll never dare to try.

> Vichyssoise, bouillabaisse,
>   Terrapin mousse,
> Cucumber hollandaise,
>   Staffordshire goose,
> Oh, the ginger, the clove,
>   Oh, the sauces well-shaken!
> But here on my stove
>   Broils the liver-and-bacon.

On idle days, on rainy days, when all the world is shut out,
I con the yellowed clippings of the recipes I've cut out.
And lovingly I memorize directions neatly pasted,
For scones and soups and savories I've never even tasted.

With eggs and with syrup,
  With herbs and with cream,
I fancy I stir up
  An epicure's dream
Of Netherland crumb cakes,
  Of sweetbreads-in-mustard;
Of pasties and plumcakes
  And Devonshire custard.

Oh, some folks dote on serious tomes, some read romances
    rippling,
But a cookbook is my Odyssey, my Shakespeare and my
    Kipling.
For while I baste the leg of lamb or stir the tapioca,
I'm visioning a vol-au-vent, or a nougat à la Mocha—

Some gossamer trifle
  That gourmets adore,
As French as the Eiffel
  (And probably more),
Like mushrooms and spices
  And artichoke hearts,
And aspics and ices
  And shortbreads and tarts,
With crusts that are thinner
  Than seafoam on top . . .
My menu for dinner?
  We're having a chop.
                              A Pocketful of Wry

Lady.—If thou be indeed a lady, remember thou art by name a cook, or at least a baker. La- means a loaf of bread; -dy means a maid; and lady means breadmaid.

                                        —E. S. DALLAS

Home Bread Maker

The expert bread maker tends to smugness. So intense is the satisfaction with the product that it promotes self-satisfaction. If you don't believe this, watch the expression on a woman's face when she announces, "It's home made."

—Dorothy Thompson

Higher Education for Haute Cuisine

For most of us, the possibility of eating well depends upon the skill and passion of the amateur cook, and learning the art should now be regarded as essential to an educated man or woman. At Oxford and Cambridge, for example, I should like to see a stove installed in every undergraduate's room and the College dining-halls transformed into supermarkets and liquor stores.

—W. H. Auden

Southern Fried Chicken
WILLIAM STYRON

Of all indigenous American culinary triumphs, probably the most put-upon, misunderstood, and generally abused is the Southern fried chicken which in its pure state almost no one ever gets to eat. The abuse is usually justifiable. What does "Southern fried chicken" ordinarily conjure up? To many people it signifies only memories of the great automobile routes wending southward from Washington, D.C., through Virginia and the Carolinas and Georgia, and those squat, slatternly roadside restaurants whose signs bid one to EAT (the noun-variant is EATS, and though our language is incontestably the noblest on earth, there is a raw anorexia-producing quality in such words that makes one understand why French is the gourmet tongue), and whose personnel and glum interiors bespeak such a basic non-interest in food that the effect—were it not for the pervasive air of commerce—is almost ascetic. In such places Southern fried chicken is invariably the specialty, and similarly a travesty and a blight; there is no wonder that Southern fried chicken has received such a bad name, considering the ignominy it has undergone in these miserable establishments.

A sullen, dark scullion-maid is sent next door (it is considered profitable to run these places in conjunction with a chicken yard*), instructed to wring the neck of the largest, most superannuated laying hen she can put her hands on. This she does, and then the enormous fowl is most cursorily plucked, eviscerated, and cut up for frying. Frying of course means something called "deep fry," which is to say that the owner has bought a large stainless steel vat, in which it is possible to allow several gallons of peanut oil to simmer for days on end without undergoing any significant evaporation. (It is the odor of rancid peanut oil, incidentally, that numbs the buds of smell, and gives to these places, all of them, such a gray, mercifully half-perceived, oleaginous aroma). Needless to say, to "deep fry"—to immerse rather than properly to fry—is not to fry at all, it is to pickle. As in the pickling process, deep frying allows for maximum permeation (in this instance, of grease) and is at the same time extremely economical, analagously resembling, let us say, the tasteless compression of frozen orange juice, or, even better, that marvel of American food technocracy which Kafka invented—the packaged breakfast cereal which is called not a breakfast food, not even a cereal, but simply "K." But worst of all is that this Southern fried chicken tastes horrible, it is both unpalatable and indigestible (at least that Kellogg product is not downright harmful); and one of our greatest national shames is that we have no central governing body, as the French have with Cognac and Roquefort, which might make mandatory certain controls over what could be, and should be, one of the greatest glories of our native cuisine. As it is, we have grease-soaked, old, pickled chicken, and I should like to venture my conviction that to rectify this disgrace is at the moment at least as

*This essay dates from *ca.* 1960. Chicken yards, which were once able to produce superior poultry, have all but vanished from the land. However, most Southern restaurants are capable of wreaking the same havoc with chickens from Perdue or Paramount. —W.S.

important as, say, the winning of the Davis cup, or possibly even a Nobel Prize for anything.

Southern fried chicken can be sublime. It is basically simple to produce, but one must be attentive and careful always. Most Southern fried chicken (I am not even thinking now of the unspeakable highway restaurants) is ruined in the home by inattentiveness, by insouciance, by the idea of—well, it's just a chicken to fry, I'll throw it in the pan. No attitude could be more disastrous, and for the production of truly great Southern fried chicken it should be remembered that at least one and a half hours of sober, selfless, undeviating effort must be spent in order to produce a satisfactory result. If this discipline be observed (and pride be taken in the fact, that this discipline must be as exacting, and can be as rewarding, as that which created *coq au vin*), the result may be a triumph. But without discipline, without attentiveness— nothing. You *cannot* go into the other room and booze it up with your waiting guests.

First, the chicken must be very young and very tender, therefore rather small—"broiler" size. Much as one might dislike the idea of frozen meat, the fact remains that most frozen chicken parts are usually smaller and more tender than those available at the butcher's counter. Certainly they are more succulent, in the final outcome, than those mammoth legs and breasts sold by the butcher as "fryers," so I suggest that unless you can get an authentic spring chicken from your butcher, you choose the frozen parts put up by Birdseye, Swanson, etc.* Secondly, the covering—the carapace. There is a school, developed mainly in the State of Maryland, which holds that, before cooking, the chicken parts should be immersed in some sort of "batter." This is absolute rubbish. Southern fried chicken should have after cooking a firm, well-developed crust—this is one of its glories—but the "batter" principle simply won't hold up after pragmatic examination. The "batter," usually made of corn meal and cream and all sorts of extraneous substances, causes a thick shell to form over the

*Again, times have changed. Fresh chicken parts are more readily available now, and are of course recommended. —W.S.

chicken after cooking, so that there is a genuine discreteness involved: "batter," carapace and chicken interior tend to fall apart from one another, whereas an indissolubility of chicken and outer covering is what is needed. Simple flour, therefore, is the answer —flour liberally laced beforehand with salt and pepper. I cannot emphasize this "no-batter" or "no–Chicken à la Maryland" principle enough. Naturally people should eat fried chicken in their fingers, and if you have ever been to a dinner where fried chicken Maryland-style was served, and have observed how the superfluous outer covering of "batter" pulls away from the chicken, without sense or savor, into people's teeth, you will understand what I mean. Flour—simple flour—on the other hand, merges and melds with the chicken in cooking, and therefore should always be used. But remember again that the flour should be seasoned with salt and pepper before dipping the chicken into it. Now we are almost ready, but here come the most critical items of all: what kind of fat? how much fat? how long should the chicken be cooked?

I'm afraid that only bacon fat will really do. Crisco or its imitators, Wesson Oil, peanut oil, and so forth, will suffice, but only pure bacon drippings—uncontaminated by any other kind of fat, especially the tallowing fat of the lamb—should be used, short of the craziest emergency. I do not know why this is so, except that chicken fried in bacon fat simply tastes better—I have tried them all—and that should do, for the purposes of this essay.*

As for the second question, it is extremely important to recognize that we are not deep frying; indeed, we are doing almost the exact opposite: we are *shallow* frying, and the more shallow the fat the better. The point is critical, as I tried to indicate earlier about "deep fry" and its consequences. Let us have no fastidiousness when we

*In one of the most humiliating notices I have ever received, the eminent food critic Craig Claiborne, reviewing the book in which this essay first appeared, belabored me severely for my recommendation of bacon fat. I could not have been more hurt had one of my novels been attacked by Edmund Wilson. In retrospect, I see that Claiborne was at least partially justified, though perhaps for the wrong reason. Claiborne, I believe, was criticizing the use of bacon fat on the grounds of palatability. I would still say that this saturated fat contributes fine taste but that we know now that it is bad for the health (besides being poorly digestible) and therefore vegetable oil is a better cooking medium. —W.S.

come to this matter: one half inch, repeat, one half inch, *at the most,* is the optimum depth of fat in the pan, and there should be an effort to maintain this depth (more or less and with considerable give and take, in spite of my strictures) throughout the entire cooking process. The possible permeation of fat is at all costs to be avoided, and one half inch, more or less, seems to represent a tolerable limit. (There is also a covered-pan vs. open-pan controversy which enters here, and is not worth dealing with: people who cook with a covered pan—"all wishfully blind," as Hopkins says—are simply not concerned with immediacy, or with the fact that the entire chicken is getting hopelessly soggy with steam.)

Medium heat throughout is best, though it may be high at the very first. There are schools which hold that the fat should be popping hot before the floured chicken parts are added to the pan, but it makes no difference whatsoever; I have seen superb Southern fried chicken emerge after the parts have been added to the cold fat. Practicality, however, dictates that, generally, speaking, the fat *will* be hot, if only because it almost invariably needs to be melted in order to cover the bottom of the pan. The cooking time itself is the most speculative aspect of the whole process. No attention should be paid to cookbooks which ordain no more than 40, or 45, or 50 minutes. Experience has taught me that a leg or a thigh, being relatively small, will usually consume no more than 30 or 35 minutes of cooking time, while a large breast may well take a full hour. Chicken livers (essential to a good giblet gravy) should take no more than eight or ten minutes. In the last analysis, the color of the chicken and the consistency of the crust should be the only determinants. The color should be a rich golden brown, and it is always better to err in favor of over-doneness, rather than that under-doneness, pale and tan in color, which can only result in a certain sogginess. Likewise, the crust itself should be firm and brittle, "crackly" in texture, and again it is better to favor a small amount of overcooking to achieve this end, if necessary. During the cooking process it must be remembered that *constant turning of the parts* is essential. I cannot emphasize this too much. Only in this way will uniformity of color, crust and general texture be achieved, and only such steady devotion can enable one to produce true Southern fried chicken which, incidentally, is best eaten with rice and giblet gravy and *always,* as I have pointed out, conveyed to the mouth with the fingers.

The Artists' & Writers' Cookbook

A MISSIONARY CHRISTMAS AT SANTA FE, 1851
WILLA CATHER

The young Bishop's pen flew over the paper, leaving a trail of fine, finished French script behind, in violet ink.

"My new study, dear brother, as I write, is full of the delicious fragrance of the piñon logs burning in my fire-place. (We use this kind of cedar-wood altogether for fuel, and it is highly aromatic, yet delicate. At our meanest tasks we have a perpetual odour of incense about us.) I wish that you, and my dear sister, could look in upon this scene of comfort and peace. We missionaries wear a frock-coat and wide-brimmed hat all day, you know, and look like American traders. What a pleasure to come home at night and put on my old cassock! I feel more like a priest then—for so much of the day I must be a 'business man'!—and, for some reason, more like a Frenchman. . . .

"To-night we are exiles, happy ones, thinking of home. Father Joseph has sent away our Mexican woman,—he will make a good cook of her in time, but tonight he is preparing our Christmas dinner himself. I had thought he would be worn out to-day, for he has been conducting a Novena of High Masses, as is the custom here before Christmas. After the Novena, and the midnight Mass last night, I supposed he would be willing to rest to-day; but not a bit of it. You know his motto, 'Rest in action.' I brought him a bottle of olive-oil on my horse all the way from Durango (I say 'olive-oil,' because here 'oil' means something to grease the wheels of wagons!), and he is making some sort of cooked salad. We have no green vegetables here in winter, and no one seems ever to have heard of that blessed plant, the lettuce. Joseph finds it hard to do without salad-oil, he always had it in Ohio, though it was a great extravagance. He has been in the kitchen all afternoon. There is only an open fire-place for cooking, and an earthen roasting-oven out in the court-yard. But he has never failed me in anything yet; and I think I can promise you that to-night two Frenchmen will sit down to a good dinner and drink your health." . . .

"Monseigneur est servi! Alors, Jean, veux-tu apporter les bougies?"

The Bishop carried the candles into the dining-room, where the table was laid and Father Vaillant was changing his cook's apron for his cassock. Crimson from standing over an open fire, his rugged face was even homelier than usual—though one of the first things a stranger decided upon meeting Father Joseph was that the Lord had made few uglier men. He was short, skinny, bow-legged from a life on horseback, and his countenance had little to recommend it but kindness and vivacity. He looked old, though he was then about forty. His skin was hardened and seamed by exposure to weather in a bitter climate, his neck scrawny and wrinkled like an old man's. A bold, blunt-tipped nose, positive chin, a very large mouth,—the lips thick and succulent but never loose, never relaxed, always stiffened by effort or working with excitement. His hair, sunburned to the shade of dry hay, had originally been tow-coloured; *"Blanchet"* ("Whitey") he was always called at the Seminary. . . .

On coming into the dining room, Bishop Latour placed his candlesticks over the fire-place, since there were already six upon the table, illuminating the brown soup-pot. After they had stood for a moment in prayer, Father Joseph lifted the cover and ladled the soup into the plates, a dark onion soup with croutons. The Bishop tasted it critically and smiled at his companion. After the spoon had travelled to his lips a few times, he put it down and leaning back in his chair remarked,

"Think of it, *Blanchet;* in all this vast country between the Mississippi and the Pacific Ocean, there is probably not another human being who could make a soup like this."

"Not unless he is a Frenchman," said Father Joseph. He had tucked a napkin over the front of his cassock and was losing no time in reflection.

"I am not deprecating your individual talent, Joseph," the Bishop continued, "but, when one thinks of it, a soup like this is not the work of one man. It is the result of a constantly refined tradition. There are nearly a thousand years of history in this soup."

Father Joseph frowned intently at the earthen pot in the middle of the table. His pale, near-sighted eyes had always the look of peering into distance. *"C'est ça, c'est vrai,"* he murmured. "But how," he exclaimed as he filled the Bishop's plate again, "how can a man make a proper soup without leeks, that king of vegetables? We cannot go on eating onions for ever."

After carrying away the *soupière,* he brought in the roast chicken and *pommes sautées.* "And salad, Jean," he continued as he began to carve. "Are we to eat dried beans and roots for the rest of our lives? Surely we must find time to make a garden. Ah, my garden at Sandusky! And you could snatch me away from it! You will admit that you never ate better lettuces in France. And my vineyard; a natural habitat for the vine, that. I tell you, the shores of Lake Erie will be covered with vineyards one day. I envy the man who is drinking my wine. Ah well, that is a missionary's life; to plant where another shall reap."

As this was Christmas Day, the two friends were speaking in their native tongue. . . . Father Joseph began gently to coax the cork from a bottle of red wine with his fingers. "This I begged for your dinner at the hacienda where I went to baptize the baby on St. Thomas's Day. It is not easy to separate these rich Mexicans from their French wine. They know its worth." He poured a few drops and tried it. "A slight taste of the cork; they do not know how to keep it properly. However, it is quite good enough for missionaries."

Death Comes for the Archbishop

TOULOUSE-LAUTREC AND HIS LOBSTER À LA DRAWING ROOM
PAUL LECLERCQ

He was a great gourmand. He always carried a little grater and a nutmeg to flavor the glasses of port he drank. He loved to talk about cooking and knew of many rare recipes for making the most standard dishes, for in this, as in all else, Lautrec had a hatred of useless frills. And like a good Southerner, the more he valued straightforward cooking, the more he despised the doubtful and pretentious chemistry of restaurants and palace hotels.

According to Lautrec, the exact amount of cooking, the quality of the butter and the spices, and a great deal of care, were the secrets of keeping a good table. He loved dishes which had been simmered slowly for hours and seasoned with perfect art. He tasted old vintages and liqueurs as a connoisseur. When he clapped his tongue against his palate and pronounced such a Burgundy to be like a 'peacock's tail in the mouth,' one was assured that the bouquet of the wine was fruity and rich.

Lautrec cooked as well as he ate. Cooking a leg of lamb for seven hours or preparing a lobster à l'Américaine held no secrets for him.

Knowing this liking for lobster, our friend, Georges Henri-Manuel, once asked him to his home to prepare one of these shellfish. Apart from Lautrec . . . I was the only guest. . . .

Henri-Manuel lived in a rather spacious apartment full of furniture and antique knick-knacks, shined and polished with all the care that only a bachelor could give them. We arrived for dinner at the Rue François at the appointed time and our host first of all wanted to show us the kitchen quarters, where everything was carefully set out for making the famous lobster dish.

Lautrec energetically refused even to put a foot inside. He declared his intention of preparing the lobster in the drawing room on an electric hot plate. . . . Georges Henri-Manuel, in great anguish because a lobster à l'Américaine has to be cut up alive, hastily covered his most precious pieces of furniture with sheets. Then, wrapped in a long white apron in which his short legs kept getting entangled, brandishing a spoon as long as himself, and moving saucepans about, Lautrec prepared the lobster à l'Américaine whose memory lingers with me yet.

He took such care in the preparation that no damage was done to the drawing room and then, and only then, did Henri-Manuel breathe again.

THE EDUCATION OF JULIA CHILD
CALVIN TOMKINS

... The Childs found a comfortable third-floor apartment on the Rue de l'Université, behind the Chambre des Députés. . . . At first, Julia spent most of her time at Berlitz, struggling with the language. Both the Childs readily concede that at this point her cooking left a good deal to be desired. Paul knew and appreciated good food, but Julia, like many American women of her background, had never really learned to cook at home, and until she married Paul she had never been interested in learning. In the fall of 1949, though, she was sufficiently interested to enroll in a special early-morning course at the Cordon Bleu cooking school, where she found herself the only woman student—the twelve others were ex-G.I.s, learning cooking on the G.I. Bill of Rights. "I would leave home at seven in the morning, cook all morning with the G.I.s, and then rush home to make lunch for Paul," Julia remembers. "I'd give him the béarnaise or the hollandaise sauce I'd just learned, or something equally rich. In about a week we both got terribly bilious. . . ."

Two of the three chefs whom Julia had as teachers were in their seventies: Max Bugnard, who had owned his own restaurant in Brussels before the war, and Claude Thillmont, for many years the pastry chef at the Café de Paris. The third was a younger man— Pierre Mangelatte, who was the chef at an excellent small restaurant in Montmartre, the Restaurant des Artistes.

"Bugnard was a marvellous meat cook, a marvellous sauce-maker, wonderful with stocks and vegetables, although not so much so with desserts," Julia recalls. "As a young man, he had known Escoffier. Chef Thillmont had worked in the twenties with Mme. Saint-Ange on her great cookbook, *Le Livre de Cuisine de Mme. Saint-Ange,* now unfortunately out of print. Those two men knew just about everything there was to know. And in the afternoons we would have demonstration classes by Mangelatte, who was a brilliant technician." Julia had just enough French by this time to keep up with the instruction. Her interest in the subject, she found, was limitless. "Until I got into cooking," she once said, "I was never *really* interested in anything."

"Good Cooking," The New Yorker, December 23, 1974

COOKING LESSONS AT DINTY MOORE'S
SHANA ALEXANDER

Dinty Moore's came floating up out of my past, all its lights ablaze, polished brass and mirrors gleaming—a gala, ghostly cruise ship bearing my childhood back to me.

Moore's was the best restaurant in New York City, and I grew up there, dining out once a week or so with my parents from the time I was old enough to hold a fork.

Moore's was a self-contained, white-tile universe, so Irish that years later when I landed in Dublin, I felt utterly at home. Ireland seemed a larger, much-diluted, open-air Moore's. The white-tiled kitchen in the rear was wide open to public view, and my sister and I had cooking lessons there after school. While our classmates were wearing white gloves and learning the right way to fox-trot, we wore big white tablecloths tied around us, waiter-style, and learned the right way to cook carrots and peas (rapidly, with a pinch of sugar) and potatoes (unpeeled, with a handful of salt).

Our teacher was the old man himself. Everyone called him "the old man," including his family. To his face he was "Mr. Moore," or "Jim." Nobody ever called him "Dinty," not even the cartoonist George McManus, who immortalized him in his abrasive comic strip "Bringing Up Father."

McManus was right about the long-smoldering warfare of the Irish household. In the Moore family nobody talked to anybody else if he could help it. Mr. Moore and his wife occupied separate floors above the restaurant and had not spoken in decades; the children rarely spoke either, except to borrow some money, or to plot against one parent or the other.

The old man believed there was only one right way to do everything. All food must be young and all ingredients perfectly fresh. The only acceptable canned food is applesauce. The only cooking sherry is Harvey's Bristol Cream. Hamburgers can only be made from prime rib. Female lobsters are sweeter. Cooking is concentration. "Watch everything on the stove," he told us, "the way you watch a piece of toast."

When the old man went to Palm Beach in winter he sent back daily postcards: "Caught a tuna today; crust on pot pie should not be too thick." "Weather beautiful; put enough barley in soup." Each vacation at least twenty-five postcards arrived, every one a reminder to prepare the food exactly as it had been prepared for a quarter century.

Mr. Moore had rigid standards. Leaving your mother and gambling were unforgivable; larceny was lower down the scale. When my mother protested that Jim should not waste his time and energy making up elaborate food hampers to send to my sister and me at camp, he told her he had to do the monthly baskets anyway "for the boys up the river."

In hot weather, you had to avoid iced drinks; sip warm soup instead. When my sister visited Jim in Florida and got a bad sunburn, he knew what to do: "Soak a large linen handkerchief in ice cubes in a silver bowl. Wring out in Gordon's gin . . . must be Gordon's . . . and apply to affected parts." She swore it worked like a charm.

In memory, the old man is a wobble of chins, an aroma of bay rum, a shirt front of creamy pongee, a fine London suit with a cuff of long underwear peeking out, a pink, just-barbered face and a few long strands of hair plastered on gleaming scalp. From him I learned inflexible rules about everything that is most important in life—food, sex, death and deportment. The sex lecture occurred when I was twelve or thirteen. One wintry night he glanced at me sharply, then bellowed, "Moran: Bring me a plate of oysters. Don't open 'em." Years before the waiter had got a $500 tip for placing a $5,000 bet on the Dempsey-Firpo fight, and surprises after that were anticlimax. Moran presented the bivalves without comment, and Mr. Moore deftly opened one with the tiny gold penknife on his watch chain. He thrust the mucid, cold object under my nose, rapped his big knuckles hard on the table to rivet my attention and said sternly, "Listen here, girlie! An oyster has everything *you* have. So don't leave your mother when her hair turns gray." So much for the facts of life. I was a woman now.

As he aged, the old man badly missed his departed cronies, and one quiet afternoon the absurdity of their absence grew intolerable. He fixed up two packages wrapped in parchment paper and tied in butcher string, climbed into the open, cream-colored, wicker-sided Packard that always stood in front of the door, and instructed his chauffeur to drive to the Hebrew cemetery. At the grave of his friend Sam Harris, the theatrical producer, the old man placed a beautiful hunk of his own corned beef and reminded him aloud how inconsiderate he had been to die young. By the time Jim had driven on to Mount Calvary and the grave of George M. Cohan, he was steaming mad. The other parcel was a fish, which he beat against the headstone. "Cohan!" he shouted. "In case you don't know, today's Friday, and I just want you to see what you're missing!"

Our world very much misses men like Jim Moore. He was more than a man with absolute standards; he was a man who lived up to those standards—publicly; like his kitchen, his life and his foibles were totally exposed. His cards were always on the table along with the food.

Talking Woman

THE ITALIAN ART OF EATING
MARCELLA HAZAN

An Italian meal is a story told from nature, taking its rhythms, its humors, its bounty and turning them into episodes for the senses. As nature is not a one-act play, so an Italian meal cannot rest on a single dish. It is instead a lively sequence of events, alternating the crisp with the soft and yielding, the pungent with the bland, the variable with the staple, the elaborate with the simple.

It takes a theme such as "fish," states it very gently in a simple antipasto of tender, boiled young squid delicately seasoned with olive oil, parsley, and lemon, contrasts it with a rich and creamy shrimp risotto, and restates it with a superbly broiled bass that sums up every pure and natural quality with which fish has been endowed. All this subsides in a tart salad of seasonal greens and closes on the sweet, liquid note of fresh sliced fruit in wine. . . .

Of course, no one expects that the Italian way of eating can be wholly absorbed into everyday American life. Even in Italy it is succumbing to the onrushing uniformity of an industrial society. In Blake's phrase, man's brain is making the world unlivable for man's spirit. Yet, it is possible even from the tumultous center of the busiest city life to summon up the life-enhancing magic of the Italian art of eating. What it requires is generosity. You must give liberally of time, of patience, of the best raw materials. What it requires is worth all you have to give.

The Classic Italian Cook Book

EATING WITH THE SWANNS
MARCEL PROUST

Upon the permanent foundation of eggs, cutlets, potatoes, preserves, and biscuits, whose appearance on the table she no longer announced to us, Françoise would add—as the labour of the fields and orchards, the harvest of the tides, the luck of the markets, the kindness of the neighbours, and her own genius might provide; and so effectively that our bill of fare, like the quatrefoils that were carved on the porches of cathedrals in the thirteenth century, reflected to some extent the march of the seasons and the incidents of human life—a brill, because the fish-woman had guaranteed its freshness; a turkey, because she had seen a beauty in the market at Roussainville-le-Pin; cardoons with marrow squash, because she had never done them for us in that way before; a roast leg of mutton, because the fresh air made one hungry and there would be plenty of time for it to "settle down" in the seven hours before dinner; spinach, by way of a change; apricots, because they were still hard to get; gooseberries, because in another fortnight there would be none left; raspberries, which Monsieur Swann had brought specially; cherries, the first to come from the cherry-tree, which had yielded none for the last two years; a cream cheese, of which in those days I was extremely fond; an almond cake, because she had ordered one the evening before; a fancy loaf, because it was our turn to "offer" the holy bread. And when all these had been eaten, a work composed expressly for ourselves, but dedicated more particularly to my father, who had a fondness for such things, a cream of chocolate, inspired in the mind, created by the hand of Françoise, would be laid before us, light and fleeting as an "occasional piece" of music, into which she had poured the whole of her talent. Anyone who refused to partake of it, saying: "No, thank you, I have finished; I am not hungry," would at once have been lowered to the level of the Philistines who, when an artist makes them a present of one of his works, examine its weight and material, whereas what is of value is the creator's intention and his signature. To have left even the tiniest morsel in the dish would have shown as much discourtesy as to rise and leave a concert hall while the "piece" was still being played, and under the composer's very eyes.

Swann's Way

TASTING

For he who rightly cares for his own eating
Will not be a bad cook. And if you keep
Your organs, sense and taste, in proper order
You will not err. But often taste your dishes
While you are boiling them. Do you want salt?
Add some;—is any other seasoning needed?
Add it, and taste again, till you've arrived
At harmony and flavor; like a man
Who tunes a lyre till it rightly sounds.
—ANCIENT GREEK

With the exception of sweet, sour, salt and bitter, all our countless gastronomic delights come to us through the sense of smell.

—HENRY T. FINCK

A cook's best friend is her nose.

—MARY AYLOTT

No mean woman can cook well. It calls for a generous spirit, a light hand, and a large heart.

—EDEN PHILLPOTTS

I don't like to say that my kitchen is a *religious* place, but I would say that if I were a voodoo princess, I would conduct my rituals there.

—PEARL BAILEY

"THEY SHOULD BUILD A STATUE"
HARRY GOLDEN

When you think of French cooking, you always think of a chef —a male. Ah, that Adolphe, you say; how wonderful that Pierre, Pea-air, and you go into ecstasies, and the same with Italian cooking. It's Luigi, how he cooks, that Luigi; and the Germans it's the same thing, the big chef with the huge apron and the chef's cap as high as a kite; and the Swiss, also—it's Oscar.

Oscar, Shmoscar; but now when you speak of KOSHER COOKING, you speak only in terms of A WOMAN—your mother, your sister, your aunt. There wasn't a man big enough to set foot into a kosher kitchen. All the philosopher, Talmudist, or scientist could do is stand on the other side of the threshold—and watch. They should build a statue in Washington to the Jewish immigrant mother and show her in bronze, standing over a stove, in the act of sprinkling or—tasting. She worked entirely by ear, like Toscanini, who used to listen to the single note coming from the most remote bass viol. If it didn't satisfy him, the whole one-hundred-and-twenty fellows had to start all over again—from the beginning, too.

But just think what America has missed; and it is our fault. Why do you suppose he spends four dollars for whiskey and fifty-five cents for lunch, which includes a hot dog or hamburger, a cola, and a B.C. headache powder? We could have reduced America's whiskey bill by one half if that fellow could sit down to a piece of nice cold gefilte fish with a strong red horseradish, followed maybe by a huge bowl of golden chicken soup with matzoh balls made of eggs, and light as a feather. And what about the Jewish potato latkes (pancakes)? What a wonderful remedy for an "Age of Anxiety."

How many of my readers remember how often they ripped their knuckles on the "reeb-eisel" as they grated the potatoes for their mothers? The hand-grated potatoes were mixed with flour and shortening and fried schmalts. But what's the use of giving the recipe? It just won't come out the same. And then how about a "symphony" like boiled flanken in horseradish sauce with a boiled potato, or a "grand opera" like holishkas—a dish which was probably invented by those alchemists of the Middle Ages who were trying to make gold out of the baser metals—ground meat and spices wrapped in cabbage leaves and cooked in a sweet-and-sour raisin sauce, which you eventually sop with a big hunk of rye bread. . . .

And what about the blintzes? How does one go about describing them? All you can do is wait for the next holiday and throw a garland in the air for those Delancey Street blintzes— those flat squares of dough folded lovingly over cottage cheese or jelly and fried in butter; and eaten as you prefer, plain or with sour cream.

And I have only touched on this wonderful culture. . . . I have spoken of "operas" and "symphonies," but I haven't even touched on the "overtures," such as kishke (stuffed goose-neck) and derma, and helzl; and what about the "nocturne" like med, a drink of hops and honey which the Jews learned about when they were still on speaking terms with Jupiter, Juno, Venus, and Adonis.

Only in America

THE INDOMITABLE FANNIE FARMER
RUSSELL LYNES

Miss Farmer was a woman of iron character who, because of physical disability, had had to conserve her time and her strength. She was by no means impatient of pleasure, or even of fanciness and frippery, and certainly not of the subtleties of decoration and taste, but she would abide no waste of her energies or anyone else's because of inexactitude. She was thirty-nine when *The Boston Cooking-School Cook Book* was published by the Boston firm of Little, Brown and Company at her own expense, and she had already had a distinguished career.

Fannie was a red-haired Boston girl, the eldest of four daughters of an editor and printer, J. Frank Farmer, and of Mary Watson Farmer, who, according to one of Fannie's very few biographers, was "a notable housewife" at a time when housewifery was not regarded as one of the prime social female virtues. When Fannie was seventeen and a junior at the Medford High School she suffered a "paralytic stroke," the exact nature of which medicine in those days did not define. It was not, however, polio, as a second stroke later in her life caused even further curtailment of her physical mobility. The first stroke ended Fannie's high-school career and, as her doctors forbade her any further formal schooling, the aspirations that she and her family had had for her going to college. Fannie was confined to staying home and ... Fannie helped with the cooking in her family's boarding house and evidenced such skill and interest in it that one of her younger sisters suggested that she go to the Boston Cooking School and learn to be a teacher of cooking.

This was sound advice. Fannie was thirty-two when she graduated, and Mrs. Carrie M. Dearborn, the director of the school, was so impressed with Fannie's intelligence, skill, and executive abilities that she invited her to become her assistant. Just two years later Mrs. Dearborn died, and the board of trustees of the school elected the impressive young Miss Farmer to take over the school as its head in spite of her physical handicaps. . . .

While she was head of the Boston Cooking School and later when she had a school of her own, Fannie spent as much time as she could going to the best restaurants that she could discover and sampling their dishes. Sometimes, when she encountered a sauce that baffled her, Fannie would take out a calling card, put a few drops of the sauce on it, fold it carefully, and take it away with her for future analysis and reference. Many of her pupils took delight in reporting their discoveries to her. One of her colleagues recalled, in an article in the *Woman's Home Companion* published shortly after Fannie's death, that the young ladies would come to her with such excitements as: "Ah, Miss Farmer, those rolls at the Holland House," or "They're serving a sausage at the Ritz-Carlton that you've nothing to match," and, the writer said, "Away would go Miss Farmer" to see for herself. Sometimes the entire faculty of the Boston Cooking School would experiment on the recipe of a baffling dish in the short snatches between classes. . . .

The red-headed Fannie was not the sort of woman who would have offered a publisher a book to which she had not given her entire intelligence or behind which she was not willing to put her personal resources. She therefore persuaded Little, Brown to publish three thousand copies on the agreement that she would pay for the printing. It is unlikely that in the entire history of the American book business any unwilling publisher ever got talked by an author into so lucrative (and at the same time so safe) a deal. . . .

The vast sale of the cookbook was only one of the ways by which Fannie's influence spread. For ten years she wrote a regular column for the *Woman's Home Companion* on topics such as "Cooking the Cheaper Meats," "The Banana in Cookery," "Twenty Good

Sandwiches" (including peanut butter mixed with orange juice, and toasted oyster sandwiches), and "The Thanksgiving Turkey." She lectured to a great many women's clubs as far from Boston as the Pacific Coast. She also wrote six shorter specialty cookery books, including *Food and Cookery for the Sick and Convalescent* (1904), *What to Have for Dinner* (1905), *Catering for Special Occasions, With Menus and Recipes* (1911), and *A New Book of Cookery* (1912).

Fannie Farmer spent the last seven years of her life in a wheel chair or on crutches. A second stroke had felled her, but she diligently followed the regime prescribed by her physicians and with the greatest exertion of will power managed to continue to lecture and spread the gospel in which she so fervently believed. "I certainly feel," she had said in the preface to the first edition of her cookbook, "that the time is not far distant when a knowledge of the principles of diet will be an essential part of one's education. Then mankind will eat to live, will be able to do better physical and mental work, and disease will be less frequent." She gave her last lecture from her wheel chair just ten days before she died at the age of fifty-eight on January 15, 1915, in Boston.

American Heritage Cookbook

If something is not right, this is due to carelessness, and it is the cook's fault. If something is good, say why, and when it is bad, pick out its faults. If one does not keep the cook in line, he becomes insolent. Before the food comes, send word down that the food tomorrow must be better.

—YUAN MEI

BAKING OFF
NORA EPHRON

Roxanne Frisbie brought her own pan to the twenty-fourth annual Pillsbury Bake-Off. "I feel like a nut," she said. "It's just a plain old dumb pan, but everything I do is in that crazy pan." As it happens, Mrs. Frisbie had no cause whatsoever to feel like a nut: it seemed that at least half of the 100 finalists in the Bake-It-Easy Bake-Off had brought something with them—their own sausages, their own pie pans, their own apples. Edna Buckley, who was fresh from representing New York State at the National Chicken Cooking Contest, where her recipe for fried chicken in a batter of beer, cheese, and crushed pretzels had gone down to defeat, brought with her a lucky handkerchief, a lucky horseshoe, a lucky dime for her shoe, a potholder with the Pillsbury Poppin' Fresh Doughboy on it, an Our Blessed Lady pin, and all of her jewelry, including a silver charm also in the shape of the doughboy. Mrs. Frisbie and Mrs. Buckley and the other finalists came to the Bake-Off to bake off for $65,000 in cash prizes; in Mrs. Frisbie's case, this meant making something she created herself and named Butterscotch Crescent Rolls—and which Pillsbury promptly, and to Mrs. Frisbie's dismay, renamed Sweet 'N Creamy Crescent Crisps. Almost all the recipes in the finals were renamed by Pillsbury using a lot of crispy snicky snacky words. An exception to this was Sharon Schubert's Wiki Wiki Coffee Cake, a name which ought to have been snicky snacky enough; but Pillsbury, in a moment of restraint, renamed it One-Step Tropical Fruit Cake. As it turned out, Mrs. Schubert ended up winning $5,000 for her cake, which made everybody pretty mad, even the contestants who had been saying for days that they did not care who won, that winning meant nothing and was quite beside the point; the fact was that Sharon Schubert was a previous Bake-Off winner, having won $10,000 three years before for her Crescent Apple Snacks, and in addition had walked off with a trip to Puerto Vallarta in the course of this year's festivities. Most of the contestants felt she had won a little more than was really fair. But I'm getting ahead of the story.

The Pillsbury Company has been holding Bake-Offs since 1948, when Eleanor Roosevelt, for reasons that are not clear, came to give the first one her blessing. This year's took place from Saturday, February 24 [1973] through Tuesday, February 27, at the Beverly Hilton in Beverly Hills. One hundred contestants—97 of them women, two twelve-year-old boys, and one male graduate student —were winnowed down from a field of almost 100,000 entrants to compete for prizes in five categories: Flour, frosting mix, crescent main dish, crescent dessert, and hot-roll mix. They were all brought, or flown, to Los Angeles for the Bake-Off itself, which took place on Monday, and a round of activities that included a tour of Universal Studios, a mini-version of television's *Let's Make A Deal* with Monty Hall himself, and a trip to Disneyland. The event is also attended by some 100 food editors, who turn it from a mere contest into the incredible publicity stunt Pillsbury intends it to be, and spend much of their time talking to each other about sixty-five new ways to use tuna fish and listening to various speakers lecture on the consumer movement and food and the appliance business. General Electric is co-sponsor of the event and donates a stove to each finalist, as well as the stoves for the Bake-Off; this year, it promoted a little Bake-Off of its own for the microwave oven, an appliance we were repeatedly told was the biggest improvement in cooking since the invention of the Willoughby System. Every one of the food editors seemed to know what the Willoughby System was, just as everyone seemed to know what Bundt pans were. "You will all be happy to hear," we were told at one point, "that only one of the finalists this year used a Bundt pan." The food editors burst into laughter at that point; I am not sure why. One Miss Alex Allard of San Antonio, Texas, had already won the microwave contest and $5,000, and she spent most of the Bake-Off turning out one Honey Drizzle Cake after another in the microwave ovens that ringed the Grand Ballroom of the Beverly Hilton Hotel. I never did taste the Honey Drizzle Cake, largely because I suspected—and this was weeks before the Consumers Union article on the subject—that microwave ovens were dangerous and probably caused peculiar diseases. If God wanted us to make bacon in four minutes, He would have made bacon that cooked in four minutes.

"The Bake-Off is America," a General Electric executive announced just minutes before it began. "It's family. It's real people doing real things." Yes. The Pillsbury Bake-Off is an America that exists less and less, but exists nonetheless. It is women who still live on farms, who have six and seven children, who enter county fairs and sponsor 4-H Clubs. It is Grace Perguson of Palm Springs,

Florida, who entered the Bake-Off seventeen years in a row before reaching the finals this year, and who cooks at night and prays at the same time. It is Carol Hamilton, who once won a trip on a Greyhound bus to Hollywood for being the most popular girl in Youngstown, Ohio. There was a lot of talk at the Bake-Off about how the Bake-It-Easy theme had attracted a new breed of contestants this year, younger contestants—housewives, yes, but housewives who used whole-wheat flour and Granola and sour cream and similar supposedly hip ingredients in their recipes and were therefore somewhat more sophisticated, or urban, or something-of-the-sort than your usual Bake-Off contestant. There were a few of these—two, to be exact: Barbara Goldstein of New York City and Bonnie Brooks of Salisbury, Maryland, who actually visited the Los Angeles County Art Museum during a free afternoon. But there was also Suzie Sisson of Palatine, Illinois, twenty-five years old and the only Bundt-pan person in the finals, and her sentiments about life were the same as those that Bake-Off finalists presumably have had for years. "These are beautiful people," she said, looking around the ballroom as she waited for her Bundt cake to come out of the oven. "They're not the little tiny rich people. They're nice and happy and religious types and family-oriented. Everyone talks about women's lib, which is ridiculous. If you're nice to your husband, he'll be nice to you. Your family is your job. They come first."

I was seven years old when the Pillsbury Bake-Off began, and as I grew up reading the advertisements for it in the women's magazines that were lying around the house, it always seemed to me that going to a Bake-Off would be the closest thing to a childhood fantasy of mine, which was to be locked overnight in a bakery. In reality, going to a Bake-Off *is* like being locked overnight in a bakery—a very bad bakery. I almost became sick right there on Range 95 after my sixth carbohydrate-packed sample—which happened, by coincidence, to be a taste of the aforementioned Mrs. Frisbie's aforementioned Sweet 'N Creamy Crescent Crisps.

But what is interesting about the Bake-Off—what is even significant about the event—is that it is, for the American housewife, what the Miss America contest used to represent to teen-agers. The pinnacle of a certain kind of achievement. The best in field. To win the Pillsbury Bake-Off, even to be merely a finalist in it, is to be a great housewife. And a creative housewife. "Cooking is very creative." I must have heard that line thirty times as I interviewed finalists. I don't happen to think that cooking is very creative—what interests me about it is, on the contrary, its utter mindlessness and mathematical certainty. "Cooking is very relaxing"— that's my bromide. On the other hand, I have to admit that some of the recipes that were concocted for the Bake-Off, amazing combinations of frosting mix and marshmallows and peanut butter and brown sugar and chocolate, were practically awe-inspiring. And cooking, it is quite clear, is only a small part of the apparently frenzied creativity that flourishes in these women's homes. I spent quite a bit of time at the Bake-Off chatting with Laura Aspis of Shaker Heights, Ohio, a seven-time Bake-Off finalist and duplicate-bridge player, and after we had discussed her high-protein macaroons made with coconut-almond frosting mix and Granola, I noticed that Mrs. Aspis was wearing green nail polish. On the theory that no one who wears green nail polish wants it to go unremarked upon, I remarked upon it.

"That's not green nail polish," Mrs. Aspis said. "It's platinum nail polish that I mix with green food coloring."

"Oh," I said.

"And the thing of it is," she went on, "when it chips, it doesn't matter."

"Why is that?" I asked.

"Because it stains your nails permanently," Mrs. Aspis said.

"You mean your nails are permanently green?"

"Well, not exactly," said Mrs. Aspis. "You see, last week they were blue, and the week before I made purple, so now my nails are a combination of all three. It looks like I'm in the last throes of something."

On Sunday afternoon, most of the finalists chose to spend their free time sitting around the hotel and socializing. Two of them— Marjorie Johnson of Robbinsdale, Minnesota, and Mary Finnegan of Minneota, Minnesota—were seated at a little round table just off the Hilton ballroom talking about a number of things, including Tupperware. Both of them love Tupperware.

"When I built my new house," Mrs. Johnson said, "I had so much Tupperware I had to build a cupboard just for it." Mrs. Johnson is a very tiny, fortyish mother of three, and she and her dentist husband have just moved into a fifteen-room house she cannot seem to stop talking about. "We have this first-floor kitchen, harvest gold and blue, and it's almost finished. Now I have a second kitchen on my walk-out level and that's going to be harvest gold and blue, too. Do you know about the new wax Congoleum? I think that's what I put in—either that or Shinyl Vinyl. I haven't had to wash my floors in three months. The house isn't done yet because of the Bake-Off. My husband says if I'd spent as much time on it as I did on the Bake-Off, we'd be finished. I sent in sixteen recipes—it took me nearly a year to do it."

"That's nothing," said Mrs. Finnegan. "It took me twenty years before I cracked it. I'm a contest nut. I'm a thirty-times winner in the *Better Homes & Gardens* contest. I won a thousand dollars from Fleischmann's Yeast. I won Jell-O this year, I'm getting a hundred and twenty-five dollars' worth of Revere cookware for that. The Knox Gelatine contest. I've won seven blenders and a quintisserie. It does four things—fries, bakes, roasts, there's a griddle. I sold the darn thing before I even used it."

"Don't tell me," said Mrs. Johnson. "Did you enter the Crystal Sugar Name the Lake Home contest?"

"Did I enter?" said Mrs. Finnegan. "Wait till you see this." She took a pen and wrote her submission on a napkin and held it up for Mrs. Johnson. The napkin read "Our Entry Hall." "I should have won that one," said Mrs. Finnegan. "I did win the Crystal Sugar Name the Dessert contest. I called it 'Signature Squares.' I think I got a blender on that one."

"Okay," said Mrs. Johnson. "The've got a contest now, Crystal Sugar Name a Sauce. It has pineapple in it."

"I don't think I won that," said Mrs. Finnegan, "but I'll show you what I sent in." She held up the napkin and this time what she had written made sense. "Hawaiian More Chant," it said.

"Oh, you're clever," said Mrs. Johnson.

"They have three more contests so I haven't given up," said Mrs. Finnegan.

On Monday morning at exactly 9 A.M., the one hundred finalists marched four abreast into the Hilton ballroom, led by Philip Pillsbury, former chairman of the board of the company. The band played "Nothin' Says Lovin' Like Somethin' from the Oven," and when it finished, Pillsbury announced: "Now you one hundred winners can go to your ranges."

Chaos. Shrieking. Frenzy. Furious activity. Cracking eggs. Chopping onions. Melting butter. Mixing, beating, blending. The band perking along with such carefully selected tunes as "If I Knew You Were Coming I'd Have Baked a Cake." Contestants running to the refrigerators for more supplies. Floor assistants rushing dirty dishes off to unseen dishwashers. All two hundred members of the working press, plus television's Bob Barker, interviewing any finalist they could get to drop a spoon. At 9:34 A.M., Mrs. Lorraine Walmann submitted her Cheesy Crescent Twist-Ups to the judges and became the first finalist to finish. At 10 A.M., all the stoves were on, the television lights were blasting, the temperature in the ballroom was up to the mid-nineties, and Mrs. Marjorie Johnson, in the course of giving an interview about her house to the Minneapolis *Star,* had forgotten whether she had put one cup of sugar or two into her Crispy Apple Bake. "You know we're building this new house," she was saying. "When I go back, I have to buy living-room furniture." By 11 A.M., Mae Wilkinson had burned her skillet corn bread and was at work on a second. Laura Aspis had lost her potholder. Barbara Bellhorn was distraught because she was not used to California apples. Alex Allard was turning out yet another Honey Drizzle Cake. Dough and flour were all over the floor. Mary Finnegan was fussing because the crumbs on her Lemon Cream Bars were too coarse. Marjorie Johnson was in the midst of yet another interview on her house. "Well, let me tell you," she was saying, "the shelves in the kitchen are built low. . . ." One by one, the contestants, who were each given seven hours and four tries to produce two perfect samples of their recipes, began to finish up and deliver one tray to the judges and one tray to the photographer. There were samples everywhere, try this, try that, but after six tries, climaxed by Mrs. Frisbie's creation, I stopped sampling. The overkill was unbearable: none of the recipes seemed to contain one cup of sugar when two would do, or a delicate cheese when Kraft American would do, or an actual minced onion when instant minced onions would do. It was snack time. It was convenience-food time. It was less-work-for-Mother time. All I could think about was a steak.

By 3 P.M., there were only two contestants left—Mrs. Johnson, whose dessert took only five minutes to make but whose interviews took considerably longer, and Bonnie Brooks, whose third sour-cream-and-banana cake was still in the oven. Mrs. Brooks brought her cake in last, at 3:27 P.M., and as she did, the packing began. The skillets went into brown cartons, the measuring spoons into barrels, the stoves were dismantled. The Bake-Off itself was over—and all that remained was the trip to Disneyland, and the breakfast at the Brown Derby . . . and the prizes.

And so it is Tuesday morning, and the judges have reached a decision, and any second now, Bob Barker is going to announce the five winners over national television. All the contestants are wearing their best dresses and smiling, trying to smile anyway, good sports all, and now Bob Barker is announcing the Winners. Bonnie Brooks and her cake and Albina Flieler and her Quick Pecan Pie win $25,000 each. Sharon Schubert and two others win $5,000. And suddenly the show is over and it is time to go home, and the ninety-five people who did not win the twenty-fourth annual Pillsbury Bake-Off are plucking the orchids from the centerpieces, signing each other's programs, and grumbling. They are grumbling about Sharon Schubert. And for a moment, as I hear grumbling everywhere—"It really isn't fair." . . . "After all, she won the trip to Mexico"—I think perhaps I am wrong about these women: perhaps they are capable of anger after all, or jealousy, or competitiveness, or something I think of as a human trait I can relate to. But the grumbling stops after a few minutes, and I find myself listening to Marjorie Johnson. "I'm so glad I didn't win the grand prize," she is saying, "because if you win that, you don't get to come back to the next Bake-Off. I'm gonna start now on my recipes for next year. I'm gonna think of something really good." She stopped for a moment. "You know," she said, "it's going to be very difficult to get back to normal living."

Crazy Salad

TARTELETTES AMANDINES
EDMÓND ROSTAND

Beat your eggs, the yolk and the white,
   Very light;
Mingle with their creamy fluff
   Drops of lime juice, cool and green;
   Then pour in
Milk of almonds, just enough.
Dainty patty pans, embraced
   In puff paste—
Have these ready within reach;
   With your thumb and finger, pinch
   Half an inch
Up around the edge of each—
Into these, a score or more,
   Slowly pour
All your store of custard; so
   Take them, bake them golden brown—
   Now sit down! . . .
Almond tartlets, Raguneau!

Cyrano de Bergerac

Cooking is like love. It should be entered into with abandon or not at all.

—Harriet Van Horne

Of Men and Cooks

The greatest crab cook of the days I remember was Tom McNulty, originally a whiskey drummer but in the end sheriff of Baltimore, and the most venerated oyster cook was a cop named Fred. Tom's specialty was made by spearing a slice of bacon on a large fork, jamming a soft crab down on it, holding the two over a charcoal brazier until the bacon had melted over the crab, and then slapping both upon a slice of hot toast. This tidbit had its points, I assure you, and I never think of it without deploring Tom's too early translation to bliss eternal. Fred devoted himself mainly to oyster flitters. The other cops rolled and snuffled in his masterpieces like cats in catnip, but I never could see much virtue in them. It was always my impression, perhaps in error, that he fried them in curve grease borrowed from the street railways. He was an old-time Model T -flat-foot, not much taller than a fire-plug, but as big around the middle as a load of hay. At the end of a busy afternoon he would be spattered from head to foot with blobs of flitter batter and wild grease.

—H. L. MENCKEN
Happy Days

Simple Cooking
RICHARD OLNEY

A grain-fed farm hen's freshly laid egg, soft-boiled, has been chosen by some, defenders of the integral, naturally determined logic of the single element, as the symbol of ultimate perfection. Others of the same school lean toward the freshly plucked, vine-ripened, sun-hot August tomato, while, for those of the rustic school, the *aligot*, a gummy but tasty enough mess of potato purée and fresh Cantal cheese, has assumed the heroic dimensions of a symbol.

One well-known journalist amuses himself by pretending that the gourmet world is broken into two camps: the eaters of the rustic *aligot*—true lovers of the good and the pure—and the eaters of the elegant woodcock in its foie-gras–tainted sauce—pretentious fools deceived by appearances and false gastronomic tradition. French writers on various regional cookings, while claiming respect for the traditions of other provinces, rarely fail to express a certain critical snobbism toward Parisian cooking, and if, in passing, the Parisian *concierge's* potato and leek soup may suffer a dig, the malice is mainly aimed at the "rootless" professional traditions. . . . *La vraie cuisine de bonne femme,* a near synonym of rustic cooking in the minds of those who fancy the phrase, is usually associated with *les plats mijotés;* stews that cook at a bare murmur for hours on end. When one of the little stews is thus denoted, one understands that it flirts with divinity—that it has reached heights of simple purity unattainable by a man's cooking. Shorn, through translation, of its mystical sheath, the phrase means "real home cooking."

. . . Consider the *cassoulet,* a voluptuous monument to rustic tradition: The beans are cooked apart, their flavor enhanced by prolonged contact with aromatic vegetables, herbs, and spices; the mutton is cooked apart, slowly, the wine and other aromatic elements refining, enriching, or underlining its character; apart, the goose has long since been macerated in herbs and salt and subsequently preserved in its own fat; a good sausage is famously allied to witchcraft. All of these separate products are then combined; a bit of catalytic goose fat—with the aid of a gelatinous pork rind —binds them together in a velvet texture, and a further slow cooking process intermingles all the flavors while a gratin, repeatedly basted, forms, is broken, reforms, is broken, a single new savor moving into dominance, cloaking without destroying, the autonomy of the primitive members.

Escoffier wrote, *"Faites simple,"* and he is often quoted. Yet, while not one to sneeze at the sun-hot tomato on the one hand nor, on the other, at the sticky *aligot* (the one representing an obvious necessity, the other a homely pleasure unrelated to his *métier*), he surely was aiming, rather, at safeguarding all that was valuable in the elaborate tradition of the nineteenth-century professional cuisine, precisely by eliminating the encumbering decorative paring that, when not merely superfluous or distracting, was often detrimental to the basic quality of a preparation.

Curnonsky, whose entire life was devoted to eating and to thinking, talking, and writing about eating, took great pride in having been instrumental in popularizing regional cooking traditions in France and, in particular, in convincing restaurant owners and professional cooks of the virtue of presenting regional specialties. On his banner were inscribed Escoffier's two famous words, but he has bequeathed us, as well, a number of maxims of his own fabrication and a throng of disciples who generally recite them. Coupled with the knowledge that Curnonsky's passion for the garden-fresh vegetable and the farm-kitchen stew failed to temper his admiration for the apparently involved refinements of the classical French tradition, these aphoristic pronouncements may shed a bit of light on what "simple food" means to a relatively complicated (gastronomic) intelligence:

En cuisine, comme dans tous les arts, la simplicité est le signe de la perfection. ("In cooking, as in all the arts, simplicity is the sign of perfection.")

Simple French Food

"Cookery Is My One Vanity"
MARJORIE KINNAN RAWLINGS

I hold the theory that the serving of good food is the one certain way of pleasing everybody. A readers' club, in advertising its wares, advises one and all to turn to books when love and liquor fail them. Love and liquor are admittedly fallible comforters, but who is to agree on books? One man's meat is another man's poison more certainly in literature than in gastronomy. Conversation is fallible, for not all want to talk about the same things, and some do not want to talk at all, and some do not want to listen. But short of dyspepsia or stomach ulcers, any man or woman may be pleased with well-cooked and imaginative dishes.

Cookery is my one vanity and I am a slave to any guest who

praises my culinary art. This is my Achilles' heel. Dorothy Parker has a delightful verse dealing with the abuse she is willing to take from her beloved, and ending, "But say my verses do not scan, and I get me another man." For my part, my literary ability may safely be questioned as harshly as one wills, but indifference to my table puts me in a rage. . . .

When we have crab meat to spare, I make a crab Newburg so superlative that I myself taste in wonder, thinking, "Can it be I who has brought this noble thing into the world?" . . . I serve it on toast points and garnish superfluously with parsley, and a Chablis or white Rhine wine is suggested as an accompaniment. Angels sing softly in the distance.

We do not desecrate this dish by serving any other, neither salad or dessert. We just eat crab Newburg. My friends rise from the table, wring my hand with deep feeling, and slip quietly and reverently away. I sit alone and weep for the misery of the world that does not have blue crabs and a Jersey cow. . . .

Cross Creek

The Woman Who First Cooked with Fire

Once upon a time men had neither sweet manioc nor fire. An old woman was given the secret of the first by the ants; and her friend, the nocturnal swallow (a goatsucker, *Caprimulgus* species), would obtain fire for her (keep it hidden in his beak), so that she could cook the manioc, instead of heating it by exposure to the sun or by putting it under her armpits.

The Indians found the old woman's manioc cakes excellent and asked how she prepared them. She replied that she simply baked them in the heat of the sun. The swallow, amused by this falsehood, burst out laughing, and the Indians saw flames coming from her mouth. They forced it open and took possession of the fire. Since then nocturnal swallows have had gaping beaks.

—Claude Lévi-Strauss
The Raw and the Cooked

"The Seasoning, the Dressing, the Garnishing"

The same Animal which hath the honour to have some Part of his Flesh eaten at the Table of a Duke, may perhaps be degraded in another Part, and some of his Limbs gibbeted, as it were, in the vilest Stall in Town. Where then lies the Difference between the Food of the Nobleman and the Porter, if both are at dinner on the same Ox or Calf, but in the seasoning, the dressing, the garnishing, and the setting forth?

—Henry Fielding
Tom Jones

Complaints to File

Nowadays, common cooks will put chickens, geese, ducks and pork all in one pot, so that all taste the same. I am afraid that their ghosts must be filing their complaints in the city of the dead.

—Yuan Mei

Man, the Cooking Animal

Man is the one amimal who can adapt himself to the changing conditions of life and the vicissitudes of climate. He can exist on every kind of food; every animal and every plant yield him their produce; all Nature is under tribute to him. It is in cooking that he is superior to other animals, for by its aid he fits to his wants much foodstuff that would otherwise run to waste. By skillful preparation and skilful cooking man enlarges his resources a thousand-fold.

—Frederick W. Hackwood
Good Cheer

To Julia—Birthday 1961
PAUL CHILD

O Julia, Julia, Cook and nifty wench,
Whose unsurpassed quenelles and hot soufflés,
Whose English, Norse and German and whose French,
Are all beyond my piteous powers to praise—
Whose sweetly rounded bottom and whose legs,
Whose gracious face, whose nature temperate,
Are only equalled by her scrambled eggs:
Accept from me, your ever-loving mate,
This acclamation shaped in fourteen lines
Whose inner truth belies its outer sight;
For never were there foods, nor were there wines
Whose flavor equals yours for sheer delight.
  O luscious dish! O gustatory pleasure!
  You satisfy my taste-buds beyond measure.

6

Chefs de Cuisine

MENU

Mousse de Foie en Brioche
Délice St. Jacques

Filet de Sole au Champag...
ou Turbot braisé au Vermou...

Poularde de Bresse Albu...
ou Pièce de Bœuf à la moe...
Gratin Dauphino...

...ou Sorbet
...ndises
...teaux
...Fruits

...Francs

AUGUSTE ESCOFFIER

Tribute is often paid to Marie-Antoine Carême, "the king of chefs and chef of kings." He is not to be ignored for many reasons, of which one of the least ignorable was neatly posed by Raymond Sokolov in The Saucier's Apprentice: "He knew exactly what he was doing—which was to conquer the world with French cooking, just as Napoleon had conquered it with the French army." Unwittingly, Carême set a pattern for twentieth-century French when he toted his pots, saucepans, and chinois from Paris to Moscow, to London and Brighton. He was peripatetic in the service of royal eaters. Chefs in the twentieth century are even more willing to pack up their batteries de cuisine for a hop across a mountain here or an ocean there, but many of them seem less enchanted with their home kitchens than with pièces montées of a jet-propelled world. Here are glimpses of a few cuisines in action.

A master cook! why, he is the man of men,
For a professor; he designs, he draws,
He paints, he carves, he builds, he fortifies,
Makes citadels of curious fowl and fish.
Some he dry-ditches, some moats round with broths,
Mounts marrow-bones, cuts fifty-angled custards,
Rears bulwark pies; and for his outer works,
He raiseth ramparts of immortal crust,
And teacheth all the tactics at one dinner—
What ranks, what files, to put his dishes in,
The whole art military! Then he knows
The influence of the stars upon his meats,
And all their seasons, tempers, qualities;
And so to fit his relishes and sauces.

CHEFS DE CUISINE   149

He has nature in a pot 'bove all the chemists
Or bare-breech'd brethren of the rosy cross.
He is an architect, an engineer,
A soldier, a physician, a philosopher,
A general mathematician.

—BEN JONSON
The Staple of News

CARÊME, THE KITCHEN MONARCH
PHYLLIS FELDKAMP

He is reckoned the father of *haute cuisine,* a title he would surely
have taken seriously, for he looked upon his calling as a sacred
trust, with himself no higher and no lower on the aesthetic scale
than any other major artistic genius whose object is to enthrall his
audience.

So Olympian were his standards for the planning, preparation,
cooking, and consumption of food that, far from regarding his
contemporary Jean Anthelme Brillat-Savarin with the reverential
awe that the author of *The Physiology of Taste* is now accorded,
Carême considered him just one more *soi-disant* gourmet. The pre-
tentions of another self-proclaimed epicure of the day, Jean-
Jacques, Duc de Cambacérès, filled Carême with disgust and despair. Perfection was his aim; at any deviation from it, in his own
work or that of others in his craft, Carême became intensely dis-
tressed, and because he tended, as have many cooks before and
since his time, to be highly emotional, he would set to moaning,
"O Momus! O Gastronomie!" and the like, personification being his
favored figure of speech.

To Carême, the fine arts were five, a number that accords with
most everyone else's way of thinking. But, elevating his own voca-
tion to the level which he believed was its due, he listed the arts
with an important appendage as consisting of "Painting, sculpture,
poetry, music, and architecture—which has as its principal branch,
pastry." Pastry? It took a sublime outlook, befitting a man who
was to go down in history as "the cook of kings and the king of

cooks," to put *pâtisserie* in such lofty company. . . .

Carême may have been the greatest chef of all time. Many authorities think so. However, about this we cannot know for certain, since he stopped cooking in the early eighteen-thirties and, as he discovered through his own researches, one century's meat is another century's poison. (After a lengthy investigation into ancient manuscripts in the Vatican library, he concluded: "The cuisine so renowned of the splendor of Rome was fundamentally bad and atrociously heavy." He did approve of the Romans' table decorations.) Also, although he gives us excellent directions for each dish and the composition of a meal himself, we no longer have Carême to prepare it.

His reputation is, however, probably not overrated. Charles-Maurice de Talleyrand-Périgord, Prince de Bénévent; King George IV, when he was Prince Regent; Czar Alexander I; and Baron James de Rothschild all fought at one time or another to keep him in their kitchens. To Talleyrand, whose house was known throughout Europe as the sanctuary of French cuisine, gastronomy was a valuable arm of diplomacy . . . If you wanted to succeed in out-maneuvering some other minister of state, there was nothing like a superlative meal, in Talleyrand's book. As he put it in his parting words to Louis XVIII before taking off for the Congress of Vienna, "Sire, I will have more need of casseroles than of written instructions."

It was Talleyrand's morning habit to fortify himself with nothing more than three or four cups of camomile tea and immediately afterward, without delay, he would go into conference from eight to nine with his cook, Carême, laying down the strategy for the daily gourmet campaign. The customary sit-down dinner of the day was for eighty or ninety, and state banquets would have twelve hundred—once, even as many as ten thousand—guests. Talleyrand's were placed at large oval tables, each seating ten to twelve persons, all of whom faced up to a formidable array of elaborate, eye-catching dishes.

The opening volley at such parties was a service of soups, followed by *relevés,* fish, entrées, roasts, *entremets,* soufflés, desserts, and concluding with a grand fanfare attack on the *pièces montées.* Each of the courses consisted of a service of numerous dishes brought in by footmen and placed on the tables at the same time. Consequently, a scramble for food ensued, and the guest who succeeded in getting something on his plate was the guest who was the most adroit and nimble and not inhibited in the use of the boarding-house reach.

. . . Carême, born in 1786 on the Rue de Bac in Paris, the son of a pieceworker, was abandoned at the age of ten by his father, who set the boy loose one dark night on the streets of Paris with these parting words which Carême never forgot: "Go, little one, go. In the world there are good careers. Leave us to suffer. Misery is our lot. We must die. These days are ones of great fortunes. All you need are the wits to make one, and you have them. Go, little one, and perhaps tonight or tomorrow some good house will open its doors for you. Give with what God has given you."

That night, Carême, who never again saw his father, his mother, or any of his brothers and sisters, knocked at the door of a grubby little eating house. Later, he moved on to a better restaurant and then to Bailly, where his employer allowed him to spend hours in the print room of the Bibliothèque Nationale to pore over the old drawings of the Italian architects Serlio, Palladio, and Vignola to get new ideas for *pâtisseries.* Afterward Carême would stay up until daybreak sketching and calculating weights and measures.

He soon had composed two hundred pastry designs, all of them, he said, *soignés,* and his great cakes, prepared for Napoleon's table, were causing a sensation. "I saw that I had arrived," wrote Carême. *"Alors,* with tears in my eyes I left the good Monsieur Bailly." . . . Seldom [thereafter] did he permit himself to fall into the hands of an employer who would not set up the most exemplary larder, and Carême knew by heart which of the hosts of his day had the most sensitive gullets.

"The eaters of my time," he stated categorically, "were the Prince de Talleyrand, Murat, Junot, Fontanes, the Emperor Alexander, George IV, Castlereagh, and the Marquis de Cussy," and Carême worked for several on this list. . . . His twelve glorious years in the service of Talleyrand put him in the pantheon of *grande cuisine.* Thanks to Talleyrand, France's reputation for magnificence and hospitality went around the world once again. Alexander

Dumas *père* tells us in his *Dictionary of Cuisine* that the refinements of cookery had spread from the Princes of Condé and the Soubises to Richelieu, to be eclipsed during the horrendous days of the Revolution and the Terror. During the Directoire, with the creations of his chef Bouché, or Bouche-Sêche, who was trained in the Condé household, Talleyrand's table became the most celebrated one in Europe. When Bouché died and Carême succeeded him, the munificence of Talleyrand's meals continued unabated. . . .

Here was a host after Carême's heart, an employer who would spare him nothing in the way of fresh seafood, pheasant, butter, and cream. Carême dedicated *The Royal Pastrymaker* to Talleyrand. "It is that Monsieur de Talleyrand understands the genius of the chef," Carême told one of his contemporaries. "It is that he respects it, and that he is the most competent judge of the delicate nuances of cuisine and that his expenditure is wise and grand at the same time.". . .

Yet in the midst of all this *gloire* Carême often labored under abominable conditions. His lungs were weakened by constant inhalations of the gases from the coal-heated ovens into which he was forced to place his head for many hours during the day. . . . But some poor cook who had had the misfortune of concocting an unfelicitous mixture could rile Careme even more. If a soup based on anise brought forth from the great chef an outburst of vocatives *("Quelle Drogue Médicinale! Quelle Mauvais Génie!"),* this would only be because Carême saw himself as the guardian and arbiter of superlative eating, with every meal an unforgettable experience in pleasure, starting with the soup, which he said, "must be the *agent provocateur* of a good dinner."

On the day he died, January 13, 1833, after a long and difficult illness, he was still preaching his mission. "Ah, it's you, thank you, good friend," he said to a student who had stopped to see him. "Tomorrow bring me some fish. Yesterday, the quenelles de sole were very good but your fish was not good. You did not season it well. Listen," said Carême, raising his right hand and moving it back and forth in the air, "you must shake the casserole." Those were his final words.

The Good Life . . . or What's Left of It

ON THE PLAINS OF VERTUS

In huge tents set up in the gardens of a nearby château, the Tsar gave a Lucullan banquet for his three hundred distinguished guests. The magnificent meal prepared by Chef Carême—lent to the Tsar for the summer—had demanded almost as much energy and organization as the maneuvers themselves. Furnaces and ovens had been hastily built in the barns and courtyards of the château, a whole ice factory bought and moved to the spot; forty cooks, a herd of cattle and innumerable wagonloads of food, wine, linen, silver, porcelain and cooking vessels—all had to be brought from Paris a week before. Among delicacies served that day were fresh oysters, truffled boar's heads in aspic, salmis of partridge in Bordeaux wine, hot and cold soups, twenty-eight different entrées and a dozen desserts. One of the harrassed chef's most difficult problems had been to prevent the incursion of Cossacks, who—used to foraging for themselves—did not mind in the least robbing the Tsar's own commissary.

—DOROTHY GIES MCGUIGAN
Metternich and the Duchess

MEDIEVAL CHEFS

In the larger establishments of the middle ages, cooks, with the authority of feudal chiefs, gave their orders from a high chair in which they ensconced themselves, and commanded a view of all that was going on throughout their several domains. Each held a long wooden spoon with which he tasted, without leaving his seat, the various comestibles that were cooking on the stoves, and which he frequently used as a rod of punishment on the backs of those whose idleness and gluttony too largely predominated over their diligence and temperance.

—ISABELLA BEETON
The Book of Household Management

In Tolstoy's Kitchen

There was the cook: Nicholas Mikhailovich, the one who played the flute in Prince Volkonsky's serf-orchestra. When asked why he had traded his flute for a cookstove he sullenly replied, "Because I lost my mouthpiece."

—HENRI TROYAT

Henri Charpentier . . . and a Story of Crêpes Suzette

GEORGES SPUNT

In the large *salle* where we were to meet . . . (Charpentier served no less than eight), a sparkling linen cloth was laid out on the table. The settings were simple but fastidious and complete. Although he served no liquor, and you were required to bring your own if you chose to drink, appropriate glasses were set for sherry, white and red wines, and champagne. The procedure . . . was that you discussed the menu with the master, who then made suggestions for the wines. A high-backed chair faced the table. As we were seated, M. Charpentier entered and took his place in the tall chair. At eighty, or thereabouts, he was a husky man with a benign but noble, unmistakably French mien. Though his skin was quite wrinkled, the coloring was fresh, and his eyes were an alert blue. . . .

As the soup plates were set before us, Monsieur Charpentier began conversing. Events that had now become part of history were related with such ease that they could only have been observed first hand.

The soup served was *potage St. Germain.* One taste of it and I immediately thought that only unmitigated slavery to preparation could have produced such a delicate marvel of flavor, such velvet texture. The *potage* was followed by *huîtres à la provençale* and superb *tripe.* (Echoing Escoffier, Charpentier deplored the habit in this country of using calves' feet instead of ox feet in preparing *tripes à la mode de Caen,* a practice, he said, that resulted in too much jelly.) The salad was a simple affair of cucumbers dressed in a light vinaigrette, and the dessert was, of course, his celebrated crêpes Suzette. . . .

When he served the *petite marmite,* he recalled that as a boy of eleven working at the Grand Hotel Frascati in Le Havre, he was assigned the task of carrying a tureen of the painstakingly prepared bouillon to a woman dressed from head to toe in black. As he came within a foot of the woman he slipped. In that perilous moment the boy remembered to reverse the tureen so that the boiling contents fell on himself. Through tears Henri tried to apologize for ruining the woman's lunch and soiling the hem of her skirt. Then she spoke in a voice that was a legend in its time. "Ah, this poor little one. See how he has burned himself, and all he thinks of is my lunch, my dress," she addressed the entire room. With one hand, using a fine *point de Venise* handkerchief, she wiped at Henri's brow, and with the other she salvaged pieces of chicken from her skirt and popped them in her mouth. Years later, when Charpentier was established at Lynbrook in Long Island, the great Sarah Bernhardt, then on a farewell tour and with one leg amputated, visited his restaurant. At the end of a sumptuous meal, which, you may be sure, began with a *petite marmite Henri VI,* Charpentier produced the lace handkerchief with which she had ministered to his burns. "How glad I am that I was kind to a little boy so many years ago," said the divine Sarah.

On and on went the stories; about Queen Victoria, Diamond Jim Brady, Teddy Roosevelt, J. P. Morgan, David Belasco, and, of course, about *l'affaire Suzette.* There are many schools of thought as to who originated these delectable pancakes. At least five famous gourmet authorities insist that it was Charpentier. The *maître* himself had a convincing anecdote to support this theory, and since I am by nature partisan, I believe implicitly that Henri, as *commis de rang* (an assistant waiter of sorts), discovered the dessert at the age of fourteen. The scene was the Café Royale in Monte Carlo, a favorite haunt of King Edward VII when he was the Prince of Wales. . . .

The basic *crêpe,* in itself, was nothing new; the French had been making thin pancakes for a long time. As Henri, in the presence of the Prince, worked in front of the chafing dish, expertly flipping his *crêpes* over and over and beginning to blend in a variety of cordials, he was startled by a sudden blaze of blue and gold flames. Acting as if this were a routine procedure, Henri proceeded to fold the *crêpes,* tossing them in the flaming liqueur. After the Prince and his party, which was comprised of men only and one little girl, had eaten the dessert, the monarch-to-be pronounced them exquisite and asked what they were called.

Deferring to His Highness, Henri said that since *crêpes* were of feminine gender, he would call them *crêpes princesse.* The Prince insisted, however, that since there was a young lady present at the conception of the dessert it should indeed be named in her honor. And so *crêpes Suzette* were born. . . . "There are many recipes for *crêpes Suzette,* some of which claim to be my original recipe," [Charpentier said]. "I have given a recipe or two for the *crêpes* to be published," he added with a wink, "but not this one." He then asked only that we never disclose his secrets in his lifetime . . . and we never did.

Memoirs and Menus

How to Learn the Secrets of a Sauce
GEORGE RECTOR

Diamond Jim had been to Paris and brought home with him glad tidings of a famous dish—fillet of sole Marguery, prepared only in the Café de Marguery. . . . I had served two years in our own kitchens and was a qualified chef. I was in Paris in less than three weeks [and] . . . I worked for eight months as an apprentice cook in the kitchens of the Café de Marguery. I learned the proper temperature of croutons, the correct humidity of consommé in an establishment where even knives and forks are laid out in true relation to the magnetic north and toothpicks have their latitude and longitude. Everything was figured out just so. The slightest swerve from ancestral routine was punished with reduction to the ranks.

But I was still far from sauce Marguery. There was another two months' sentence to serve as bus boy to a venerable waiter who smoothed out a tablecloth as lovingly as an operating surgeon pats his apron. I learned to move silently and swiftly. Then came my promotion to a journeyman waitership with ceremonies befitting a coronation. But I had a good deal still to learn about a nation that has the culinary art drawn so fine it can detect the difference between the juice of the clam during times of unrest and the same juice extracted from the clam at a period when the franc is at par. . . . The slightest error is detected by an epicure, and resented.

My time being over, I was then sent to the Café de Marguery kitchen to get the hang of the famous sauce. It required two months of close application in the kitchens before I felt qualified to say I had absorbed the technical details of fillet of sole with sauce Marguery. During those entire sixty days, for fifteen hours a day I experimented with sole and sauce, until I managed at last to produce a combination which was voted perfect by a jury of seven master chefs. It was a dish that even Brady might sop or a dunker dunk. . . .

I took the boat for America and bade farewell to France . . . the sole American carrying the secrets of centuries of European civilization. I was greeted on the wharf by Rector's Russian Orchestra, my father and Diamond Jim Brady, whose first words were, "Have you got the sauce?" An elaborate dinner was tendered to me that evening by my father. I was the guest of honor and also the cook. . . . I prepared fillet of sole with sauce Marguery. Diamond Jim dipped a spoon into it, sipped it, smacked his lips and said, "It's so good I could eat it on a Turkish towel!"

The Girl from Rector's

Cooking is a fickle and faltering art. Didn't Rembrandt ever ruin a picture? Then why shouldn't I have the right to ruin a dish?
—Chef Raymond Oliver, Restaurant Le Grand Véfour

ESCOFFIER REMEMBERED
JULIAN STREET

At dinner on the evening of October 28, 1946, we produced our one remaining magnum of eighteen-year-old Pierre-Jouët and asked our guests to join in drinking to the memory of August Escoffier. . . . Born on that day one hundred years earlier, he practiced his art actively for sixty-two years—an all-time record, we believe, for a chef—and after his retirement continued, as dean of culinary elder statesmen, to work, experiment, travel, and advise until in 1935, at the age of eighty-eight, he took his place in history, having done more than any other chef who ever lived to promote throughout the world the glory of the French cuisine.

He was eighty-four when we met him in 1930, and he had come from his home in Monte Carlo to New York for the opening of the Hotel Pierre, where Charles Scotto, frequently mentioned as Escoffier's favorite pupil, was chef. Scotto was a fine fellow and a great creative cook. Through the years we had many a fine meal with and by him, and of all these the only one to which we failed to give strict heed was a little supper à trois, served in a small room off the hotel kitchen, to which Scotto invited us so that we might become acquainted with the slender, aquiline, handsome, perceptive little man with the brilliant dark eyes and snowy hair and mustache who was humbly addressed by Scotto and many another chef of the first rank as "Master."

Escoffier was great partly because of his qualities as a human being and an artist, and partly because he was born into this world at exactly the right time. His early beginnings might have been those of any one of a thousand other French cooks. His native town, Villeneuve-Loubet, not far from Monte Carlo, is too small to be on any map we have. At the age of thirteen he became sauce boy in the kitchen of his uncle's hotel in Nice. There, beginning at the bottom of the ladder, he learned to cook while going to school at night. In 1865, when he was nineteen, he went to Paris and he became an under-cook in a fashionable restaurant on the Champs-Elysées. The name of the place was Le Petit Moulin Rouge—not to be confused with the Montmartre music hall—and once when the young Prince of Wales, destined later to reign as Edward VII, was dining there, the young Escoffier managed to peep at him. (As Escoffier was later to prepare many a meal for the Prince, this seems to call for a "little-did-he-think" paragraph, but we regret to say we haven't any left in stock.) In three years or so he became chef at this restaurant, but pretty soon came 1870 and the Franco-Prussian War, and he was called to the colors. After the war he worked for several years more at Le Petit Moulin Rouge, then at the Casino de Boulogne, and after that at the Restaurant Maire in Paris. And then, in 1882, when he was thirty-six years old, Opportunity came in the guise of the gifted César Ritz, who employed him as chef at one of his early luxury hotels, the Grand National at Lucerne.

The alliance with Ritz settled Escoffier's future. The two understood each other and also understood the times. Thenceforward Escoffier was Ritz's man, spiraling upward with him in a brilliant sybaritic world that seemed to be made to order for them—unless perhaps they were made to order for it.

Each was a genius in his line; each stamped his talent like a trade mark on everything he touched. Better, probably, than anyone else then living, Ritz knew how to gather in grandees; and equally well Escoffier knew how to feed them. And so in 1889, when Ritz assumed management of the newly built Savoy Hotel in London, Escoffier commanded the cuisine. And so again, when Ritz left the Savoy and in 1899 opened the new Carlton, Escoffier accompanied him. . . .

Escoffier had been chef at the Carlton only a few years when he published his masterly *Guide to Modern Cookery,* the most important of his seven or eight books. In his preface he attributed the principles of modern cookery to Carême, but pointed out that dining, along with other ways of life, was in the process of tremendous change. "A gradual but unquestionable revolution" was affecting ancestral English customs. Long and massive dinners served in pompous splendor by liveried footmen in the majestic halls of manor houses and palaces now belonged to state occasions. Meals in the great homes of fashionable society were becoming lighter, more French, and less formal; fashionable society was turning to the sumptuous hotels and restaurants where food was fine, the service brisk, the music gay, and the women, from peeresses to chorus girls, generally good-looking. It was, in short, the Edwardian Era—an era in which the social pace was set by the Prince of Wales, who was a gourmet and wine-lover, a racing-man and connoisseur of feminine charm. The Prince and his set liked to dine and sup in public places. First the Savoy, then the Carlton profited by this predilection, and the benefit continued even after 1901, when Edward, as King, began to practice greater circumspection.

When Escoffier felt that the Hotel Carlton kitchens could run along without him, he would take a leave of absence every now and then to set up a French kitchen staff in some new great hotel. These journeys took him to different parts of Europe and the Americas, to Africa and even India. Also he engaged to install Ritz-Carlton restaurants on new Hamburg-Amerika liners as they came out. Charles Scotto was the first chef sent to sea in this special service, and the ship was the *Amerika.* In 1905, before she sailed on her maiden voyage, Escoffier came from London and supervised a banquet on board at which Kaiser Wilhelm and many German notables were guests. . . .

That night at the Pierre, when it came time to say good-by to the two great chefs, a question popped into our mind, and we put it to them.

"You have spent your lives in striving for perfection of cuisine and service; but, no matter how one tries, things can't always go exactly right. What is the worst mishap you remember?"

They looked at each other and smiled.

"It was at the Carlton," said Monsieur Escoffier, "at supper on one of those fashionable Sunday nights we used to have, and it happened at a table where there were four couples, very smart. A young waiter was serving green peas to one of the ladies. Someone bumped his arm, and a helping of peas went down the front of her very low-cut gown.

"The poor devil of a waiter—he was just a youth—went all to pieces. Apologizing frantically in broken English, he began picking the peas from her *décolletage.* Whereupon, to complete the catastrophe, the lady's husband leaped to his feet and knocked the wretched boy down." . . .

Legend says the delectable dessert Peach Melba—most famous of modern dishes invented by the most famous of modern chefs—was the result of inspiration felt by him when he heard her sing in the opera *Lohengrin*.

When asked about this, his eyes twinkled and he said: "I often discussed with Mme. Melba the menus for her supper parties at the Savoy and the Carlton, but I am very much afraid I never heard her sing."

Table Topics

AN EVENING WITH TROISGROS PÈRE
ISRAEL SHENKER

Jean Baptiste Troisgros is making his nightly entrance into the dining room of the Restaurant Troisgros, of which he is the founding father; he is good-naturedly known as *patron* (boss). Monsieur Troisgros is stocky, well-dressed, and wears lightly-smoked glasses.

The *patron* is very much at home here. He approaches a table at which two guests are starting their dinner. Without a word the *patron* pours himself a little wine from their bottle.

"Undrinkable!" he exclaims, screwing his face into an expression of extreme distaste. "Are you *paid* to drink that? It's wood—all stalk and no grape—the wood of a cadaver. You like cadavers? Not possible!"

Peremptorily, he summons the sommelier and sends back the bottle, explaining that these guests are indignant at being served this atrocious wine. The maître d'hotel, who has enjoyed years of the *patron's* caprices, smoothly whisks away the offensive bottle and quickly returns with a different vintage. . . .

The *patron* is now smiling triumphantly—until he notices the tomato salads that his two new friends are about to savor. He gestures in despair, and without a word, reaches for a plate and pours off most of the *sauce vinaigrette*. "It's a swimming pool," he complains, and then, as they are about to eat the drained version, he stands by to lecture them on the art of preparing parsley. "Don't cut the parsley," he warns, "Tear off little bits—like this. Slight adjustments. Like coming home at eight o'clock and saying to your wife, 'Let's go to the theatre.' She was all dressed, and she'd carefully made up her face, but she'll still go off to make some adjustments to her face. Well, the same is true here. You add a little, make a slight adjustment."

Since the *patron* eats at the Troisgros every night, his critical faculties on the *qui vive,* his complaints briskly audible, *this* chapel of faithful gastronomy keeps getting better. "Eat the perch with a spoon," the *patron* is saying to two guests. "A spoon is more feminine. You caress the perch. A fork is so masculine—it's a nail, a spike, a *member.*"

The *patron* calls the sommelier back, and orders a white Sancerre and a red Margaux. "Try the Sancerre with the fish," the *patron* urges. "Now try the Margaux. Now the Sancerre. When you buy a suit you need to choose among several. You don't want to go into a store that offers you only one suit. Now tell me which is acid, and which is tender and fits your mouth."

Picking up his courage, the guest suggests that the Sancerre tastes acid, while the Margaux goes wonderfully with the fish. The *patron* looks pleased, as though a promising pupil had done well on his first examination. "The reason people in France drink white wine with fish is that somebody laid down the rule centuries ago, and he was stronger than everybody else," says the *patron.* "Look at the perch with the onions, carrots and parsley. It's tricolor—like our flag. The tomatoes simple, the perch simple."

He looks about the restaurant, then goes off to speak with other guests. But he returns in time for the cheese course—to stare at the cheese, and then at a man buttering his bread before he puts cheese on it. "Butter and cheese don't marry," the *patron* warns. "You don't go to the doctor when you're not sick, and when the cheese is fresh you don't need to *doctor* it with butter. Anyway, it just loads up your stomach. The cheese, however, helps digestion, because there are ferments in it. Cheese is like love—you mustn't throw yourself at it. 'Speak to me, I'll caress you, we have all the time in the world.' Don't hurry. Eat the cheese slowly. Now your mouth is full, fat. But the cheese doesn't irritate, does it?"

He looks on approvingly until—when the dessert is served—he discovers the waiter lavishly pouring raspberry sauce onto the strawberry sherbet. "No, no!" the *patron* shouts. "Not so much! Put it on like salt and pepper—just the right amount. . . . But the sherbet is too cold. Take your spoon and massage the sherbet—like a muscle, give it air. Give it soul. What does a meal require? Harmony. With a woman there's the hair, the dress, the stockings, the shoes, the bag. If you have a red dress, you don't put on yellow shoes. In a menu you have to succeed at harmony, and then your stomach is proud of you. It says, 'You're intelligent. What you've done is right.' "

The New York Times, June 3, 1973

A Way of Cooking

In Eugènie I plan to keep in close touch with the local people. One always learns from them. Last week some neighbors killed a pig and invited us for *la fête.* The neighbors had done fine things with their pig—*andouille, boudin noir, boudin blanc,* made exactly as their parents and grandparents made them. Modern butchers in our cities wouldn't approve of their methods—though they're methods that preserve the true flavor of the pork. Now there are modern factories where these things are made "scientifically," hygienically—but the true flavors are lost. Many people in the cities don't even known about those flavors. No one talks about them in the *charcuterie* factory. It's very sad.

Some people call me a dilettante, even a charlatan. . . . I do things that many people can't understand. Actually, I'm trying to bring back some things that existed a long time ago. If you go back far enough, you realize that you are not an inventor, only a recreator.

Somewhere I read that Claude Monet once said he would like to paint the way the birds sing. Sometimes I wish I could cook the way the birds sing.

—Michel Guérard

A Chef Named Otto Goes Shopping
JOHN McPHEE

. . . For all his rampant eclecticism—and the wide demands of his French-based, Continentally expanded, and sometimes Asian varietal fare—he knows where the resources of his trade are virtually unlimited. Mondays, when the inn is dark, he leaves his Herman boots in his bedroom—his terry-cloth hat, his seam-split dungarees—and in a dark-blue suit like a Barclays banker he heads for New York City. "In a few square blocks of this town are more consumer goods than in the whole of Soviet Russia," he remarked one time as he walked up Ninth Avenue and into the Salumeria Manganaro, where he bought a pound of taleggio ("It's like soft fontina") and was pleased to find white truffles. "They're from Piedmont. Grate them on pasta and they make it explode." At Fresh Fish (498 Ninth), he bought river shrimp from Bangladesh weighing up to a quarter of a pound each. He bought sausage flavored with provolone and parsley at Giovanni Esposito (500), and at Bosco Brothers (520) he stopped to admire but not to purchase a pyramid of pigs' testicles, which he said were delicious in salad. "Texas strawberries, you know. They're wonderful. They're every bit as good as sweetbreads. Boil them tender. Dry them. Dredge them in flour. Pan-fry them." At Simitsis International Groceries & Meat (529), he bought a big chunk of citron in a room full of open bins and buckets full of nuts and peppers, of great open cannisters of spices and sacks full of cornmeal, hominy grits, new pink beans, pigeon peas, split peas, red lentils, semolina, fava beans, buckwheat kasha, pearl barley, Roman beans, mung beans. "This place is fabulous. If I had a restaurant in New York —oh, boy! New York has everything you could possibly want in food. If you look hard enough, you'll find it all." At Citarella (2135 Broadway, at Seventy-fifth), he admired but did not buy a twenty-pound skate. He had walked the thirty-five blocks from Simitsis to Citarella. He prefers to walk when he's in town. I have seen him on the street with a full side of smoked salmon, wrapped in a towel, tied to a suitcase like a tennis racket. . . . "You poach skate and serve it with capers and black butter," he said. "It's a wonderful fish, completely underrated. I shot a big electric one in the Caymans." Citarella had flounder roe for eighty-five cents a pound. "You pay four dollars a pound for shad roe," said Otto. "Flounder roe is every bit as good. Shad roe has the name." He stopped for tea, ordering two cups, which he drank simultaneously. At Zabar's (Eightieth and Broadway), he bought thin slices of white-and-burgundy Volpi ham. "It's from St. Louis and it's as good as the best jamón serrano." At Japanese Food Land (Ninety-ninth and Broadway), he bought a couple of mounds of bean threads and four ounces of black fungus. On the sidewalks and having a snack, he ate twelve dried bananas. "That's, actually, nothing," he remarked. "I once et thirty-six sparrows in a bar in Spain. Gorriones, you know—spitted and roasted."

He tried to prove to himself not long ago that with United States ingredients he could duplicate the taste of chorizo, a hard Spanish sausage. He had to throw a good part of it away, because he failed to pack it tight enough and "fur grew inside." Casa Moneo, on Fourteenth Street between Seventh and Eighth, "is the best place for chorizos," he says. "They're made in Newark. They're as good as you can get in Spain."

He also buys chorizos at La Marqueta—a series of concession stalls housed below the railroad tracks on Park Avenue in Spanish Harlem. Chorizos. Jamón serrano. Giant green bananas—four for a dollar. Dried Irish moss. Linseed. Custard apples. "When they're very ripe they get slightly fermented. Mmm." He will buy a couple of pounds of ginger, a bunch of fresh coriander, a couple of pounds of unbleached, unpolished rice—letting go the dried crayfish and the green peanuts, the Congo oil and the pots of rue, letting go the various essences, which are in bottles labelled in Spanish: Essence of Disinvolvement, Essence of Envy and Hate. Breadfruit. Loin goat chops. "OHIO STATE UNIVERSITY" shopping bags. "Goat is milk-white when it's young. I don't want to get into an argument with these people, but that is not kid, it's lamb." Seeing a tray of pigs' tongues, he calls them "beautiful." And high-piled pigs' ears: "You slice them thin." . . .

He has lieutenants—certain fish merchants from his general neighborhood—who shop for him at the Fulton Market. But often he goes there himself, his body, at 4 A.M., feeling what he calls the resaca—"when the tide goes out and leaves the dry sand." He loves this world of rubber boots and bonfires, wet pavement and cracked ice, and just to enter it—to catch the bright eye of a fresh red snapper—is enough to cause his tides to rise. "There is no soul behind that eye," he says. "That is why shooting fish is such fun." Under the great illuminated sheds he checks everything (every aisle, bin, and stall), moving among the hills of porgies and the swordfish laid out like logs of copper beech, the sudden liveliness in his own eyes tempered only by the contrast he feels between the nonchalance of this New York scene and the careful constructions of the Algeciras wholesale fish market, where "they display the food with a lot more love."

"You never know what is going to be good. You have to look at everything," he says, and he looks at bushels of mussels, a ton of squid, bay scallops still in their shells. "Make sure they're not Maine mussels," he remarks, almost to himself. "If they are, forget it. I've had Maine mussels in Le Cygne. They're awfully tough. You just want the big squid." He looks at a crate of lobsters. They are dragons—up into their salad years—and three of them fill the crate, their heads seeming to rest on claws the size of pillows. "People think they're dragons because they look like dragons, but they're called that because they are caught in drag nets," he says, picking one up and turning it over, then the second, and the third. The third lobster has many hundreds of green pellets clinging like burrs to its ventral plates. "Eggs. They're better than caviar," says Otto. "They're so crunchy and so fresh-tasting—with lemon juice, and just enough bland vegetable oil to make them shine. You remove them from the lobster with a comb."

Baskets of urchins disappoint him. "See all the white spots? The freckles? See how the spines are flat? If the spines are standing, the creature is very much alive." For many months, he and his legates have been on the watch for urchins that are up to his standards. They must be very much alive because their roe, which is what he wants, is so rich and fragile that it soon goes bad.

He views with equal scorn a table of thin fresh herrings. He serves herring fillets in February, and this is not February. "That's the only time of the year when we can get big fat herrings. They're sensational then, maybe a day or two out of the sea. You have et bottled herring, have you? Awful. Herring, or salmon, in sour cream. They don't use crème fraiche. They use a sauce with dubious taste but with better keeping qualities." Otto never prepares herring the same way twice, but his goal is the same if his ingredients are not. He uses, say, vinegar and dill with peppercorns and onions, and his goal is to give the herring "a taste so clean it's lovely."

He feels the flanks of sand eels, each no longer than a pencil. "You dredge them with flour, drop them into deep fat, and eat them like French fries." And he presses the columnar flank of a swordfish, pleased to have it back in the market. He quotes Ted Williams. It is Williams' opinion that the surest way to save the Atlantic salmon is to declare the species full of mercury and spread the false word. "Swordfish is a bummer in the freezer," Otto says. "But there are all sorts of fish you *can* freeze. Shrimp are better frozen properly on a ship than carried for days to market unfrozen. In properly frozen shrimp there's never a hint of ammonia. Scallops freeze well, too—and crabmeat, octopus, striped bass, flounder, conch, tilefish, grouper. Red snapper frozen is no good. It gets watery, waterlogged. A soft-fleshed fish like sea trout is no good frozen. Freezing tuna or bluefish precipitates the oily taste. No frozen fish is better than fresh, but well-frozen fish is better than fish a week old."

Groupers—weighing thirty, forty pounds—face him in a row, like used cars. "You can split those big heads," he says. "Dredge them in flour and pan-fry them. Then you just pick at them—take the cheeks, the tongue."

There are conger eels the size of big Southern rattlesnakes. "With those I make jellied eel, cooked first with parsley, white wine, and onions. Almost no one orders it. I eat it myself."

As he quits the market, he ritually buys a pile of smoked chub, their skins loose and golden. "Smoked chub are so good," he says. "They just melt like butter. You can eat half a dozen quite happily on the way home in the car."

"Brigade de Cuisine," The New Yorker, February 19, 1979

FERNAND POINT
QUENTIN CREWE

His passionate concern was for the produce which he was going to cook. "If the Creator took the trouble to give us these exquisite things, it was so that we should prepare them with care and serve then with ceremony." Obviously any good, old-fashioned chef was always interested in buying good produce, but the very nature of the elaborate cuisine of the first twenty years of this century meant that a slightly less than perfect chicken might not taste very different from a perfect one by the time a chef had finished with it.

Point believed, above all else, that a chicken on a customer's plate should taste of chicken—the very best, most perfect chicken, the most carefully bred, the healthiest chicken, in its prime, kept for four or five days in the refrigerator after being killed, prepared with infinite care and cooked in such a way that nothing of its essence be lost. Every ingredient of a dish was subjected to precisely the same scrutiny and the same meticulous preparation, so that no vegetable should lose its juice, no fish its firmness. Nothing should be done one minute before it had to be done. It was one of Point's most rigid rules that, "Every morning must start from scratch, with nothing on the stoves. That is cuisine."

Cooking, for Point, was to capture the taste of the food and then to enhance it, rather as a composer may take a theme and then delight us with his variations, so that the sauce was never something used to conceal or mask a deficiency, but the supreme complement to bring out the perfection of his materials. "It is the sauce that distinguishes a good chef. The *saucier* is a soloist in the orchestra of a great kitchen."

It was not elaboration which was the mark of Point's cooking, but rather the most luxurious and polished simplicity. "Butter. Give me butter and then more butter," he said. It was the challenge of simple things which intrigued him, the apparently simple being often the hardest to achieve. "Take a *béarnaise* . . . what is it? A yolk of egg, a shallot, some tarragon. But, believe me, it takes years of practice before the result is perfect. Let your eyes wander for a moment and the sauce is unusable."

Point used to be in his kitchen by 5:00 every morning, and he would not finish until 11:00 at night, taking only two hours rest in the afternoon. The whole establishment was run with the greatest precision. 'The meal times of the staff in a restaurant must be as regular as a railway time table,' he wrote in his little white notebook. Cuisine, he decided, was a pitiless profession. 'A man is not a machine and a chef gets tired—but the clientele must never know it.'

Within three years of his marriage, the *auberge de campagne* had become world-famous. He had won three Michelin stars. Prince Curnonsky said, 'La Pyramide is one of the great restaurants of the world. There are people who have crossed the earth to eat one dish *chez* Point. It is the summit of culinary art.'

It was not until forty years later that everyone would start talking of *la nouvelle cuisine* and the publicity machines would puff out news of chefs in the same breathless tone accorded to film stars and pop-singers. But it was at Vienne that it began, without the questionable benefits of advertising and promotions. Point would never have lent his name to anything. He refused even to take over the kitchens for the maiden voyage of the *Normandie.* He was happy only at home.

At home he was an impressive figure—a large man knowing exactly what he wanted, somewhat eccentric and deferring only to one person—his wife, Mado. In some ways, he seemed autocratic. If people arrived for lunch after 2:00, he would say politely that it was too late. If they said it didn't matter what they ate, he would say that in that case it wouldn't matter where they ate it—but it wouldn't be at La Pyramide. If anyone started smoking before the cheese, Point at once brought them coffee and, if they protested, said amiably, "Oh, I thought you had finished."

He was not prompted by vanity. In his notebook he wrote that even if the clients made a face at the soup, one must keep on smiling. What mattered to him was that his food should reach the client in the best possible condition, and that the client should be in a condition to eat it. If the client then didn't like it, that was painful but also a matter of individual taste. But the point of it all was enjoyment. 'At table people enjoy one another; above all when one has managed to enchant them.'

Point enchanted everyone by the immense warmth of his personality. He refused to make any distinction between famous clients and those who were unknown, giving always of his best, so that La Pyramide became known as much for its friendliness as for the quality of its food. This informality appealed particularly to actors and writers like Cocteau, Colette, and Sacha Guitry, who enjoyed Point's extravagant style and his bizarre sense of humour.

Point had, to the fullest degree, that love of practical jokes which, for some reason, seems to be the characteristic of great chefs. He was always putting the lights out in the cellar when people were down there. He used to hide the brushes of the barber who came to shave him every morning. His friend and cellarman, Pierre Chauvon, was a great fisherman who looked forward, every year, to the opening of the fishing season. When the day came, he would find, as often as not, that his boat had disappeared. It would eventually be discovered up a tree, on the station platform, or in some improbable place to which Point had removed it. When he took visitors to the kitchen, he often kept them standing by the serving counter, holding their attention with anecdotes, while the young *commis* would creep under the counter and paint the visitors' shoes in lurid colours. One April 1, the staff cloakroom caught fire and Point telephoned the fire brigade. They just laughed, for they had been caught too often, and quite a lot of damage was done before they could finally be persuaded to come.

He was a believer in the living of life to the full. "Whenever I go to a restaurant I don't know, I always ask to meet the chef before I eat. For I know that if he is thin, I won't eat well. And if he is thin and sad, there is nothing for it but to run." But he would add, wryly, "Before misjudging a thin man, one should make an enquiry or two—he may be a formerly fat man."

Great Chefs of France

7
Hosts and Hostesses

Tempting things often seem better when they are shared. Good food is good enough alone, but it takes on eminence when there is host, or hostess—preferably both—with undiluted love for the act of hospitality, and guests to match. I don't mean that word in any sense of playing a role or impersonation, but as a mode of conduct and commitment. Generous people are good hosts. They are not simply well intended, but openly giving; not, come to think of it, as self-involved as Mr. Woodhouse in Jane Austen's Emma: *"His own stomach could bear nothing rich, and he never could believe other people to be different from himself." Uninterested in what food his guests might appreciate, Mr. Woodhouse was no great shakes as a host. "What was unwholesome to him he regarded as unfit for anybody. . . ." That is decidedly not the way to please, at least not those who love to eat. Hosts and guests must find common enthusiasms, gastronomically as well as otherwise. If they don't, things unpredictable may occur—as witness an incident here and there among the following glimpses of hostesses and hosts.*

A Hostly Use of Oranges
JOHN McPHEE

Before 1500, European orange growers mainly grew Bitter Oranges, because they were more aromatic, better as seasoning, and hence more valuable. Dinner guests could measure their importance in the regard of their hosts by the number of oranges that came to the table. One fourteenth-century cookbook, describing a dinner given by an abbot of Langy for his superior, the Bishop of Paris, indicates how impressive a meal it was by noting that the roast fish was seasoned with powdered sugar and Sour Oranges. In 1529, the Archbishop of Milan gave a sixteen-course dinner that included caviar and oranges fried with sugar and lemon, brill and sardines with slices of orange and lemon, one thousand oysters with pepper and oranges, lobster salad with citrons, sturgeon in aspic covered with orange juice, fried sparrows with oranges, individual salads containing citrons into which the coat of arms of the diner had been carved, orange fritters, a soufflé full of raisins and pine nuts and covered with sugar and orange juice, five hundred fried oysters with lemon slices, and candied peel of citrons and oranges.

Oranges

BRILLAT-SAVARIN—HE TOOK CARE
NOT TO BE CLEVERER
JOSEPH WECHSBERG

Brillat-Savarin did more than any other man for the evolution and theory of *la grande cuisine.* He wasn't a practicing cook, and the famous chefs of his time didn't like him because he was difficult, fastidious, and often pretentious. Antonin Carême, who died seven years after Brillat-Savarin, had little use for this "dilettante" who, it was rumored, ate too much and fell asleep at the table. But he and Carême curiously complement each other. Brillat-Savarin was the great philosopher of the art of gastronomy, and Carême became the founder of *la grande cuisine,* the practitioner who codified its laws and wrote its recipes. Only in France could two giants of the same art have lived at the same time. . . .

Jean Anthelme Brillat-Savarin was born on April 1, 1755, in Belley, a small town in the district of Bugey, now in the *département* of the Ain. (The 1969 *Michelin* features a single one-star restaurant in Belley, Pernollet, which had the good sense *not* to name its *specialité de la maison* after Brillat-Savarin.) His father, Marc Anthelme Brillat, was a distinguished lawyer and *procureur du roi*

(king's counsel). He later added his second name from Mademoiselle Savarin, a rich old aunt, who made this the condition of
leaving him her money. Brillat-Savarin's mother was Claudine-
Aurore Récamier. (The famous Madame Récamier that fascinated
Napoleon was Brillat-Savarin's cousin.) . . .

Young Jean Anthelme grew up in the comfortable house at 62,
Grande Rue, studied law, and became a well known lawyer at the
court of Belley. In 1789 he was elected to the Constituent Assem-
bly as deputy for the districts of Bugey and Valromey. These were
politically difficult times. Brillat-Savarin was a middle-of-the-
roader. Returning to his *département* he was named President of the
Tribunal of the Ain. He lost his posts in 1793, during the Reign
of Terror, and went home to Belley. There he was elected mayor,
but he didn't enjoy his new position for long. He was accused of
being a federalist and a member of certain royalist "front groups."
The Revolution was getting worse, and the guillotine was working
overtime. One night a friend came to warn him that "they" would
soon come to his home to arrest him.

Brillat-Savarin was no fool. He walked out of his house and kept
walking, with short interruptions, until he had crossed the Swiss
border near Geneva, some fifty miles away. He stayed for a while
in Lausanne but wasn't happy there, and he took a boat to America
"to find refuge, work and peace." Refugee Brillat-Savarin made
fast adjustments in New York. Later, he wrote: "That I prospered
in America was chiefly due to this: that from the day of my arrival
among the Americas, I spoke their language, dressed like them,
took care not to be cleverer than they, and praised all their ways:
thus repaying the hospitality I met with.". . .

He returned to France in 1796. His name had been removed from
the blacklist of émigrés, and he became secretary on the staff of the
French Army in Germany under Augereau. Later, he became commissary of the government of the *département* of Seine-et-Oise, and
he was made a counselor in the Court of Appeals. He was one of the
highest judges in France, and somehow he managed to keep his
position during the various political eras that followed. His father's
estate and a small vineyard had been confiscated when he went to
America, but he was indemnified and bought a nice house in Vieu,

which is still there. On the mantelpiece of the salon is his bust, made by Vermare. He looks satisfied with the world and with himself. Occasionally, his pupils and friends would meet there to celebrate with a lunch in his honor. Tendret remembers Brillat-Savarin, "with his round face, bright eyes, small forehead, short nose, full lips and well-rounded chin . . . truly an heir of gourmandism."

Brillat-Savarin uses the term "gourmandism" in the sense of "gastronomy," but doubtless he was both a gourmet and a gourmand in today's sense of these words. Apparently he was able, physically and financially, to enjoy Gargantuan meals. . . .

Brillat-Savarin never married. He would spend ten months of the year in Paris, and he usually came to his country home for his birthday. His unmarried sisters, known as "la Marion" and "la Padon," lived there all year round. A chronicler reports that "the ladies stayed in bed ten months and got up only two days before the arrival of their brother." Brillat-Savarin would receive his guests there and give the wonderful dinners he later wrote about. It was a fine place for a practicing gastronome. . . .

Brillat-Savarin had both good taste and a great deal of money. The pleasures of gastronomy were never inexpensive. When he was not giving dinners for his friends, he would be dining in their homes. He was able to eat two copious meals a day, and in between he would write legal opinions, preside in court, play his Stradivari, and work on his books. He didn't believe in physical exercise. He was already well known as the "serious" author of legal and historical essays when he published his great work. Perhaps he had some second thoughts about his high position because he put out *Physiologie du goût* anonymously, and at his own expense, calling himself *"le professeur."* After his death the publisher Sautelet, a smart fellow, offered to buy all the book rights from Brillat-Savarin's heirs, a brother (who was an army colonel) and a nephew. The colonel said, "What the devil should we do with Anthelme's book?" and the nephew said, "Let's get rid of it." They sold the book rights for fifteen hundred francs. . . .

The book consists of "gastronomical meditations." In the chapter "On the Senses," the Professor adds to the customary five a sixth, "physical desire, which draws the two sexes together," and he concludes, ". . . although each sex possesses everything necessary to produce this reaction of desire, male and female must be together before they can attain the end for which it was created." So he *did* give some thought to matters other than the table! The Professor defines gastronomy as "the intelligent knowledge of whatever concerns man's nourishment . . ." and claims it is part of natural history, physics, chemistry, cookery, business, and even political economy, "because of the sources of revenue which gastronomy creates. . . ." He even wrote about "political gastronomy," because "Meals have become a means of governing." He may have written these lines during the Congress of Vienna, when Talleyrand is said to have achieved at the dinner table, with the help of his chef, Carême, what he failed to do at the conference table. Brillat-Savarin later became a sort of gastronomic adviser to Talleyrand, who paraphrased one of the Professor's aphorisms, "The first duty of a statesman is to look well after his liver." Judging by the dour, dyspeptic countenance of some of our leading statesmen, they don't know their first duty. . . .

"I am happier than I imagined possible to be able to give to my readers a wonderful bit of news," Brillat-Savarin writes in the chapter, "Inevitable Longevity of Gourmands." "Good living is far from being destructive to good health . . . all things being equal, gourmands live much longer than other folk. This has been mathematically proven in a very well-constructed essay which was read just lately at the Academy of Sciences by Dr. Villermet."

More power to Dr. Villermet—and especially to our Professor, who died at the age of seventy-one, of pneumonia.

JUDGE TRUAX AND THE FLIGHTY GOOSE
CAROL TRUAX

The round dark mahogany dining table . . . just right for the four of us . . . could be magically lengthened for the large dinner parties Father liked to assemble. He had twenty-two real Chippendale chairs to set around the table, with seats upholstered in red brocade velvet, proportioned to accommodate the broad bottoms of heroic trenchermen in an earlier age. They just fitted Father.

Red velvet portières to match divided the dining room from the parlor. There were gold drapes on the parlor side, and the sliding doors ran in the space between.

Since those doors were habitually kept open, that space was just right for a small girl to lurk in. I was never invited to Father's dinner parties, but now and then I managed to be an unseen and unsuspected guest. It was exciting to curl up between the portières and see the guests go past me into the dining room. . . .

Thus I was among those present when my Father committed one of his rare social errors. He was carving a large goose, when suddenly the resisting bird with a great slide took wing and landed squarely in Mrs. Dugro's broad embroidered lap. I heard the shocked exclamations, and the ensuing horrified hush as the whole table waited to see how the Judge would apologize for such a monumental *faux pas.*

Did my Father apologize? Not he. He drew himself up with the portentous frown he had learned to assume on the bench.

"Madam," he said sternly, "I'll trouble you for that goose!"

Father Was a Gourmet

THE GREATEST GASTRONOMER
LATELY THOMAS

Just as Sam Ward had been accorded the title "King of the Lobby," so, in the seventies and eighties, was he recognized as America's premier authority on matters pertaining to food and wine. His principal renown, then and since, rests upon his eminence as a connoisseur of the *haute cuisine,* its preparation and service. . . .

According to Sam, the preparation of a dinner must begin with the marketing; the ingredients must be of the choicest quality, and a host should attend to this matter himself. Siro Delmonico, of the famous family, did his own marketing every day, and Sam wrote poems to Siro Delmonico. The next step was to *compose* the menu, and this should be done in consultation with the cook. Ward McAllister [his cousin] reported Sam's practice. First, the chef should be brought to "fever heat by working on his ambition and his vanity. Impress upon him that this particular dinner will give him fame and lead to fortune." At this point—according to McAllister—Sam would "bury his head in his hands and (seemingly to the chef) rack his brain, seeking inspiration, fearing lest the fatal mistake should occur of letting two white or two brown sauces follow each other in succession, or truffles appear twice in the dinner. The distress his countenance wore as he repeatedly looked up at the chef, as if for advice and assistance, would have its intended effect on the culinary artist, and *his* brain would at once act in sympathy." . . .

In his own writings Sam Ward laid down the broad rules that should govern the organization and presentation of a dinner of merit. In the first place, "the host must feel that for the nonce he is Aladdin served by the genii of the lamp, in his own palace." Next: "The menu is the plan of campaign, dependent upon the numbers of the enemy who will be reduced to capitulation by the projected banquet. The host will inspect it and suggest changes, often an abridgment, but if wise, rarely an enlargement. People who have come into an unexpected fortune, or have stolen a railroad, may take needless pride in exuberant, costly, and ostentatious plenteousness. But the elect require an early inspection of the plan, and ponder thoughtfully the affinities of its details, the harmony of the ensemble, and the selection and distribution of the wines, which may be likened to the application of algebra to geometry. The whole should be suitable to the prevailing season, and last, not least, to the temperaments of the guests."

Sam took pride in his menus. Many of these he filed away, with a methodicity unusual in him, in a folder labeled: *"Menus of a few of the dinners wherein the Honbl. Samuel Ward took part—or partook of, as you like it."* The menu cards were elaborate. The card for a banquet at the Union Club on St. Patrick's Day, 1877, for example, was decorated with a water color from Tiffany's studios. Another, for a dinner given on June 14, 1879, at Pinard's restaurant, by the eminent New York attorney, Charles O'Connor, in honor of Chief Justice Morrison R. Waite, was printed on gilt-edged parchment embellished with a songbird in feathers. Sam planned this affair and sat at the speakers' table with such worthies as Joseph Choate, S. L. M. Barlow, August Belmont, Samuel J. Tilden, James B. Keene, and William Waldorf Astor (Sam's nephew by marriage). Secretary of State [William M.] Evarts, regretting that he had been detained in Washington, the next day congratulated Sam upon a "magnum opus," as reported in the *New York World*. . . .

Sam preferred to dine in company, although even when he sat alone at table, he could not be said to be dining without a friend, for between courses he would pull from his pocket the slim volume of Horace's poems, explaining, "When I have no other friend present, I invite my Horace." . . .

It was the combination of this social adaptability and his peerless purveyance as an epicure that distinguished Sam as host. His own eating habits were classically simple. He tasted with relish, but sparingly, the many-course repasts which custom prescribed for public functions, but when dining alone he usually preferred a plain chop, or a single dish, such as a *rouleau* of truffles *en serviette*, washed down with a glass of sound wine. His breakfast ordinarily was a baked apple and tea, about the brewing of which he was extremely particular. He imported his own tea, China, usually. He would place a liberal quantity of leaves in a preheated earthen pot, pour on boiling water, let it stand a very few moments, then decant the tea into a second pot. About coffee he was just as exacting, storing it green and roasting it at the time of brewing. To this temperate eating he attributed his being able to slim down to one hundred seventy-four pounds towards 1880,—the first time he had tipped the scales at that figure in twenty years. His digestion remained incorruptible. "To think that I can go through such a banquet as Mr. Evarts gave last Monday," he told his niece Daisy Terry, "twenty-two courses, and wake up singing like a lark, and that he, after a dinner at the club with me, should have suffered torments that still rack him!" . . .

The evidence is ample of Sam's preeminence in the American hierarchy of the table, ranking second to none, and his scattered writings affirm his worthiness of association with the brightest luminaries of the French firmament. Although time and circumstances have given him less fame posthumously, it may be said safely that, as a host, Sam Ward was no bit inferior to Grimod de la Reynière, and as a *raisonneur* and illuminator of gastronomy, he was on a par with his engaging contemporary, Charles Monselet. But none of the gastronomes of French renown were endowed with "Uncle Sam's" grace and wit (Talleyrand alone excepted), and not one possessed his unique power of personality, his charm.

Sam Ward, King of the Lobby

INVITING A FRIEND TO SUPPER

BEN JONSON

Tonight, grave sir, both my poore house, and I
   Doo equally desire your companie:
Not that we thinke us worthy such a ghest,
   But that your worth will dignifie our feast,
With those that come; whose grace may make that seeme
   Something, which, else, could hope for no esteeme.
It is the faire acceptance, Sir, creates
   The entertaynment perfect: not the cates.
Yet you shall have, to rectifie your palate,
   An olive, capers, or some better sallade
Ushring the mutton; with a sort-leg'd hen,
   If we can get her, full of egs, and then,
Limons, and wine for sauce: to these, a coney
   Is not to be despair'd of, for our money;
And, though fowle, now, be scarce, yet there are clarkes,
   The skie not falling, thinke we may have larkes.
Ile tell you of more, and lye, so you will come:
   Of partrich, pheasant, wood-cock, of which some
May yet be there: and godwit, if we can:
   Knat, raile, and ruffe too. How so ere, my man

Shall read a piece of VIRGIL, TACITUS,
  LIVIE, or some better booke to us,
Of which wee'll speake our minds, amidst our meate;
  And Ile profess no verses to repeate:
To this, if ought appeare, which I not know of,
  That will the pastrie, not my paper, show of
Digestive cheese, and fruit there sure will bee. . . .

WALLACE STEVENS COMES TO DINNER

My friend Phil May asked to bring his friend, Wallace Stevens, the poet, to dinner at Cross Creek. The great man was on a strict diet, he wrote, and must be served only lean meat, a green salad and fruit. I planned my best baked-in-sherry-ham for the rest of the company, and wracked my brains for a method of making of lean meat a delicacy. I decided to prepare the heart of a Boston pot roast of beef in an individual casserole, with sherry. The poet proved delightful but condescending. He began on his beef, looked over at the clove-stuck ham, and announced that he would partake not only of that, but of all the other rich dishes on the table. His diet, it seemed, was not for the purpose of health, but for vanity. He was, simply, reducing. I snatched his sherried beef from him, pulled out the bone and tossed it on the hearth to my pointer dog.

—MARJORIE KINNAN RAWLINGS
Cross Creek Cookery

THE INVITATION

. . . and pondering on the food,
How cold it was, and how it child my blood;
I curst the master; and I damn'd the souce;
And swore I'de got the ague of the house.
Well, when to eat thou dost me next desire,
I'le bring a Fever, since thou keep'st no fire.

—ROBERT HERRICK

Setting the Table

Prepare the table according to the season: in warm, well-closed places in the winter, in cool and apt ones in the summer. Spring should find you in a large hall, and you should sprinkle flowers about the table. In the fall burn perfumed woods. During the summer the floor should be strewn with fragrant fronds from trees, vines, and willows, which placed together will perfume the air, and make the place fresh and new. During the fall decorate with pears and apples and grapes attached with wire.

—Platina, 1508

"If You Do Not Ever Afterwards Prefer My Table"
PLINY

How happened it, my friend, that you did not keep your engagement the other night to sup with me? But take notice, justice is to be had, and I expect you shall full reimburse me the expense I was at to treat you; which, let me tell you, was no small sum. I had prepared, you must know, a lettuce apiece, three snails, two eggs, and a barley cake, with some sweet wine and snow: the snow most certainly I shall charge to your account, as a rarity that will not keep. Besides all these curious dishes, there were olives from Andalusia, gourds, shallots, and a hundred other dainties equally sumptuous. You should likewise have been entertained either with an interlude, the rehearsal of a poem, or a piece of music, as you liked best; or (such was my liberality) with all three. But the luxurious delicacies and Spanish dancers or a certain—I know not who, were, it seems, more to your taste. However, I shall have my revenge of you, depend upon it—in what manner, shall be at present a secret. In good truth it was not kind thus to mortify your friend,—I had almost said yourself;—and, upon second thoughts, I do say so: for how agreeably would we have spent the evening, in laughing, trifling, and deep speculation! You may sup, I confess, at many places more splendidly; but you can nowhere be treated with more unconstrained cheerfulness, simplicity and freedom; only make the experiment; and if you do not ever afterwards prefer my table to any other, never favour me with your company again. Farewell.

Letter to Septimius Clarus

DINNER GUEST FOR RENT
ART BUCHWALD

A few years ago I wrote about the shortage of guests on the Riviera, and pointed out that while everyone had a villa or a yacht, the natural resources in house guests and boat guests were drying up fast, and unless a guest conservation program was instituted, the people along the Riviera would soon find themselves dining and sailing alone. Well, they scoffed at my warning, but this year the Riviera is facing its worst guest shortage since Elsa Maxwell tried to get a passenger list together for a cruise of the Greek islands.

The profiteering in guests this year is unimaginable.

I know, because that's how I was paying for my vacation. It happened by accident, but if a fellow doesn't take advantage of a situation, he'll wind up spending his own money on the Riviera, and who wants to do that?

It seems that fellow columnist John Crosby showed up in Monte Carlo and innocently asked me if I could get him invited to the Red Cross dinner and gala at which Sammy Davis, Jr., was going to entertain.

I pretended it would be difficult but said I'd do my best. What I knew but John didn't was that the ratio of women to men along the Riviera was six to one, and hostesses were willing to pay anything for a single man to sit at one of their tables.

An hour later I was down at the beach making discreet inquiries. I was tipped off that a Mrs. Max Kettner of New York had three extra women for the gala evening and was getting desperate.

"How would you like to have Crosby at your table?" I asked her.

"Bing Crosby?" she asked.

"Listen," I said, "if I had Bing Crosby I wouldn't be here—I'd would be negotiating at the Palace with Princess Grace.

"My boy's John Crosby, but he's been a helluva dinner guest in his time. He's eaten at Bill Paley's house, he's broken bread with Mrs. Leland Hayward, he's had coffee with Desi and Lucy twice. This guy is no bum—he's Yale '36, and that gives a presold table audience right there."

Mrs. Kettner wet her lips. "How much are you asking for him?"

"It depends," I said. "Do you want him for cocktails before the dinner?"

"What's the difference?" Mrs. Kettner wanted to know.

"Well, I can book him for cocktails before the gala at the Hotel de Paris with another party, and that would cut down the price for you. He could join you for dinner around ten o'clock."

"I think I should have him for cocktails," Mrs. Kettner said. "But I'd better warn you that I don't want to pay more than $1,500 for the evening."

"Fifteen hundred dollars?" I said. "Why, I turned down $2,000 from Sam Spiegel for Crosby to lunch with him on his yacht, and Crosby didn't have to put on a black tie either. If you're going to start talking chicken feed I'd rather have Crosby stay in his room tonight."

"I'll pay $1,750," Mrs. Kettner said.

"This is ridiculous. I couldn't get you a golf caddy for $1,750 tonight. Look, Crosby's a syndicated columnist, he's a name. You pair him up with one of your female guests and she's going to be impressed—the guy's got class. I'm not going to sell him out for a song."

"Well, how much do you want?" Mrs. Kettner said.

"The same as Sammy Davis, Jr., is getting for entertaining tonight," I said.

"But that's outrageous!" Mrs. Kettner replied.

"Look. Entertainers are a dime a dozen," I said. "Where are you going to find dinner guests at this late date? After all, Davis will only be on stage entertaining; Crosby will actually be at your table sitting with you."

Mrs. Kettner finally agreed, provided Crosby also would come for cocktails.

I pocketed the money and then rushed back to tell Crosby the news I had managed to get him invited to the gala.

Tears of gratitude poured from his eyes. "How can I ever thank you?" he said.

"Forget it, kid," I said, punching him lightly in the shoulder. "You can do a favor for me sometime."

To this day Crosby doesn't know how much he is worth. He still thinks I did him a good turn. If I only had three Crosbys a season, I could make enough dough to retire for the rest of the year.

Is It Safe to Drink the Water?

To invite a person to your house is to take charge of his happiness as long as he is beneath your roof.

—BRILLAT-SAVARIN

A boastful Welshman was bragging that when his father once entertained twelve guests he had twelve cooks to provide for them. "Ah!" was the rejoinder, "I suppose every man toasted his own cheese."

—ANONYMOUS

The confidences of the dinner-table are held to be inviolable— the Romans always placed a vase of roses in the center of the table as the emblem of silence, to signify that what was heard *sub rosa* ("under the rose") was not to be lightly repeated elsewhere.

—FREDERICK W. HACKWOOD

Conversation is but carving:
Give no more to every guest
Than he's able to digest;
Give him always of the prime,
And but little at a time;
Give to all but just enough,
Let them neither starve nor stuff,
And that each may have his due,
Let your neighbour carve for you.
—SIR WALTER SCOTT

COPING ON SHORT NOTICE
REV. JAMES WOODFORDE

Feb. 29, 1788—Mr. Taswell sent early to me this Morning that
he would take a Family Dinner with us to-day and desired us to
send to Mr. Custance that they might not wait dinner for them.
. . . At 11 o'clock this Morning I sent Briton to Weston House to
let them know that Mr. Taswell was to take a Family Dinner with
us to-day, Briton returned pretty soon and informed us that Mr.
and Mrs. Custance, Lady Bacon and Son and Master Taswell
would also come and partake of the Family Dinner, and they sent
us some Fish, a wild Duck and a Sallad. It occasioned rather a
bustle in our House but we did as well as we could—We had not
a bit of White Bread in House, no Tarts whatever, and this Week
gave no Order whatever to my Butcher for Meat, as I killed a Pigg
this Week. We soon baked some white bread and some Tartlets
and made the best shift we could on the whole. About 3 o'clock
Mr. and Mrs. Custance, Lady Bacon and Son, Mr. Taswell and
Nephew arrived and they dined, drank Coffee and Tea and returned home about 7 o'clock this Evening to Weston House.
. . . We gave the Company for Dinner some Fish and Oyster Sauce,
a nice piece of Broiled Beef, a fine Neck of Pork roasted and Apple
Sauce, some hashed Turkey, Mutton Stakes, Sallad, etc., a wild
Duck roasted, fryed Rabbits, a plumb Pudding and some Tartlets.

Desert, some Olives, Nuts, Almonds, and Raisins and Apples. The whole Company were pleased with their Dinner, etc. Considering we had not above 3 hours notice of their coming we did very well in that short time. All of us were rather hurried on the Occasion.

Diary

DR. ALBERT SCHWEITZER, HOST
JOHN GUNTHER

At 6:30 P.M. a bell announces the end of the day; at 7:30 comes the dinner bell and at 8:30 a final bell after which the *indigènes* are now allowed out of doors. Europeans, too, seldom stir outside after this hour, because of the danger from mosquitoes. But once we joined the whole staff at the riverbank, when Schweitzer celebrated a saint's day by building a large fire of palm fronds and watching it burn fiercely. That was all that happened, but it was a beautiful and impressive ceremony. The Doctor's face was rapt, and the flames sounded like surf.

The dining table is long enough to hold twenty or more people, and is lit by a row of kerosene lamps. Schweitzer's cook is a Swiss lady, and the meals are simple, ample, and altogether delicious. At breakfast pots of tea and coffee are waiting, with toast and several kinds of jam made out of local fruit. At lunch there will be a vegetable or fruit stew—for instance of papaya and carrots mixed together—plain boiled sweet potatoes in their jackets, noodles, breadfruit fritters, palm nuts, fresh salad, and steamed bananas. Once we had meat—some lamb sent over by a neighboring mission. Eggs or fish are served every day, sometimes twice a day. At dinner tureens of healthy thick soup are placed on the tables as the company assembles, and this is followed by rice or macaroni, other vegetables, and great bowls of fresh fruit cut up into a macédoine.

Schweitzer sits at the middle of the long table flanked by Miss [Emma] Haussknecht and Miss [Matilde] Kottmann, with guests of honor opposite. Gently the two nurses offer him special delicacies, like radishes from his preciously tended garden, tidbits of salad, or brown beans. At each meal, including breakfast, Schweitzer eats steamed bananas. Sometimes he puts food into a soup plate, and eats with a spoon. When fresh fruit is served he pulls a large penknife out of his pocket, and peels an orange or grapefruit with it.

Immediately before each meal Schweitzer says a brief grace in French; immediately after dinner (no meal takes more than half an hour) he announces a hymn in a decisive voice, and hymn books are passed around. He walks to an upright piano at one end of the room, and plays briefly with great vigor and precision as the company sings. He returns to his place at the table, inspects carefully a list of Bible passages, slowly opens the Bible, and reads a few lines from scripture. . . .

After dinner doctors and nurses gather at one end of the long room, and have cinnamon tea or some similar mild stimulant. Schweitzer may, or may not join them. . . . Always on leaving the dining hall he takes with him odd bits of food, which he gives to the antelopes.

Inside Africa

A CODE OF CONDUCT FOR A FRENCH GUEST

Hélène had her opinions, she did not for instance like Matisse. She said a frenchman should not stay unexpectedly to a meal particularly if he asked the servant beforehand what there was for dinner. She said foreigners had a perfect right to do these things but not a frenchman and Matisse had once done it. So when Miss Stein said to her, Monsieur Matisse is staying for dinner this evening, she would say, in that case I will not make an omelette but fry the eggs. It takes the same number of eggs and the same amount of butter but it shows less respect, and he will understand.

—GERTRUDE STEIN
The Autobiography of Alice B. Toklas

Byron Fakes a Monkish Appetite

Neither Moore nor myself had ever seen Byron when it was settled that he should dine at my house. . . . When we sat down to dinner I asked Byron if he would take soup? "No, he never took soup."—"Would he take fish?" "No, he never took fish."—Presently I asked if he would eat some mutton? "No, he never ate mutton."—I then asked if he would take a glass of wine. "No, he never tasted wine." It was now necessary to inquire what he *did* eat and drink; and the answer was, "Nothing but hard biscuits and soda-water." Unfortunately, neither hard biscuits nor soda-water were at hand; and he dined upon potatoes bruised down on his plate and drenched with vinegar.—My guest stayed till very late discussing the merits of Walter Scott and Joanna Baillie.—Some days after, meeting Hobhouse, I said to him, "How long will Lord Byron perservere in his present diet?" He replied, "Just as long as you continue to notice it." I did not know then, what I now know to be a fact—that Byron, after leaving my house, had gone to a club in St. James's Street, and eaten a hearty meat-supper.

—Samuel Rogers
Table Talk

Don't Close Your Lips

If you wish to imitate the French or the English, you will put every mouthful into your mouth with a fork; but if you think, as I do, that Americans have as good a right to their own fashions as the inhabitants of any other country, you may choose the convenience of feeding yourself with your right hand, armed with a steel blade: and provided you do it neatly, and do not put in large mouthfuls, or close your lips tight over the blade, you ought not to be considered as eating ungenteelly.

—Mrs. John Farrar
The Young Lady's Friend, 1838

THE HOSPITALITY OF CHARLES DICKENS
EDGAR JOHNSON

Life at Gad's Hill reflected a routine of genial if strenuous hospitality on the part of its host. Breakfast was between nine and ten-thirty. . . . In the dining room, bright with mirrors, Dickens gave a morning greeting and recommended some savory dish from the sideboard, perhaps kidneys with an appetizing dressing, although he was an abstemious eater himself, and seldom took more than a rasher of bacon, an egg, and a cup of tea. After breakfast, Dickens wrote all morning, either in his study or in the chalet, while his guests could please themselves, smoking cigars, reading the papers, strolling in the garden among its clambering honeysuckle, clumped nasturtiums, red geraniums, mignonette. . . .

At one o'clock Dickens emerged for lunch, a substantial meal, though again he himself ate little, usually confining himself to bread and cheese and a glass of ale. The dinner menu was always on the sideboard at lunchtime, and Dickens would discuss the items. "Cock-a-leekie? Good, decidedly good; fried soles with shrimp sauce? Good again; croquettes of chicken? Weak, very weak; decided want of imagination here." For the rest of the day he devoted himself to his guests. . . .

After taking a shower bath, which he loved, Dickens would be as fresh at dinner as any of his guests. Though he was not a glittering conversationalist, he sparkled with the pleasure of companionship. He was sometimes so comical that he convulsed the servants. . . . But, better than a brilliant talker, he was a brilliant listener, who stimulated others to their best, filled everyone with the conviction that Dickens delighted in his company, and allowed no man to be a bore.

Charles Dickens, His Tragedy and Triumph

MRS. CHARLES DICKENS, HOSTESS
MARGARET LANE

I sometimes turn over the pages of a little-known volume called *What Shall We Have for Dinner?* It was published when Isabella Beeton was sixteen, written under a pseudonym, Lady Maria Clutterbuck, and was the sole literary production of Mrs. Charles Dickens. (She had played the minor part of Lady Maria in an amateur theatrical production two years before.) It consists almost entirely of dinner menus, designed for two, four, six, and up to twenty-four persons, offers no advice, contains only a handful of recipes, and gives a terrifying picture of Victorian hospitality. It is easier to understand Jane Carlyle's nasty remarks about the vulgarity of Dickens's dinner parties when one has studied these bills of fare. "Such a getting up of the steam is unbecoming to a literary man. . . . The dinner was served up in the new fashion, not placed on the table at all, but handed round—only the dessert on the table and quantities of artificial flowers—but such an overloaded dessert! pyramids of figs, raisins, oranges—ach!"

When entertaining, the Victorian table was expected to groan; the status symbol was a superfluity of dishes, and the menus in Mrs. Dickens's book belong to the period of Dickens's established prosperity, when he was living with his numerous family at 1 Devonshire Terrace and beginning to entertain the comparatively famous. Every course must offer at least an alternative, and nobody shrank from sickening repetition. For a little dinner for eight or ten persons Mrs. Dickens recommends three soups, four fish dishes, eleven separate dishes of meat and game, three different cream puddings and a savoury. When lobsters are in season she offers boiled salmon with lobster sauce *and* filleted lobster for the first course, lobster cutlets in the second, and, after the usual three puddings and a savoury, lobster salad. . . .

Mrs. Dickens's menus are singularly repetitive in their puddings, and more meals than one would have thought possible end with bloaters. A Yarmouth bloater, like toasted cheese, was a favourite savoury at Devonshire Terrace, but to find it recommended again and again for a 'dinner for four or five people,' at the end of a substantial meal and following, say, apple fritters or a boiled batter pudding, suggests almost an obsession.

The emphasis on rich and starchy dishes, as well as the monotony of Mrs. Dickens's collection, makes one wonder whether Dickens's growing distate for his marriage, which culminated in the famous breach and in prolonged unhappiness for both parties, may not have been—at least partly—due to the fact that while still young she became mountainously fat. . . . Her Italian Cream, to take a recurring example, begins—"Whip together for nearly an hour a quart of very thick scalded cream, a quart of raw cream . . . with ten ounces of white powdered sugar, then add half-a-pint of sweet wine and continue to whisk until it is quite solid. . . ."

Poor lady, she would have done better to follow the advice of Mrs. Beeton, but alas, she was born too soon; the cookery books of her time thought nothing of gallons of cream and quantities of beaten yolks and powdered sugar. . . .

Purely for Pleasure

ENTERTAINING WILLIAM FAULKNER
ANTHONY WEST

William Faulkner was not an easy man to know. He liked keeping a lot of himself to himself, and wherever I found him . . . [in] his own place in Oxford, Mississippi, or in my own house in the country, he was the same self-contained, immaculate, and untouched figure. The great mystery about him was that his silences —he could spend an entire day with you without speaking, if he felt like it—were as full as most people's conversation. One just felt more alive when he was around. His compact, neat person radiated something stimulating. Though I don't get much sense of what his people eat when I read his books, I always found him very responsive to a good meal. He would thaw out, or emerge from his shell, and deliver a rich stream of reminiscence when he had eaten well. . . .

The flavor of his after-dinner talk comes through in some parts of his work with extraordinary directness. Some passages in his books, long codas in which comic invention is piled on top of comic invention—such as the yarn in *Mosquitoes* about the bayou farmer whose sheep got crossed with alligators—were, in fact, set pieces that he talked for the sheer pleasure of reeling them off when he was in the mood. I am almost certain that they originated that way.

One of the things I used to cook for him was steak *poivrade.* This is a matter of slices of filet mignon cut between a half and a quarter of an inch thick. Before they go into the frying pan they should be slightly scored on both sides with a sharp knife, salted, rubbed all over with the cut face of a garlic clove, and finally coated with very coarsely ground or cracked peppercorns. While you are doing this a tablespoonful of butter and a like measure of olive oil should be heating in the pan, which should be one of those heavy cast-iron affairs coated with enamel. When the mixture is beginning to bubble you should be about ready with the slices of meat, which are done to my taste after they have had a minute and a half on each side.

I used to give Mr. Faulkner his steak *poivrade* with a potato dish that involved about two or two-and-a-half pounds of boiled potatoes, sliced wafer thin, a couple of onions sautéed in olive oil until they were softened and beginning to turn brown, a handful of diced ham, two eggs, and a pint of milk. The sliced potatoes are put in a well-buttered Pyrex dish in layers, and every second or third layer is given a sprinkling of onion, diced ham, pepper, and salt. The eggs are then beaten into the milk and the mixture is poured into the dish, which cooks for thirty-five to forty minutes at 350°F. As a rule, the top layer of the potatoes rises out of the milk and a few knobs of butter should be put on it so that the dish will be topped with a pleasant, crisp brown crust when it is served. I used to give this combination to Mr. Faulkner together with a salad of undressed cos lettuce and a bottle of Lynch-Bages or Brane-Cantenac. We would finish up with a wedge of Brie and a good pear, or, when the season was right, a blissful invention of my wife's, mulberries washed in kirsch. After such a meal Mr. Faulkner was very likely to lean back and talk.

Remembering William Faulkner

"The Key to Open the Heart"

I recall a French painter, Fernand Léger, who, when he found his French friends too unhappy in New York during the war, would invite them to his studio to dine on a *pot-au-feu* that he prepared himself after the Norman country fashion. The beef melted in the mouth; coarse salt, mustard and horse-radish accompanied it; for dessert there was an apple pie washed down with an old Calvados. For an evening one could believe oneself back in France. In the same way I have been touched when Italians have served me the best tagliatelli, dusted over with the finest Parmesan, followed by a perfect zabaglione; or when, one evening in Kansas City, some exiled Russians gave me a Russian dinner with caviar, sturgeon and vodka. One sense wakens another, and the mouth may be the key to open the heart.

—ANDRÉ MAUROIS
Cooking with a French Touch

DINNER WITH MR. JEFFERSON
MARSHALL FISHWICK

There was no greater special prize in the early days of the United States than an invitation to have dinner with Thomas Jefferson in the White House. It wasn't only that he was President. It wasn't only the assurance of dining well—dining magnificently, as a matter of fact. It wasn't only the beautiful surroundings. The pleasure centered on the man himself. He was wonderful. He was surrounded by an aura of charm, and he charmed all those around him. He was an inventor, a diplomat, a philosopher, a musician, an architect, a gardener, a scientist, an aristocrat, a democrat—and a gourmet.

An invitation went to the Rev. Mr. Manasseh Cutler to have dinner at the White House on February 6, 1802. He was asked not by the "President" but by Mr. Jefferson. The author of the Declaration of Independence abhorred titles and snobbery. He believed all men were created equal.

When Mr. Cutler arrived at 4 P.M.—the usual dinner hour—other guests were on hand, fifteen others, and the lively talk, which was as delectable as the food and wine, had begun. So had the music, which Mr. Jefferson called "the passion of my life." Among the six musicians was a violinist; Mr. Jefferson played a violin himself, though never when he was host. We don't know what music he chose that night, but can guess that "the Italian mode" was favored, as on other evenings.

And we can guess that, as on many other mornings, Jefferson had been up before dawn to go with his steward Lamar to the Georgetown market. "He often took fifty dollars to pay the marketing used in a day," Lamar recorded. "Mr. Jefferson's salary did not support him while he was President." This is borne out by the meticulous figures Jefferson kept; so is the relative importance of wine in his overall budget. . . .

While Jefferson greeted his guests, the eleven servants he has brought up from Monticello (his Virginia manor house) were preparing to serve the elaborate dinner "in the French style." This means there were separate "covers" (we say courses) for soup, salad, meats and vegetables, desserts, cheeses and fruits.

That night rice soup was served. The salad contained whatever vegetables his dawn trip to Georgetown could produce: he favored "cucumbers, cress, endive, lettuce, chives, cabbage, and peppergrass." But especially in the winter months, when greens were hard to come by, the gastronomic weight fell heavily on the meats: beef, turkey, mutton (always a particular Jeffersonian favorite), ham, loin of veal and cutlets of veal.

To assure such range and variety of meat, Jefferson had not only to spend liberally for available stores but also to plan ahead for future dinners. Hence a letter to his Monticello overseer contained these instructions: "Keep it in deer, rabbits, guinea, pigeons, etc. Let it be an asylum for hares, squirrels, pheasants, and partridges."

Such lists should not lead today's reader, who seldom has such choices of food even at banquets, to conclude that the Sage of Monticello was a glutton. "He was never a great eater," his steward, Edmund Bacon, wrote, "but what he did eat he wanted to be very choice. He often told me that the meat I gave one servant for a week would be more than he would use in six months." Bacon also recalled that peas were Jefferson's favorite vegetable; he raised thirty varieties and took special pride in serving the first dish of green peas each spring.

The unusual item that caught the guests' eyes on that February 6 was "a pie called macaroni." This was one of the items Mr. Jefferson discovered in Europe, and brought back after making careful notes of the ingredients and recipes. On other nights he served "French fries" with beefsteak—a novelty which invariably brought comments from the guests. Desserts were another area in which the ingenious Mr. Jefferson loved to experiment. Here Mr. Cutler's account is so revealing that we might best quote him exactly:

"Ice cream very good, crust wholly dried, crumbled like thin flakes; a dish somewhat like a pudding—inside white as milk or curd, very light and porous, covered with cream sauce—very fine. Many other jim cracks, a great variety of fruit, plenty of wine, and good."

The group sat at the table until about six. Then the ladies retired, leaving the men to their cigars and men's talk. (Jefferson might have complained, as he did often in 1801, that Mr. Hamilton had made government finances so complicated that neither Congress nor President understood them. He had plans to straighten this out.) The ladies returned about seven, when the tea tray was brought in. There was laughter and more good talk until about ten, when the guests left the warm, friendly atmosphere for the streets of Washington.

The next day, in all probability, there would be another dinner party. "Jefferson dines a dozen every day," said his predecessor, John Adams. If that was meant as criticism, Mr. Jefferson didn't take it that way. He was a Virginia gentleman, and hospitality was in his heritage. He himself said, "Man was destined for society."

No wonder those who went to dinner at the White House with Mr. Jefferson remembered and commented on it. So did another President, 160 years later. Dining with a group of leading twentieth century minds, John F. Kennedy said: "This is the most extraordinary group of intellectuals that has sat at this table—with the possible exception of when Mr. Jefferson had dinner alone!"

Ford Times

A WHITE HOUSE DINNER WITH ANDREW JACKSON
MARQUIS JAMES

If compensatory economies marked the management of the White House, they were invisible to a boy from Ohio who, reporting for his first cruise as a second lieutenant of Marines, viewed everything in the capital with fresh, astonished eyes. A note from Mr. Van Buren [the vice president] had procured an invitation to partake of a family dinner at the Mansion, served at the proper Tennessee hour of four o'clock [on December 29, 1834]. . . .

Walking very erectly in his new, high-collared uniform, Lieutenant Caldwell met the other guests in what he described as an "anti-chamber." After a little the President entered, greeted everyone and chatted for fifteen minutes. Then a "porter" announced that the meal was served. "Led by the porter we pass through a spacious Hall and entered another finely furnished room which was darkened by the window curtains and blinds and contained two tables richly laden with fine plate and dishes and tall splendid lamps—around one table were chairs, so we were seated— What attracted my attention first was the very nicely folded napkin on each plate with a slice of good light bread in the middle of it." Light bread, made of wheat flour, was so designated to distinguish it from ordinary or corn bread. "Well, all being seated the Gen. asked the blessing, then the servants about the table, I believe one to every man, commenced—'Will you have some roast beef?—some corn beef?—some boiled beef?—some beef stake?'

"Well, the beef being through with, away goes your plate and a clean one comes. 'Will you have this kind or that kind or the other kind of fish?' Fish being through, a new plate & then comes some other dish. Then a new plate comes and some other dish—

then a new plate and the pies— then the dessert— then & in the mean time the wines— sherry, madaira & champagne. . . . [We] drink one another's health— then after so long a time, all of which made very agreeable by miscellaneous conversation, we retire again to the Chamber whence we had come, where being seated, in comes a servant with a dish of coffee for each of us. . . . Directly aside looking at my watch [and] find[ing] it almost 7 o'clock I conclude to retire. So I takes the Prest. by the hand and says Gen, I bid you good-night and it will always be my pride to do you honor.' "

The Life of Andrew Jackson

BUCHANAN IN THE WHITE HOUSE
JOHN UPDIKE

BUCHANAN *(alone)*: There is a profound wisdom in a remark of La Rochefoucauld with which I met the other day—"Les choses que nous desirons n'arrivent pas, ou, si elles arrivent, ce n'est, ni dans le temps, ni de la manière qui nous auraient fait le plus de plaisir."

HARRIET *(his niece, bustling through)*: Oh, Nunc, let's have my French lesson later; the company's about to arrive! Only Southerners and Secretary Black, nobody north of Philadelphia will come to the White House any more! I don't care, Mr. Seward and Douglas were so short I could never decide what lady to let them take in!

BUCHANAN: What is the menu?

HARRIET: It is *glo*rious. Oysters and terrapin from the Chesapeake, shad from the James, venison from Virginia, mutton from Vermont, and from Lancaster County, roast shoulder of pork, stuffed with sauerkraut and garnished with cinnamon apples! For dessert, your favorite, gooseberry tart, not to mention sweetmeats and syrupy wines imported from France and Spain, admitted under the low tariff the Southern Democrats wouldn't raise for you, after you broke your heart over Lecompton for *them,* and poor Aaron Brown died of the postal deficit! To end up, for those still awake, port and brandy, chartreuse and crème de cacao, and English mints just like we used to buy on Marylebone Road!

BUCHANAN: Banquet enough, for the edge of an abyss.

Buchanan Dying

ENTERTAINING A ROYAL COUPLE
W. E. RUSSELL

A royal couple [during the Victorian period] arranged to pay a two-nights' visit to a country house of which the owners were friends of mine. For reasons of expediency we will call the visitors the duke and duchess, though that was not their precise rank. When a thousand preparations too elaborate to be described here had been made for the due entertainment of them and their suite and their servants, the private secretary wrote to the lady of the house, enclosing a written memorandum of his royal master's and mistress's requirements in the way of meals. I reproduce the substance of the memorandum—and in these matters my memory never plays tricks. The day began with cups of tea brought to the royal bedroom. While the duke was dressing, an egg beaten up in sherry was served to him, not once, but twice. The duke and duchess breakfasted together in their private sitting room, where the usual English breakfast was served to them. They had their luncheon together with their hosts and the house party, and ate and drank like other people. Particular instructions were given that at a 5 o'clock tea, there must be something substantial in the way of eggs, sandwiches, or potted meat, and this meal the royalty consumed with special gusto. Dinner was at 8:30, on the limited and abbreviated scale which the Prince of Wales introduced—two soups, two kinds of fish, two entrées, a joint, two sorts of game, a hot and cold sweet, and a savory, with the usual accessories in the way of oysters, cheese, ice and dessert. This is pretty well for an abbreviated dinner. But let no one suppose that the royal couple went hungry to bed. When they retired, supper was served to them in their private sitting room, and a cold chicken and a bottle of claret were left in their bedroom, as a provision against emergencies.

Reminiscences

DON VICTORIANO OF VERACRUZ
DIANA KENNEDY

Don Victoriano, who had taught the cooks in the famous little restaurant . . . came shuffling quickly into the room in his worn leather huaraches. He was of medium build, slim; his tightly curling black hair was receding and tinged with grey at the temples; his eyes were a lively blue-grey and his dark skin was mottled with pink. He was dressed like the fishermen of the town, in baggy blue pants and a white sweatshirt. He welcomed me in the open, friendly manner typical of the coast, as though I were an old friend and he had been expecting me.

No formal introduction seemed necessary. I loved good food; I loved to cook and wanted to learn about the regional specialties. "Come to lunch tomorrow at one o'clock. I am just cooking a *galápago en moste,* and by tomorrow it will be well seasoned and ready to eat."

The dish he had described, terrapin in a black sauce, sounded too good to miss, and the hollow, toneless church bell was just striking one o'clock when I returned the following day. Don Victoriano welcomed me by rushing out from the kitchen, noisily punctuating his greeting by sucking at the pineapple pulp that was lodged between his lower lip and teeth. We were very soon joined by an old lady and her companion, both carrying big black umbrellas against the afternoon sun.

Don Victoriano proudly ushered us into his new dining room, which was also the kitchen. The burners were set into a countertop that ran the width of the room and was completely tiled. The whole room, in fact, was covered with highly glazed blue and white tiles—floors, walls, buffet, stove, even the table.

The meal began. The fresh rolls that he himself had brought from the bakery only minutes before were carried into the room, along with a pile of carefully wrapped tortillas and a jug of iced, crushed papaya drink. The maid brought in large plates of shrimp soup—the small, sweet shrimps from the river, which reminded me of those I used to eat at home in England—then white rice and fried plantain. These were followed by the *pièce de résistance, galápago en moste quemado.*

The terrapin was delicious. Gelatinous and much more tender than sea turtle, it had been cooked in a thin, blackish sauce that had a musky flavor and was colored by the burnt, ground leaves of the *moste* bush that he had by his back door. "This dates from Zapotec times," said Don Victoriano.

I was beginning to feel very full—and then another steaming, fragrant dish was brought in. Don Victoriano apologized profusely for not serving something more elegant; apparently relatives had arrived unexpectedly, and because he had served them breakfast at ten-thirty that morning he couldn't get out to the market. He said the new dish was a duck in *lo que queda sauce.* I soon realized it was literally *lo que queda;* "that which was left over" had gone into the sauce, which resembled a light *pipián,* or pumpkin-seed sauce.

A huge mountain of sliced pineapple was now placed on the table, along with cookies made of unrefined sugar and grated fresh coconut, but the real dessert was on the buffet: enormous portions of a light egg custard thickened with finely ground almonds and topped with swirls of beaten egg white.

After the meal was over . . . our lunch companions dozed, their heads bent over peacefully while their chairs rocked. . . .

Recipes from the Regional Cooks of Mexico

SOME THOUGHTS ON GUESTS FOR DINNER
KAY BOYLE

There is always a question as to whether a woman should or should not reveal the secrets which distinguish her. I do not know the answer entirely, but I do know that I am as loath to receive guests without my earrings on as I am to have my guests sit down to dinner without having my Ratatouille Rowayton in the oven with a generous sprinkling of freshly-grated cheese encrusting the top. I have never divulged the recipe for this dish, and I do not intend to do so now. But put the ingredients together, and you will have prepared one of the most satisfactory casseroles that ever accompanied a meat dish (preferably broiled chicken or baked ham), or—with fresh, briefly-boiled shrimp added—ever constituted an entire dinner in itself.

In either case, a garden of raw peas, lettuce and spinach leaves, tossed with olive oil, garlic, and lemon juice, must be present, as fresh and inevitable as apple blossoms in May.

1. Seeds. White and long-grained and beloved in China. 2. Thistlelike herbs. Drab green, hearts of, and they may be frozen, their natural habitat, France or Italy. 3. Capsicums. Emerald green and varnished (come in red, if you prefer). 4. Undeadly nightshade. Bright red, and should be skinned for participation in the Ratatouille. 5. Italian squash. Green, mottled like snakes. They might be taken for cucumbers by the undiscerning. 6. Fleshy fungi. Golden, and filled with forest darkness and evening dew. Take a squirrel's advice on the edible varieties.

Number 5 must first be washed slightly in cold water, hand-dried, and sliced. Number 3 must be gutted of seeds and chopped fine. Number 2 may be split in two, broken hearts being more tender than others. Now boil 1, 2, 3, 4, and 5 in a minimum of salted water for precisely fifteen minutes. Remove from fire and add Number 6, which has been previously broiled in butter. Place entire mixture in a glass casserole so that the colors show, sprinkle with Parmesan, and place in the middle of oven. Bake at 350° for fifteen minutes, broil for time required to brown the Parmesan. Serve with Beaujolais, 1959.

The Artists' & Writers' Cookbook

"A HOST TO SNATCH FOOD FROM A GUEST!"
ARNOLD BENNETT

Cyril's guests ranged in years from four to six; they were chiefly older than their host; this was a pity, it impaired his importance; but up to four years a child's sense of propriety, even of common decency, is altogether too unreliable for a respectable party. . . .

Cyril, while attending steadily to the demands of his body, was in a mood which approached the ideal. Proud and radiant, he combined urbanity with a certain fine condescension. His bright eyes, and his manner of scraping up jam with a spoon, said: "I am the king of this party. This party is solely in my honour. I know that. We all know it. Still, I will pretend that we are equals, you and I." He talked about his picture-books to a young woman on his right named Jennie, aged four, pale, pretty, the belle in fact, and Mr. Critchlow's grand-niece. The boy's attractiveness was indisputable; he could put on quite an aristocratic air. It was the most delicious sight to see them, Cyril and Jennie, so soft and delicate, so infantile on their piles of cushions and books, with their white socks and black shoes dangling far distant from the carpet; and yet so old, so self-contained! And they were merely an epitome of the whole table. The whole table was bathed in charm and mystery of young years, of helpless fragility, gentle forms, timid elegance, unshamed instincts, and waking souls. [Cyril's parents] Constance and Samuel were very satisfied; full of praise for other people's children, but with the reserve that of course Cyril was *hors concours*. They both really did believe, at that moment, that Cyril was, in some subtle way which they felt but could not define, superior to all other infants.

Some one, some officious relative of a visitor, began to pass a certain cake which had brown walls, a roof of cocoa-nut icing, and a yellow body studded with crimson globules. Not a conspicuously gorgeous cake, but a cake to which a catholic child would be likely to attach particular importance; a good, average cake! Who could have guessed that it stood, in Cyril's esteem, as the cake of cakes? He had insisted on his father buying it at Cousin Daniel's, and perhaps Samuel ought to have divined that for Cyril that cake was the gleam that an ardent spirit would follow through the wilderness. Samuel, however, was not a careful observer, and seriously lacked imagination. Constance knew only that Cyril had mentioned the cake once or twice. Now by the hazard of destiny that cake found much favour, helped into popularity as it was by the blundering officious relative who, not dreaming what volcano she was treading on, urged its merits with simpering enthusiasm. One boy took two slices, a slice in each hand; he happened to be the visitor of whom the cake-distributor was a relative, and she protested; she expressed the shock she suffered. Whereupon both Constance and Samuel sprang forward and swore with angelic smiles that nothing could be more perfect than the propriety of that dear little fellow taking two slices of that cake. It was this hullaballoo that drew Cyril's attention to the evanescence of the cake of cakes. His face at once changed from calm pride to a dreadful anxiety. His eyes bulged out. His tiny mouth grew and grew, like a mouth in a nightmare. He was no longer human; he was a cake-eating tiger being balked of his prey. Nobody noticed him. The officious fool of a woman persuaded Jennie to take the last slice of the cake, which was quite a thin slice.

Then everyone simultaneously noticed Cyril, for he gave a yell. It was not the cry of a despairing soul who sees his beautiful iridescent dream shattered at his feet; it was the cry of the strong, masterful spirit, furious. He turned upon Jennie, sobbing, and snatched at her cake. Unaccustomed to such behaviour from hosts, and being besides a haughty put-you-in-your-place beauty of the future, Jennie defended her cake. After all, it was not she who had taken two slices at once. Cyril hit her in the eye, and then crammed most of the slice of cake into his enormous mouth. He could not swallow it, nor even masticate it, for his throat was rigid and tight. So the cake projected from his red lips, and big tears watered it. The most awful mess you can conceive! Jennie wept loudly, and one or two others joined her in sympathy, but the rest went on eating tranquilly, unmoved by the horror which transfixed their elders.

A host to snatch food from a guest! A host to strike a guest! A gentleman to strike a lady!

Constance whipped up Cyril from his chair and flew with him to his own room, where she smacked him on the arm and told him he was a very, very naughty boy and that she didn't know what his father would say. She took the food out of his disgusting mouth—or as much as she could get at—and then she left him, on the bed.

The Old Wives' Tale

Free Eats
Marjorie Kinnan Rawlings

The pilau is almost a sacred Florida dish, and for making a small amount of meat feed a large number, it has no equal. A Florida church supper is unheard of without it. Bartram found the dish here those many years ago, and called it "pillo," and once "pilloe." We pronounce the word purr-loo. Almost any meat, but preferably chicken or fresh pork, is cut in pieces and simmered in a generous amount of water until tender. When it falls from the bones, as much rice is added as is needed for the number to be fed, and cooked to a moist flakiness. . . .

Word came that Fatty Blake, a snuff and tobacco salesman, and Anthony's richest citizen—wealth at Anthony, as elsewhere, is relative—was having a big doings on a certain Thursday night. The world was invited. Fatty himself stopped at the village store to verify the invitation. He was inviting two counties to his doings, and all was free. There would be squirrel pilau and Brunswick stew. Fatty couldn't likker folks, as he would like to do, but if you brought your own 'shine, and were quiet about it, why, he'd meet you at the gate for a drink, and God bless you.

"I got boys in the woods from can't-see to can't-see," he said, "getting me squirrels for that pilau. I got a nigger coming to stir that pit of rice all day long. And my wife, God bless her, is walking the county, getting what she needs for Brunswick stew, the kind her mammy made ahead of her in Brunswick, Georgia."

Cars and wagons and lone horses and mules began coming in to Anthony long before dark. They brought women in homemade silks and in ginghams, men in mail-order store clothes with stiff collars and men in blue pin-checks of the day's work. Children screamed and played all over the swept sand about Fatty's two-story house. The wives of Anthony bustled up and down a forty-foot pine-board table. Each had brought her contribution, of potato salad made by stirring cut onion and hard-boiled eggs into cold mashed potatoes, of soda biscuits and pepper relish, of pound cake and blueberry pie. Back of the house a Negro stirred rice in a forty-gallon iron kettle with a paddle as big as an oar. It grew dark and the crowd was hungry.

At seven o'clock Mrs. Jim Butler played three solo hymns on the Blakes' parlour organ, moved out to the front porch for the occasion. Then she lifted her shrill soprano voice in the opening strains of "I know Salvation's free," and the crowd joined in with quivering pleasure. At seven-thirty the Methodist preacher rose to his feet beside the organ. He lauded Fatty Blake as a Christian citizen. He prayed. Here and there a devout old woman cried "Amen!" And then the parson asked that anyone so minded contribute his mite to help Brother Blake defray the expense of this great feast.

"Will Brother Buxton pass the hat?"

The hat was passed, and as the pennies and nickles clinked into it, Fatty Blake made his address of welcome.

"I've done brought all you folks together," he shouted, "in the name of brotherly love. I want to tell you, all at one great free table, to love one another.

"Don't just stick to your own church," he pleaded. "If you're a Baptist, go to the Methodist church when the Methodists have preaching Sunday. If you're a Methodist, go help the Baptists when their preacher comes to town.

"Now I want to tell you this meal is free and I had no idea of getting my money back, but as long as our good parson here has mentioned it, I'll say just do what your pocket and your feelings tell you to, and if you feel you want to do your share in this big community feed, why, God bless you.

"Now, folks, we've all enjoyed the entertainment, and I know you're going to enjoy the rations just as much. There's all you can eat and eat your fill. Don't hold back for nobody. Get your share of everything. . . . It smells the best of any pilau I've ever smelt. It's got forty squirrels in it, folks, forty squirrels and a big fat hen. And my wife herself made that Brunswick stew, just like she learned it at her mother's knee back in Brunswick, Georgia. Now go to it, folks, but don't rush!"

The crowd packed tight around the table, weaving and milling. The pilau and stew were passed around in paper dishes. The passing hat reached a lean, venerable farmer just as he had completed a tour of exploration through his pilau.

"No!" he shrilled, with the lustiness of an old man with a grievance.

"No, I ain't goin' to give him nothin'! This here was advertised as a free meal and 'tain't nothin' but a dogged Georgia prayer-meetin'. Get a man here on promises and then go to pickin' his pocket. This food ain't fitten to eat, dogged Georgia rations, Brunswick stew and all. And he's done cooked the squirrel heads in the pilau, and that suits a damned Georgia cracker but it don't suit me.

"I was born and raised in Floridy, and I'm pertikler. I don't want no squirrel eyes lookin' at me out o' my rations!"

Cross Creek

VIRGINIA HOSPITALITY

The welcome comes from back in the days when we were slaves. For over two hundred years we were told where to live and where to work. We were given husbands and we made children, and all these things could be taken away from us. The only real comfort came at the end of the day, when we took either the food that we were given, or the food that we raised, or the food that we had caught, and we put it in the pot, and we sat with our own kind and talked and sang and ate.

—RUTH L. GASKINS
A Good Heart and a Light Hand

"MY DINNER WAS GREAT"

Home to dinner, whither by and by comes Roger Pepys, Mrs. Turner and her daughter, Joyce Norton, and a young lady, a daughter of Coll. Cockes, my uncle Wight, his wife and Mrs. Anne Wight. This being my feast, in lieu of what I should have had a few days ago . . . for which the Lord make me truly thankful. Very merry at, before, and after dinner, and the more for that my dinner was great, and most neatly dressed by our own only maid. We had a fricassee of rabbits and chickens, a leg of mutton boiled, three carps in a dish, a great dish of a side of lamb, a dish of roasted pigeons, a dish of four lobsters, three tarts, a lamprey pie (a most rare pie), a dish of anchovies, good wine of several sorts, and all things mighty noble and to my great content.

—SAMUEL PEPYS
Diary, March 4, 1663

NOTES IN A DIARY: A HOST'S CRITIQUE
ANDRÉ L. SIMON

Menu: Crème Nantua; Suprême de Barbue Gallieni; Baron d'Agnelet à la broche; Croûte aux morilles; Parfait Glace Savoy; Café. Wines: Amontillado; Pommery Extra Sec; 1865 Château Lafite Magnum; 1921 Chateau d'Yquem; 1812 Fine Champagne.

The occasion was to celebrate the successful publishing of *The Art of Good Living,* and my return to London.

The Bisque d'écrevisses was just right, creamy, spicy and served very hot. The Sherry was not exceptional, but it was just the right sort of dry, almost tart, wine to act as a tonic and a mouth-wash.

The Barbue was also perfect and without any trace of fishiness; it provided an excellent background for the slightly acid sorrel sauce. The Champagne was young and lively; not too serious, but just the thing at this early stage of the dinner.

The lamb was the tenderest lamb ever put on a spit; but good as it was it was unobtrusive; its part was to show off the Claret and it played its part admirably. The two Magnums of *Lafite* were wonderful—both. The wine was deep and true, deep of colour and true to breed. No superfluous flesh about it; as firm as any young vintage could be, but with that wonderful softness that age alone can give. A truly wonderful wine.

The lamb was so modest that the first Magnum of 1865 captured all the limelight. But the second Magnum, although every bit as perfect as the first, had to share the honours with the most deliciously fragrant 'Morilles' I have ever tasted. Their perfume was not assertive—far from it—but it was as persistent as it was discreet: it refused to be ignored.

Then came an ice, which was not too cold, and some Fraises des bois, which had reached London by air at 6 o'clock to-night. They had been *rafraíchies* with just a little Barsac and were simply delicious. The *'21 Yquem* was magnificent and a perfect anti-climax. It was served at the right temperature, not too cold. It closed in a charming manner a memorable chapter of "The art of good living."

Tables of Content

8

Potpourri

Anyone who grew up in a family in whose dining room an unabridged dictionary, mounted on a cast-iron easel, stood at the ready knows the satisfaction of having word books at hand—a point to be made in respect to the use above of potpourri. *Its meanings include, according to one gastronomic dictionary, "a stew made of several kinds of meat, vegetables and seasonings"; and, according to a dogeared Webster's, "a medley, sometimes an anthology." There is a stewlike quality to the ingredients employed in this section: meaty extracts with provenance of great variety, chunks of color, salty aphorisms, peppery one-liners. In the view of Crosby Gaige, there are "essences as precious as phrases from Keats." This medley is, much as Webster asserts, "a composition of passages and scraps," and the selections—be prepared for a surprise from Adolf Hitler—often are enough to make a word person (and many others, perhaps) aware of a kind of hunger within.*

I wonder if the cabbage knows
He is less lovely than the Rose;
Or does he squat in smug content,
A source of noble nourishment;
Or if he pities for her sins
The Rose who has no vitamins;
Or if one thing his green heart knows—
That self-same fire that warms the Rose?
—ANONYMOUS

"Essences as Precious as Phrases from Keats"
CROSBY GAIGE

While still miles at sea, sailors know when they are approaching the spice islands in an eastern ocean by the scented breath of the welcoming breezes. Even thus guests at Watch Hill Farm, up the Hudson, if they be blessed with sensitive nostrils, can tell that they are nearing my kitchen laboratory. However closely the ground-glass stoppers guard the bottled mysteries of leaf, seed and bark in scores of jars, fragrant hints do escape.

The sine qua non of my culinary atelier, of course, is its tall and capacious spice closet. There is nothing skimpy about that department, there are no gaping spaces. Spices have always been a symbol of opulence, and it is fitting that the crowded closet should convey a sense of plenitude. Row upon row of jars shoulder to shoulder, with other bottles straining to peep over their proud heads. Rare spices, esoteric blends, dried herbs in leaf, stalk and powder; private mixtures and essences as precious as phrases from Keats or poems from the Chinese. A few jars hold an ounce or two of some rare powder, a stick or two of some gnarled root, as if to emphasize their preciousness. . . .

If you are one of those prosaic people to whom pepper is just pepper, you will only smile at my enthusiasm. The ordinary spice closet in America is, alas! a routine affair of tin cans and commercial bottles, and even our best restaurants use no more than a pitiful fraction of the rainbow range of spices and herbs, while the subtler shadings of flavor are unused and unknown.

But if you are aware that there are about forty kinds of pepper and that each of them has a different gustatory message for the cultivated palate, you may yield more willingly to my high mood. You will then realize that the possession of a dozen or so peppers is no mean treasure—not merely the black, white, red and cayenne peppers, but their subtler versions of Tellicherry or Malabar, Achin or Mangalore, Mombassa or Siam. . . .

My peppers are jostled by self-important jars of cinnamon, ginger, saffron, coriander, turmeric, allspice, cardamon, nutmeg, mace, paprika, cloves and others, all in various shadings and varieties.

There is the extract of the manioc root, called cassareep, which provides me with an exciting new note in stews and ragoûts, and which I can replenish only by direct import from London. There is ajinomoto, the white powder that the canny Japanese extract from wheat and which suggests the delicate flavor of beef juice in certain sauces and gravies. Above all, there are the special mixtures that defy the dictionary for description and give many dishes their unique counterpoint of flavor. . . .

A few grains of golden brown mace, for instance, if intelligently distributed, raise a Welsh rarebit from the level of the ordinary to the plane of gastronomic novelty. The use of ground cinnamon in egg drinks, cocoa, fudge, oatmeal and tapioca cream is worth the trouble of experiment. The subtle flavor in my goulash is derived, in part, at least, from six or seven cloves imbedded in an onion. If your taste is of the analytic sort you will detect ginger, cloves and cinnamon in my steamed brown bread, and if it is not analytic you will enjoy the unusual overtones without knowing their names. I can think of no dish, offhand, whose message cannot be heightened and refined by the magic of some spice or herb.

Fit for a King

"Trust Your Taste"

Some years ago I dined in an elaborately decorated and expensive restaurant in Atlanta. I was so surprised to see *gazpacho* on the menu that I ordered it, and this cold soup was beautifully served in a silver tureen, accompanied by minced onions and croutons. As I began to eat the soup, I had the most peculiar impression about its taste, which was later confirmed by a friendly waiter: I was sitting a long way from home, eating canned tomato juice out of a bowl with a spoon.

If there was a lesson to be learned from this incident, it is to trust your own reaction to whatever you taste. . . .

—ALEXIS BESPALOFF
Guide to Inexpensive Wines

WOODSY FILLIP

The nuttiness of nuts has almost universal appeal. We pay a high compliment when we ascribe a "nutty" flavor to such disparate items as cereals, certain cheese, broiled bacon, browned butter, whole-wheat bread, wild rice or dry sherry. There are many ways to add this woodsy fillip to foods of otherwise conventional flavor. Good cooks endow brook trout, filet of sole, frog's legs, soft-shelled crabs and other seafood with a golden brown sauce of melted butter and roasted almonds. Chopped walnuts or pecans are an inspired addition to green beans or spinach fresh from the garden. A light sprinkle of roasted salted peanuts works wonders with such bland foods as cream soups, whipped potatoes, mashed turnips or broccoli. And, as any sweet-toothed teen-ager realizes, crisp, buttery nuts add excitement to a plate of ice cream.

—SILAS SPITZER

AN INVITATION TO BREAKFAST

Dear Moore,

I have a breakfast of philosophers to-morrow at ten *punctually*. Muffins and metaphysics; crumpets and contradiction. Will you come?

—SYDNEY SMITH

ON TASTING OYSTERS
ELEANOR CLARK

The sign says Bar—Crêperie—Dégustation d'Huîtres, and the word dégustation means what it says: not "consumption of" but "tasting," "savoring." It does not mean having a snack, with no suggestion beyond feeding your face. You are in the country of the art of good food, and this dégustation is very like what you do in an art gallery, unless your soul is lost; it is essential to be hungry but impermissable to be merely that; you have to take your time, the imagination must work; the first rule is to pay attention to what you are doing.

There is a certain expression that comes on a middle-to-upper income bracket Frenchman's face when he is about to déguster something really good, cheese, wine, any sort of culinary specialty, that starts out as a sudden interior break in the train of conversation. Silence; he is about to have a gastronomic experience. Then as the fork or glass nears his mouth, his eyes and ears seem to have blanked out; all is concentrated in the power of taste. There follows a stage when the critical faculties are gathering, the head is bent, eyes wander, lips and tongue are working over the evidence. At last comes the climactic moment of judgment, upon which may hang the mood of the meal and with it who knows what devious changes in the course of love, commerce or the body politic. The thing was poor or indifferent; the man shrugs, applies his napkin as though wiping out the whole experience, and goes on with what was interrupted, not quite relaxed; some sense of letdown, a slight disgruntlement lurks in the conversation. It was good, excellent, perfect, and oh what an expansion of frame and spirit; the chair will hardly hold him; he is not smiling, not just yet, but life is as he sits back gravely nodding, eager to look his companion and all the world in the eyes, and this time the napkin touches his lips like a chaste kiss, or a cleaning rag on an objet d'art.

It might be argued that this approach not only has a class angle to be considered but is old-fashioned. The Snack and the Snack Bar have appeared; the characters in the more fashionable French novels of recent years don't take any such view of food and in fact mostly don't seem to go in for it at all. Obviously, if you don't love life you can't enjoy an oyster. But ennui and social injustice are nothing to what the art of food has survived many times before in this country. The odors issuing from any boulangerie, from almost any provincial doorway at noon any day of the week can stir longings in an American, of which a sudden acuity of appetite is only the beginning.

Or consider the formidable directions printed on the menu of a cafe at La Trinité on how to déguster ice cream: first warm each bite slightly in the spoon as you would warm a brandy glass, to bring out the flavor; eat nothing with it but one of the two specified kinds of wafer or gauffrette, and so on.

In this fashion you approach, and ultimately consume, an oyster. . . .

The Oysters of Lacmariaquer

It is true that I live almost entirely on bivalves. I prefer them as they are—and I think that oysters *au naturel* are as much a mental as a material enjoyment: you are eating the whole ocean.

—ISAK DINESEN

THE GREAT SUMMONS
CH'Ü YUAN

O Soul come back to joys beyond all telling!
Where thirty cubits high at harvest-time
The corn is stacked;
Where pies are cooked of millet and bearded maize.
Guests watch the steaming bowls
And sniff the pungency of peppered herbs.
The cunning cook adds slices of bird-flesh,
Pigeon and yellow-heron and black-crane.
They taste the badger-stew.
O Soul come back to feed on foods you love!

Next are brought
Fresh turtle, and sweet chicken cooked with cheese
Pressed by the men of Ch'ü.
And flesh of whelps floating in liver-sauce
With salad of minced radishes in brine;
All served with that hot spice of southerwood

The land of Wu supplies.
O Soul come back to choose the meats you love.

Roasted daw, steamed widgeon and grilled quail—
On every fowl they fare.
Boiled perch and sparrow-broth—in each preserved
The separate flavor that is most its own.
O Soul come back to where such dainties wait!

WHO'S TO CRITICIZE?

George Bernard Shaw was right. "Clearly a critic should not belong to a club at all," he wrote. "He should not know anybody: His hand should be against every man, and every man's hand against his." Hmmmph. That was easy enough for Shaw to say. He was a vegetarian.

—GAEL GREENE

"CAVIAR HAS ALWAYS BEEN WITHIN MY REACH"
LUDWIG BEMELMANS

In Paris there was a great gourmet who had Cartier construct a little gold ball which he wore on the other end of his watch chain. He would go to one of the good restaurants, have his plate heaped with caviar and then drop the golden sphere from a foot above the plate. If it passed through the caviar without effort, he pronounced it first rate. If the ball got stuck in its passage and did not reach the bottom of the plate, he sent the plate and the black stuff back to the kitchen.

I have never been quite this fussy when eating caviar, though I do not blame the gentleman for performing the ritual. Caviar has always been within my reach, since I was born into the hotel trade and raised therein. It was available in various grades in all the cold-food departments of the many establishments for which I worked.

The best caviar I ever found was in the old Ritz in New York, and to avail myself of some, I and several bus boys in the Banquet Department invented a system of thievery which worked very well for a while. The *garde-manger,* as the man in charge of caviar and other delicatessen is called, carefully weighed the cans of caviar, before and after each banquet. We overcame this problem by burying in the bottom of the can some object—usually a silver peppermill—which equaled in weight a large coffee cup of the stuff. The caviar was later enjoyed, in a corner of the magnificent Ritz ballroom, under a darkened crystal chandelier against priceless tapestry, and with some millionaire's leftover wine. Like all stolen things, it tasted wonderful. Those were the best caviar days I can remember.

La Bonne Table

There is more simplicity in the man who eats caviar on impulse than in the man who eats grapenuts on principle.

—G. K. CHESTERTON

"MY FILL OF CAVIAR"
RUSSELL JONES

Once I went down to Astrakhan, the old Tartar city in the delta of the Volga River where it flows into the Caspian Sea. It is from this delta that about 80 per cent of all the caviar in the world comes. My expedition started by taking a small hydrofoil boat about fifty miles down one of the Volga's main channels to a collective enterprise where fishermen were casting their nets to catch the sturgeon—the roe of the giant sturgeon is the only true caviar—on their way up river to spawn. There, while we watched, a small power boat dragged the 800-foot net out into the channel, then swept back to shore with its tons of struggling fish.

To one who spent much of his boyhood on the banks of a Minnesota river waiting, mostly in vain, for a sunfish or a crappie to take the hook it was almost unbelievable. But there they were: hundreds of Beluga sturgeon which are the largest in size and produce the biggest eggs, and hundreds of Sevruga and Osotra sturgeon which are somewhat smaller and sometimes yield roe a darker shade than the gray-to-black eggs of the Beluga. In the same net were herring, carp, perch-pike and bream.

During the working day I spent with the fishermen they caught in this manner about four tons of sturgeon with a yield of eight hundred pounds or more of caviar that would be worth, they said, about $40,000 at wholesale prices. The sturgeon were taken from the net and thrown into boats half filled with water to keep them alive on the way to the processing plant back at Astrakhan. On arrival they were knocked on the head and put on conveyor belts to be carried to the plant. There a woman worker, wielding a knife shaped like a hook, ripped open the bellies and another woman scooped out the roe into an aluminum collander. Washed of blood and cleaned of membrane, the caviar was then slightly salted— hence the word *malasol* which appears on labels—and was put into jars or cans.

In Czarist times, the great nobles carried in their pockets small, personal spoons made of gold or silver or even semi-precious stone especially for the eating of caviar. No bread or crackers or chopped onions or even lemon juice for them. Then as now, they ate their caviar plain, whether it was Beluga or Sevruga or Osotra. Then as well as now, there was the very rare white caviar that was called the Czar's caviar and was reserved for the imperial court. I saw some of this in Astrakhan and was told it all goes to the Kremlin, as does the gold or amber-colored caviar which is just about as rare.

Regardless of color, according to the fishermen of Astrakhan, the roe of sturgeon is the ideal treatment for loss of blood; it's the best thing to take for ulcers. And if you're a drinker, one tablespoon of caviar, the men insisted, will balance more than six ounces of alcohol. What's more, the best way to clarify fish soup is to put in a little caviar to collect the sediment.

The fishermen produced that caviar-clarified soup at a lunch they gave me aboard their boat, and I must say it was something very special. But there was also something about that lunch that was without comparison. In addition to the soup and the various kinds of smoked and cured fish, the six of us at the table shared four and a half pounds of Beluga, the very best. My spoon was neither gold nor silver nor even semi-precious stone. It was with an ordinary spoon that for the first time—and probably the last time in my life—I ate my fill of caviar.

A Journey to Astrakhan

PLAINT OF A PERVERSE PALATE
GEORGE SLOCOMBE

I have dined too long off delicate food:
I am now in far too coarse a mood:
Bring me a thick beefsteak *saignant,*
A mountain cheese and an onion,
Garlic soup and a smoking mess
Of fish unknown to *bouillabaisse!*
My palate is perversely off
Dinde *truffée,* sauce Stroganoff,
Suprême and Mornay and Cardinal,
Dubarry and Hollandaise *et al,*
Give me coarse black bread and *boeuf tartare,*
I am sick to death of caviare.

If only Luther had been allowed to eat game on Fridays there would have been no Reformation and no Protestant schism.

—MARQUIS DE CUSSY

THE BAKER'S TALE

They roused him with muffins—they roused him with ice—
    They roused him with mustard and cress—
They roused him with jam and judicious advice—
    They set him conumdrums to guess.

                   —LEWIS CARROLL

THE PENGUIN GOURMET
LAURENS VAN DER POST

It did not take the food-conscious Dutch [settlers] long to discover what an excellent delicacy penguins' eggs were. They collected eggs in their thousands and although they were not unusual in my youth at the Cape I never realized the passion they aroused in colonial palates at the beginning, until searching through South African archives I found recipes for making even omelettes out of penguins' eggs for whole families—and Cape families were as large as their appetites. In my youth, however, the penguin population was in some danger of extinction and one considered oneself lucky to be offered in due season a penguin's egg as an *hors-d'oeuvre* once or, at the most, twice a week. Today the Government, quite rightly, has severely limited the number of eggs allowed to be collected for sale to private individuals. People who love them have to watch the newspapers for a Government announcement inviting them to send whatever the market price may be to an appropriate official address and the penguin gourmet, if he is lucky, will receive a case containing two dozen at most, or his money back.

There are many schools of thought as to how so rare a dish can be made to give its best. The classical way is to boil the eggs for at least twenty minutes. They must then be removed from their shells quickly so that they do not lose any of their heat; I have known penguin-egg lovers to keep special gloves for the purpose. The extracted egg, burning hot, is dropped in a hot tumbler, mashed quickly with a fork in fresh butter, a little pepper, salt, and sometimes a drop or two of wine vinegar or lemon. It is then whisked quickly into a sort of soufflé consistency. I have eaten it also cold, at an hotel which specialised in penguins' eggs and stood almost in the surf on Blueberg Strand with a superb view over the bay towards Devil's Peak, Table Mountain, Signal Hill and Lion's Head. There, the mildest of salad dressings was served with the cold eggs and the result was good, but the egg is best left to itself except for butter and salt and a trace of pepper. Coming as it does from one of the oldest forms of life it has a savour so remote and tenuous that it must not be corrupted by modern substances. Moreover there is nothing at all fishy in the taste of the penguin egg. It is far, far superior to any of the plover or gulls eggs so popular as an *hors-d'oeuvre* in parts of Western Europe. I prefer it even to caviare.

First Catch Your Eland

"IMAGINE A LILLIPUTIAN RABBIT!"

I and sister are just returned from Paris! We have eaten frogs. It has been such a treat! You know our monotonous tenor. Frogs are the nicest little delicate things—rabbity-flavoured. Imagine a Lilliputian rabbit! They fricassee them; but in my mind, dressed seethed, plain, with parsley and butter, would have been the decision of Apicius.

—CHARLES LAMB

I eat everything that nature voluntarily gives: fruits, vegetables, and the products of plants. But I ask you to spare me what animals are forced to surrender: meat, milk, and cheese. Thus from animals, eat only eggs!

—ADOLF HITLER

THE POETRY OF BUTTER

The well-fed Bressois are surely a good-natured people. I call them well fed both on general and on particular grounds. Their province has the most savory aroma, and I found an opportunity to test its reputation. I walked back into the town from the church (there was really nothing to be seen by the way), and as the hour of the midday breakfast had struck, directed my steps to the inn. The *table d'hôte* was going on, and a gracious, bustling, talkative landlady welcomed me. I had an excellent repast—the best repast possible—which consisted simply of boiled eggs and bread and butter. It was the quality of these simple ingredients that made the occasion memorable. The eggs were so good that I am ashamed to say how many of them I consumed. "La plus belle fille du monde," as the French proverb says, "ne peut donner que ce qu'elle a"; and it might seem that an egg which has succeeded to being fresh has done all that can reasonably be expected of it. But there was a bloom of punctuality, so to speak, about these eggs of Bourg, as if it had been the intention of the very hens themselves that they should be promptly served. "Nous sommes en Bresse, et le beurre n'est pas mauvais," the landlady said, with a sort of dry coquetry, as she placed this article before me. It was the poetry of the butter, and I ate a pound or two of it; after which I came away with a strange mixture of impressions of late gothic sculpture and thick *tartines*.

—HENRY JAMES
A Little Tour of France

Manius Curius lived frugally and happily on turnips all his life —when the Sabines sent him a gift of hundreds of gold pieces he said he had no need of wealth while he lived on such food.

—ANONYMOUS

Nero Wolfe on American Inventiveness
Rex Stout

Wolfe, facing me, was sitting up in bed with four cushions at his back, displaying half an acre of yellow silk pajamas. On the bedstand beside him were two empty beer bottles and an empty glass. He appeared to be frowning intently at my socks as he went on:

". . . but the indescribable flavor of the finest Georgia hams, the quality which places them, in my opinion, definitely above the best to be found in Europe, is not due to the post mortem treatment of the flesh at all. Expert knowledge and tender care in the curing are indeed essential, but they are to be found in Czestochowa and Westphalia more frequently even than in Georgia. Poles and Westphalians have the pigs, the scholarship and the skill; what they do not have is peanuts."

He stopped to blow his nose. I shifted position. He resumed: "A pig whose diet is fifty to seventy percent peanuts grows a ham of incredibly sweet and delicate succulence which, well-cured, well-kept and well-cooked, will take precedence over any other ham the world affords. I offer this as an illustration of one of the sources of the American contributions I am discussing, and as another proof that American offerings to the roll of honor of fine food are by no means confined to those items which were found here already ripe on the tree, with nothing required but the plucking. Red Indians were eating turkeys and potatoes before the white man came, but they were not eating peanut-fed pigs. Those unforgettable hams are not gifts of nature; they are the product of the inventor's enterprise, the experimenter's persistence, and the connoisseur's discrimination. Similar results have been achieved by the feeding of blueberries to young chickens, beginning usually—"

"Hold it. Not chickens, poultry."

"Chickens are poultry."

"You told me to stop you."

"But not to argue with me."

"You started the argument, I didn't."

He showed me a palm. "Let's go on . . . Beginning usually at the age of one week. The flavor of a four months old cockerel, trained to eat large quantities of blueberries from infancy, and cooked with mushrooms, tarragon and white wine—or, if you would add another American touch, made into a chicken and corn pudding, with onion, parsley and eggs—is not only distinctive, it is unique; and it is assuredly haute cuisine. This is an even better illustration of my thesis than the ham, for Europe could not have fed peanuts to pigs, since they had no peanuts. But they did have chickens—chickens, Archie?"

"Poultry."

"No matter. They did have chickens and blueberries, and for centuries no one thought of having the one assimilate the other and bless us with the result. Another demonstration of the inventiveness—"

Too Many Cooks

A clever cook can make . . . good meat of a whetstone.
—ERASMUS

You will eat, bye & bye,
In that glorious land above the sky;
Work and pray, live on hay,
You'll get pie in the sky when you die.
—ANONYMOUS

THE DUKE AND DUCHESS OF WINDSOR DINE AT HOME
INEZ ROBB

I had an anxious call from His Royal Highness. Would I, he begged, as a great favor to himself and the Duchess, not mention the fact that she often cooked their Sunday night supper—and sometimes their Sunday luncheon—on an electric two-burner plate they had smuggled into their suite in the Waldorf-Astoria?

POTPOURRI   231

(On such occasions, the Duke told me, it was his job to put up the card table and set it properly.)

Only a day or two before, the Duke confessed, the Duchess, a famous cook, had been unable to resist cooking on both burners to speed things up. As a result, every fuse in their apartment blew. They had been hard put to explain the matter to the hotel authorities, since cooking by guests in the hotel is strictly forbidden.

"Since then," said the Duke conspiratorially, "we put the card table right by the stove and service is direct from burner to consumer." Please, the former King-Emperor petitioned, would I strike out all reference to the outlaw stove! "If the hotel found out, it might dispossess us," he said with genuine concern. "And it does give us such pleasure to have a meal at home."

Don't Just Stand There!

We may live without friends; we may live without books;
But civilized man cannot live without cooks.
—OWEN MEREDITH

THE GOURMET
JUDITH VIORST

My husband grew up eating lox in New Jersey,
But now he eats saumon fumé.
The noshes he used to nosh before dinner
He's calling hors d'oeuvres variés.
And food is cuisine since he learned how to be a gourmet.

He now has a palate instead of a stomach
And must have his salad après,
His ris de veau firm, and his port salut runny,
All ordered, of course, en français,
So the waiter should know he is serving a full-fledged gourmet.

No meal is complete without something en croûte, a-
Mandine, béchamel, en gelée,

And those wines he selects with the care that a surgeon
Transplanting the heart may display.
He keeps snifting the corks since he learned how to be a
    gourmet.

The tans some folks get from a trip to St. Thomas
He gets from the cerises flambés,
After which he requires, instead of a seltzer,
A cognac or Grand Marnier,
With a toast to the chef from my husband the noveau
    gourmet.

The words people use for a Chartres or a Mozart
He's using to praise a soufflé.
He reads me aloud from James Beard and Craig Claiborne
The way others read from Corneille.
And he's moved by a mousse since he learned how to be a
    gourmet.

But back in New Jersey, whenever we visit,
They don't know from pouilly-fuissé.
They're still serving milk in the glass from the jelly.
They still cook the brisket all day.
And a son who can't finish three helpings is not a gourmet.

People and Other Aggravations

INSTEAD OF LUXURY

It is not luxury in the ordinary sense of the word that is demanded. I have had luxurious meals at the Hotel Splendide and the
Hotel Glorieux which were costly rubbish. I have lunched on
bread, and cheese, and beer to admiration; but then the bread, and
cheese, and beer were the best of their kind: a good Caerphilly
cheese is better than a raw, unripe, stinging Stilton; as a decent,
honest beer—if you can get any—is infinitely above third-rate
champagne.

—ARTHUR MACHEN

My mother keeps in two big books
The secrets of the things she cooks.
If I could ever learn to bake,
I'd send my brother Bill a cake.
But Mother says it's hard to learn
How to bake cakes that never burn.
—MOTHER GOOSE RHYME

A WELSH CAWL

A good chicken and a noble piece of ham, with a little shoulder
of lamb, small to have the least of grease, and then a paste of the
roes of trout with cream, a little butter, and the yolk of egg,
whipped tight and poured in when the chicken, proud with a
stuffing of sage and thyme, has been elbowing the lamb and the
ham in the earthenware pot until all three are tender as the heart
of a mother. In with the carrots and turnips and the goodness of
marrow bones, and in with the potatoes. Now watch the clock and
every fifteen minutes pour in a noggin of brandy, and with the first
a pint of home-brewed ale. Two noggins in, and with the third,
throw in the chopped bottoms of leeks, but save the green leaves
until ten minutes from the time you sit to eat, for you shall find
them still a lovely green.

Drink down the liquor and raise your eyes to give praise for a
mouth and a belly, and then start upon the chicken.
—RICHARD LLEWELLYN
How Green Was My Valley

A VERY VEAL DINNER

At a dinner given by Lord Polkemmet, a Scotch nobleman and
judge, his guests saw, when the covers were removed, that the fare
consisted of veal broth, a roasted fillet of veal, veal cutlets, a veal

pie, a calf's head, and calf's-foot jelly. The judge, observing the surprise of his guests, volunteered an explanation.—"Ou, ay, it's a' cauf; when we kill a beast, we just eat up ae side, and doun the tither."

—Isabella Beeton
The Book of Household Management

"My Dear, How Ever Did You Think Up This Delicious Salad?"

OGDEN NASH

This is a very sad ballad
Because it's about the way too many people make a salad.
Generally they start with bananas,
And they might just as well use gila monsters or iguanas.
Pineapples are another popular ingredient,
Although there is one school that holds preserved pears or
      peaches more expedient,
And you occasionally meet your fate
In the form of a prune or date.
Rarely you may chance to discover a soggy piece of tomato
      looking very forlorn and Cinderella-ry,
But for the most part you are confronted by apples and celery,
And it's not a bit of use at this point to turn pale or break out
      in a cold perspiration,
Because all this is only the foundation,
And the further we go into the subject the quicker you will
      grow prematurely old along with me,
Because the worst is yet to be,
Because if you think the foundation sounds enticing
Just wait until we get to the dressing, or rather, the icing.
There are various methods of covering up the body, and to
      some, marshmallows are the pall supreme,
And others prefer whipped cream,
And then they deck the grave with ground-up peanuts and
      maraschinos

And you get the effect of a funeral like Valentino's
And about the only thing that in this kind of salad is never
      seen
Is any kind of green,
And oil and vinegar and salt and pepper are at a minimum,
But there is a maximum of sugar and syrup and ginger and
      nutmeg and cinnamum,
And my thoughts about this kind of salad are just as
      unutterable
As parsnips are unbutterable,
And indeed I am surprised that the perpetrators haven't got
      around to putting buttered parsnips in these
      salamagundis,
And the salad course nowadays seems to be
A month of sundaes.

The Primrose Path

An Arab when asked by an arrogant Englishman why he didn't eat his rice with a spoon instead of with his fingers, said: "My fingers have never entered any mouth but mine; can you say that of your spoon?"

—ANONYMOUS

"FISHIEST OF ALL PLACES"
HERMAN MELVILLE

Upon making known our desires for a supper and a bed, Mrs. Hussey, postponing further scolding for the present, ushered us into a little room, and seating us at a table spread with the relics of a recently concluded repast, turned around to us and said— "Clam or Cod?"

"What's that about Cods, ma'am?" said I, with much politeness.

"Clam or Cod?" she repeated.

"A clam for supper? a cold clam; is *that* what you mean, Mrs.

Hussey?" says I; "but that's a rather cold and clammy reception in the winter time, ain't it, Mrs. Hussey?"

But being in a great hurry to resume scolding the man in the purple shirt, who was waiting for it in the entry, and seeming to hear nothing but the word "clam," Mrs. Hussey hurried towards an open door leading to the kitchen, and bawling out "clam for two," disappeared.

"Queequeg," said I, "do you think that we can make out a supper for us both on one clam?"

However, a warm savory vapor from the kitchen served to belie the apparently cheerless prospect before us. But when the smoking chowder came in, the mystery was delightfully explained. Oh, sweet friends! hearken to me. It was made of small juicy clams, scarcely bigger than hazel nuts, mixed with pounded ship biscuit, and salted pork cut up into little flakes; the whole enriched with butter, and plentifully seasoned with pepper and salt. Our appetites being sharpened by the frosty voyage, and in particular, Queequeg seeing his favorite fishing food before him, and the chowder being surpassingly excellent, we despatched it with great expedition: when leaning back a moment and bethinking me of Mrs. Hussey's clam and cod announcement, I thought I would try a little experiment. Stepping to the kitchen door, I uttered the word "cod" with great emphasis, and resumed my seat. In a few moments a savory steam came forth again, but with a different flavor, and in good time a fine cod-chowder was placed before us. . . .

Fishiest of all fishy places was the Try Pots, which well deserved its name, for all the pots there were always boiling chowders. Chowder for breakfast, and chowder for dinner, and chowder for supper, till you began to look for fish-bones coming through your clothes.

Moby Dick

Ther ought t'be some way t'eat celery so it wouldn't sound like you wuz steppin' on a basket.

—KIN HUBBARD
The Sayings of Abe Martin

Soup for a Fledgling Tenor

I went into the artillery and my major wanted to know who was that fellow who was singing all the time. . . . One great day he took me to a friend, a wealthy amateur musician, who listened to me and taught me the tenor roles in *Cavalleria Rusticana* and *Carmen.* One day I did not sing at all. The major sent for me.

"Why do you not sing today, Caruso?"

"I cannot sing on greasy soup."

"Next day my soup was strong and there was no grease on it."

—ENRICO CARUSO, IN A NEWSPAPER INTERVIEW

The Bride-Cake

This day my Julia thou must make
For Mistresse Bride, the wedding Cake;
Knead but the Dow and it will be
To paste of Almonds turn'd by thee:
Or kisse it thou, but once, or twice,
And for the Bride-Cake ther'l be Spice.

—ROBERT HERRICK

Fadiman's Law of Optimum Improvement
CLIFTON FADIMAN

Two scrambled eggs was what I ordered from the pleasant-faced drugstore counterman.

"On buttered toast," he declared firmly. "White, rye, gluten. Marmalade or jam."

"Just two scrambled eggs," I muttered.

He eyed me with suspicion. A pause. Then, "Potatoes on the side," he stated.

"Just two scrambled eggs."

Another pause. "Nothing on the side?"

Down but still twitching, I said, "Eggs."

"Coffee now or later?"

"No coffee. Eggs."

Lost in misgivings, he prepared the eggs and was about to crown them with a generous bouquet of parsley, when I quavered, "Just the eggs—no parsley."

The eggs were fine. Asking for salt and pepper helped to patch things up a little, but I know I left the counter under a cloud.

Man, boy, and Master of Ceremonies, I have worked in radio and television for over fifteen years. During this period—such is the public's good sense—I have drawn weighable fan mail only once. That was when, through the courtesy of an obliging network, I explained the difficulty I had always met in getting a ham sandwich. By a ham sandwich I meant a ham sandwich—a slice of ham between two pieces of buttered bread, minus lettuce, parsley, olives, pickles, carrots, shredded cabbage, mayonnaise, whipped cream. My open confession attracted many heartfelt letters, all from males.

"Man wants but little here below," the poet Goldsmith tells us. But try to get it. Try to get potatoes without parsley. A Martini without the olive. An Old Fashioned without the cherry. . . .

Party of One

No Challenge to the Chef Is Too Great

It was Scott Fitzgerald who ordered shredded wheat at Voisin's, and on one occasion made a meal there of hors d'oeuvres; so they put a notice on their menu saying hors d'oeuvres would not be served without two other dishes.

—Mrs. E.C.N. of Chicago, in a letter to Julian Street

Peas

I eat my peas with honey,
I've done it all my life,
It makes the peas taste funny,
But it keeps them on the knife.

—Anonymous

New Mexican Fire

At the El Sombrero restaurant Isabel asked for eggs ranchero. She's very In is Isabel and has had eggs ranchero at the Hotel Bamer in Mexico City and at the Fonda del Sol in New York so she says "huevos rancheros." This dish is subject to wide variations; sometimes the fried eggs are on tortillas with the sauce on top and sometimes the eggs are on rice with the sauce circulating around freely but essentially it is fried eggs with a "Spanish" sauce made of tomatoes, onions, peppers, and stuff.

I guess where she went wrong was the peppers.

"Do you want red peppers or green peppers?" asked the waitress.

"Green peppers," Isabel, who is never at a loss for a quick answer, replied.

After awhile the waitress delivered Isabel a bowl of green soup with some green eggs floating in it.

Isabel shoved her spoon in and took a big mouthful, did a take like Patsy Kelly, and grabbed for the water glass. "Ooooh," she said, gasping and drinking everybody's water. So we all twitted her and tried it.

Well the fact is, a white anglo-saxon protestant can't *eat* eggs ranchero in Gallup because they have a patent there on comestible liquid fire. You might as well go to Carnegie Illinois Steel and ask them to fill your pannikin at Furnace Number 2.

—Richard Bissell
How Many Miles to Galena?

THE BREAKFAST FOOD FAMILY
BERT LESTON TAYLOR

John Spratt will eat not fat,
    Nor will he touch the lean;
He scorns to eat of any meat,
    He lives upon Foodine.

But Mrs. Spratt will none of that,
    Foodine she cannot eat;
Her special wish is for a dish
    Of Expurgated Wheat.

To William Spratt that food is flat
    On which his mater dotes.
His favorite feed—his special need—
    Is Eata Heapa Oats.

But Sister Lil can't see how Will
    Can touch such tasteless food.
As breakfast fare it can't compare,
    She says, with Shredded Wood.

Now, none of these Leander please,
    He feeds upon Bath Mitts.
While sister Jane improves her brain
    With Cero-Grapo-Grits.

Lycurgus votes for Father's Oats;
    Proggine appeals to May;
The junior John subsists upon
    Uneeda Bayla Hay.

Corrected Wheat for little Pete;
    Flaked Pine for Dot; while "Bub"
The infant Spratt is waxing fat
    On Battle Creek Near-Grub.

To be wanting in the sense of taste is to have a stupid mouth, just as one may have a stupid mind.

—Guy de Maupassant

WAITING FOR NAPOLEON

General Bisson, who was issued triple rations in the field by Napoleon, is said to have consumed eight bottles of wine for breakfast every day. On one occasion, summoned to Malmaison by Napoleon, the general was kept waiting in an antechamber from four to ten P.M., suffering increasing hunger. From time to time a lackey would enter and deposit a roast chicken on the table. Every fifteen minutes or so he would remove it and replace it with another (Because Napoleon did not like to wait and had no fixed hours of eating, his chef had a roast chicken ready every fifteen minutes.) After observing the arrival and departure of several chickens, General Bisson succumbed and ate one. Though surprised on bringing the next to find the previous one gone, the servant continued to bring a chicken every fifteen minutes. That evening the chamberlain informed Napoleon that three of the chickens brought to his table had mysteriously disappeared. It was no mystery to Napoleon, who immediately identified General Bisson as the guilty one, adding that the general would need an entire steer to make a few sandwiches.

—Barbara Norman
Tales of the Table

The sameness of food, served day after day and month after month, caused battles in homes, riots in institutions and rebellions in armies. A continued diet of bread and water is no worse than a prolonged existence on quail. Either one will get you in the end.

—G. Selmer Fougner

CHRISTMAS BEHIND BARS
BRENDAN BEHAN

Yes. I smiled a bit and whispered to Charlie that from this good day it would be getting better, instead of worse, and we could smell the dinner coming up, and it smelt great.

It was as good as its smell. Usually the screws shouted out, "Bang out your doors" the minute we took the diet can off the tray, but this day I took my diet can into the cell, put it on the table, and banged out the door.

In the top shallow tier of the can were three lovely golden-brown roasted potatoes with chopped green vegetable and in the long part was roasted meat, a piece of Yorkshire pudding, at least that's what I thought it was, and gravy, and all roasting hot with steam running in pearls down the side of the can.

I was looking at it with delight and already had eaten with my eyes when the screw came back to the cell.

"Don't you want your duff?"

He turned to someone else on the landing outside and said, "Paddy, 'ere, 'e doesn't want 'is duff," and went to walk off.

"I do, I do," I shouted, and hoping to Christ he would not go off.

But he'd only been joking, and opened the door. It was the old Cockney, and there was a great smell of beer off him. He smiled as he handed me my duff and poured custard on it from the ladle.

"There you are, Paddy. That'll put 'air on your chest. We was forgetting all about you, we was." He smiled again and nodded to the orderly to take the tray and can of custard.

"A happy Christmas to you, sir," said I, on an impulse of liking.

He looked at me for a second and then said, "And the same to you, son, and many of 'em."

I banged out the door and got out the dinner on the plate. It lay hot and lovely, the roast potatoes, the Yorkshire pudding, the chopped greens and the meat, and a big piece of bread to pack up with, and it wasn't long before I had it finished, and the plate clean (not that I left anything on it) for the duff and the custard.

Borstal Boy

Musical Spits

The most singular spit in the world was that of the Count de Castel Maria, one of the most opulent lords of Treviso. This spit turned one hundred and thirty different roasts at once, and played twenty-four tunes, and whatever it played, corresponded to a certain degree of cooking, which was perfectly understood by the cook. Thus, a leg of mutton *à l'Anglaise* would be excellent at the twelfth air; a fowl *à la Flamande* would be juicy at the eighteenth, and so on. It would be difficult, perhaps, to carry farther the love of music and gourmandising.

—Frederick W. Hackwood
Good Cheer

In the early eighteenth century little strips of salted hard cheese were sold to New York City theater audiences who could eat them or throw them at the actors. They did both.

—Anonymous

"Americans Do Not Respect Their Palates"

Of cooking-school marms, of course, we have a-plenty, and we also have a vast and cocksure rabble of dietitians, some of them more or less scientific. But it must be obvious that the cooking-school marm knows very little about voluptuous eating, and that the dietitian is the enemy. The marm, indeed, seldom shows any sign that the flavor of victuals interests her. The thing she is primarily interested in, to borrow a term from surgery, is the cosmetic effect. In the women's magazines she prints pretty pictures of her masterpieces, often in color. They look precisely like the dreadful tidbits one encounters in the more high-toned sort of tearooms, and at wedding breakfasts. One admires them as spectacles, but eating them is something else again.

Moreover, the marm is primarily a cook, not an epicure. She is interested in materials and processes, not in gustatory effects. When she invents a new way to utilize the hard heel of a ham, she believes that she has achieved something, though even the housecat may gag at it. Her efforts are to the art of the cordon bleu what those of the house painter are to those of a Cezanne. She is a pedagogue, not an artist. The fact that she is heeded in the land, and her depressing concoctions solemnly devoured, is sufficient proof that Americans do not respect their palates.

—H. L. MENCKEN
Victualry as a Fine Art

This is every cook's opinion,
No savory dish without an onion,
But lest your kissing should be spoil'd,
Your onions must be thoroughly boiled. . . .
    —JONATHAN SWIFT

SNAILS

DR. G. C. WILLIAMSON

Snails are strange creatures, especially with regard to reproduction, as they are hermaphrodite, and copulate reciprocally. Their eyes are of extreme beauty, at the end of their long horns, and they can move them about in all directions, when they take up the effect of light in a marvellous fashion, as they are faceted like a wonderful gem.

In Alsace, the snail is stewed in white wine, baked and served with cabbage, anchovy, bacon and spice. In Burgundy, he is generally grilled and stuffed with garlic, parsley and shallots, sometimes in ordinary white wine, more especially in Chablis. He is also served *sauté,* chopped up with chives; or else eggs are filled with chopped snails, mixed with the yolk, and served with a thick red wine sauce.

In Provence, there are tasty snail fritters that are highly appreciated, and the snail finds a place in the national dish of bouillabaisse. Snails in Provence are also simmered in bouillon, and served with onions and tomatoes.

Languedoc is, however, the province of France in which snails are best understood, and where they are regarded as one of the greatest delicacies that can be served. They are stewed in spiced bouillon with butter and served with boiled watercress, celery and spinach. They are also cooked with various spices and lemon, and served with onions and ham.

In Narbonne and in Nîmes, snails are served with mayonnaise and almonds, or cooked in milk and served with anchovies, onion, ham and a thick buttery sauce. In Bas Languedoc, they are often served with a sauce piquante, shallots, onions and walnuts; in Toulouse they are fried in oil and served as hot as they possibly can be eaten, with chopped onions and a small portion of garlic.

In Paris, and occasionally in London, escargots are served grilled in hot milk soup. In any of these forms they are extremely delicious, and the French people are very definite as regards their health-giving qualities, particularly recommending them in cases of lung trouble and pronouncing them, in hot milk soup, as a sure specific against tuberculosis.

RECEIPT TO ROAST MUTTON

Gently stir and blow the fire,
    Lay the mutton down to roast,
Dress it quickly, I desire,
    In the dripping put a toast
        That I hunger may remove—
        Mutton is the meat I love.

On the dresser see it lie;
   Oh! the charming white and red.
Finer meat ne'er met the eye,
   On the sweetest grass it fed:
     Let the jack go swiftly round,
     Let me have it nicely brown'd.

On the table spread the cloth,
   Let the knives be sharp and clean,
Pickles get and salad both,
   Let them each be fresh and green;
     With small beer, good ale, and wine,
     O ye gods! how I shall dine!
                —ENGLISH FOLK SONG

FOOD AND WORLD AFFAIRS
MICHAEL FIELD

. . . Ambassador and Mme. Michalowski invited Frances and me
to a formal dinner at which the dishes would be prepared in the
authentic style, and which, I was delighted to learn, would be
cooked by wives of the embassy's staff.

Everything I had felt about Polish food was confirmed for me
that night. The hors d'oeuvre—Polish ham thinly sliced, a whole
pike in glistening aspic, a salad of finely cut sauerkraut mixed with
carrots, apples and caraway seeds—were delicious; the meat course
—a braised beef stuffed with Polish mushrooms and accompanied
by a sour-cream sauce—a tour de force; the pastries—tortes
masked with butter cream or coated with nuts and fruits, and four
different kinds of *mazurki*—superb beyond belief. Yet there was
not the slightest hint of pretentiousness or ostentation that one
might have expected at a dinner such as this. And during a lively
and entertaining afterdinner discussion about food and cooking in
different parts of Poland—the influences upon it, what was a true
Polish dish and what was not—in which Ambassador Michalow-

ski revealed himself as most knowledgeable, I found myself re-flecting briefly on world affairs and couldn't help thinking rather wistfully: would that all debates in the world's embassies were limited to arguments about food.

A Quintet of Cuisines

No one could make pot-pourri like my grandmother. She knew the fragrance value of such combinations as sweet briar, bay, myr-tle, lavender and thyme. And she knew to the last fraction of an ounce how much cinnamon, cloves, lemon rind, nutmeg and orris root should be added to the bay salt and saltpetre in which the leaves were "pickled."

MAURA LAVERTY
Never No More

GARLIC

A SPANISH COUNTRYMAN'S REPAST

At noon he took his lunch, composed of ten raw tomatoes, half a loaf of bread, a piece of raw ham, and a large bulb of garlic consisting of a score of bulblets, which he took one at a time to flavor his portions. It is doubtful if he expected another meal that day, and in watching him a brilliant theory came to my mind:— perhaps the poor classes in Spain are so fond of garlic for the reason that they have so little to eat; for, as it takes several days to digest a bulb of it, they always feel as if they had something in their stomachs.

—HENRY T. FINCK

"Nothing to Equal a Few Pieces of Raw Garlic"

Garlic I consider a most valuable article of food in a hot climate, especially eaten raw. I never travelled without a supply of garlic, and I found its beneficial effects on the stomach and system most marked. When very hungry and fatigued, I have found nothing to equal a few pieces of raw garlic, eaten with a crust of bread or a biscuit, for producing a few minutes after a delightful sensation of repose, and that feeling of the stomach being ready to receive food, generally absent when excessive emptiness or exhaustion is the case.

—Charles Monteire

Henry of Navarre (Henry IV of France) had his lips rubbed the moment he was born with a clove of garlic—a time-honoured custom in his native place.

—E. S. Dallas

What do you think? Young women of rank actually eat—you will never guess what—*garlick!* Our poor friend Lord Byron is quite corrupted by living among these [Italian] people. . . .

—Percy Bysshe Shelley to Leigh Hunt

In this country [the Dauphine] I was almost poisoned with garlic, which they mix in their ragouts and all their sauces; nay, the smell of it perfumes the very chambers, as well as every person you approach.

—Tobias Smollet
Travels in France and Italy

No cook who has attained mastery over her craft ever apologizes for the presence of garlic in her productions.

—RUTH GOTTFRIED
The Questing Cook

In provincial inns garlic is no doubt used too freely, but no harm can come to those who cannot stomach it, since its warning appeals as distinctly to the nose as the rattlesnake's does to the ear.

—HENRY T. FINCK
Food and Flavor

The honest flavor of fresh garlic is something I can never have enough of.

—JAMES BEARD
Beard on Food

Cookery in Périgord is done with lard or walnut oil, further south with olive oil, and everywhere with garlic. Those who do not like garlic can ask for it to be left out; but it must be said that the best cooks use it with discretion, almost imperceptibly.

—FREDA WHITE
Three Rivers of France

If Leekes you like, but do their smell dis-like,
Eat Onyons, and you shall not smell the Leeke;
If you of Onyons would the scent expell,
Eat Garlicke, that shall drowne the Onyons' smell.

—DR. WILLIAM KITCHINER
The Cook's Oracle

Everybody knows the odor of garlic except the one who has eaten it and wonders why everybody turns away from him. Athenaeus says that no one who had eaten garlic could enter the sacred temple of Cybele. Virgil refers to it as useful to restore the strength of reapers, against the heat, and the poet Macer says that it was used to prevent people who feared being attacked by snakes from falling asleep. The Egyptians worshipped it. The Greeks detested it. The Romans ate it with delight. Horace, who suffered indigestion on the very day of his arrival at Rome, from a sheep's head prepared with garlic, had a horror of it.

—ALEXANDRE DUMAS PÈRE
Le Grand Dictionaire de Cuisine

It is not really an exaggeration to say that peace and happiness begin, geographically, where garlic is used in cooking.

—MARCEL BOULESTIN

Garlicks, tho' used by the French, are better adapted to the uses of medicine than cookery.

—AMELIA SIMMONS
American Cookery

Today we do not, like the ancient Greeks, compel criminals to eat garlic to purify themselves of their crimes or, like the Romans, press the juice from artichoke hearts to use as a lotion for restoring the hair.

—JUNE OWEN

Garlic is the Fifth Element. As important to our existence as earth, air, fire and water. Without garlic I simply would not care to live.

—Chef Louis Diat

To the Editor of the *Daily Telegraph*

Sir, Your [editorial] writer stresses insufficiently the virtues of garlic.

I once served in France with a Belgian major, aged seventy-five, who made his breakfast entirely off this strange food. He was the fittest man, among twenty different nationalities, on the Pyrenees frontier. He climbed the mountains daily.

For twelve months I sat with this gallant major on the opposite side of my office table without wearing a gas mask, and I have never been so fit before or since. And I have never had such few visitors to bother me.

Yours faithfully,
A. M. Cree, Capt.
R.N. (ret'd)

* * *

He Was a Meat and Potatoes Man, a Milk and Hoecake Man
EVAN JONES

He was a meat and potatoes man, a milk and hoecake man, a watermelon and clabber man. He was, after all, as American as the food he liked best, and in more than one book he paused in the course of his story to interject his enthusiasm. "A man accustomed to American food and American domestic cookery would not starve to death suddenly in Europe," he wrote nostalgically in *A Tramp Abroad*, "but I think he would gradually waste away, and eventually die."

The writer of such words would not have been Mark Twain had he not resisted the blandishments of cuisines he considered too exotic for sanity. "There is here and there an American who will say he can remember rising from a European table d'hôte perfectly satisfied; but we must not overlook the fact that there is also here and there an American who will lie."

However, Mark Twain himself would not lie when he discovered the gustatory solace of a British mixed drink. "Livy my darling," he wrote his wife in 1874, "I want you to be sure to have in the bathroom, when I arrive, a bottle of Scotch whisky, a lemon, some crushed sugar, & a bottle of *Angostura bitters.* Ever since I have been in London I have taken in a wine-glass what is called a cock-tail (made with those ingredients) before breakfast, before dinner, & just before going to bed. . . . To it I attribute the fact that up to this day my digestion has been wonderful—simply *perfect.* . . . Now my dear, if you will give the order *now,* to have those things put in the bath-room & left there till I come, they will *be* there when I arrive. Will you? . . . I love to picture myself ringing the bell, at midnight—then a pause of a second or two—then the turning of the bolt, & 'Who is it?'—then ever so many kisses—then you & I in the bath-room, I drinking my cock-tail and undressing, & you standing by—then to bed, and—everything happy & jolly as it should be."

In those post-bellum years he was to label the Gilded Age, Sam Clemens of Hannibal, Missouri, matured from a connoisseur of wild fruit to a Yankee *bon vivant.* "I know the look of an apple that is roasting and sizzling on a hearth on a winter's evening," he wrote in his sixties, "and I know the comfort that comes of eating it hot, along with some sugar and a drench of cream. . . . I know how the nuts taken in conjunction with winter apples, cider, and doughnuts, make old people's old tales and old jokes sound fresh and crisp and enchanting. . . . I know the look of Uncle Dan'l's kitchen as it was on the privileged nights, when I was a child. . . ."

Especially when he was traveling in foreign countries was he haunted by the tastes and smells of kitchens he remembered, and in Paris during the summer of 1879 he turned his memory back over four decades to compile a bill of fare that includes dozens of "nourishing" dishes—a modest, private dinner, which he said he would have "all to myself" and which must "be hot when I arrive."

Mark Twain, his wife and children once spent a year and a half in Europe, and pater familias, at least, was literally fed up. He said that after a few months' exposure to the coffee served in a European hotel a man's mind was apt to weaken. Even the bread was "unsympathetic" because it was cold, and the butter, "made of goodness knows what," had no salt. Asserting that the commonest American breakfast consisted of coffee and beefsteak, he stormed over the inadequacy of European meat, calling it dry, insipid, and usually "as overdone as a martyr."

Sam Clemens began complaining about food when he was a fifteen-year-old apprentice on a weekly newspaper in Hannibal. The invariable diet of thin stew and boiled cabbage drove him and a fellow apprentice to steal onions and potatoes from the editor's cellar and to cook them at night on the printshop stove. When offered a job on another newspaper, owned by his brother, he readily accepted. But with subscribers paying in cordwood and turnips rather than in cash, the paper failed, and Sam left home for good.

Much of his life was to be spent in travel—to New York when he was seventeen, up and down the Mississippi as a steamboat pilot, roughing it in western mining camps. From his first overseas voyage to Hawaii in 1866 to his last to Bermuda just before his death in 1910, he spent much of his time on the road as a lecturer —perforce in hotels and restaurants—and he was never persuaded that home-cooked food, southern style, could be outmatched.

He grudgingly admitted that European provincial fare was better than that to be had in "our minor cities." But even in lunching with Andrew Carnegie and other tycoons who were his friends, he preferred to take his companions to his family dining room. "The main splendor," he once said in some rapture, was in the way that food was cooked at home. And at the mention of beef he could work up a fine disdain for European notions about preparing and serving a piece of meat.

"Then there is the beefsteak. They have it in Europe, but they don't know how to cook it. Neither will they cut it right. It comes on the table in a small, round, pewter platter. It lies in the centre of this platter, in a bordering bed of grease-soaked potatoes; it is the size, shape, and thickness of a man's hand with the thumb and fingers cut off. It is a little overdone, is rather dry, it tastes pretty insipidly, it rouses no enthusiasm.

"Imagine a poor exile contemplating that inert thing," he sniffed scornfully; "and imagine an angel suddenly sweeping down out of a better land and setting before him a mighty porter-house steak an inch and a half thick, hot and sputtering from the griddle; dusted with fragrant pepper; enriched with little melting bits of butter of the most unimpeachable freshness and genuineness; the precious juices of the meat trickling out and joining the gravy, archipelagoed with mushrooms; a township or two of tender, yellowish fat gracing an outlying district of this ample county of beefsteak; the long white bone which divides the sirloin from the tenderloin still in its place; and imagine that the angel also adds a great cup of American home-made coffee, with the cream a-froth on top, some real butter, firm and yellow and fresh, some smoking hot biscuits, a plate of hot buckwheat cakes, with transparent syrup—could words describe the gratitude of this exile?"

When the Clemens family first went to live in London they took Katy Leary with them to supervise the children and to pinch-hit occasionally for the English cook. As the Clemens housekeeper for a quarter-century, Katy had her troubles with the food, "because the English," she said in her own story of Mark Twain, "they didn't half cook things through, specially the vegetables." She added that she was able finally to educate a London cook to some extent, but that there was no one in England who could be taught to make creamed potatoes—a regular Sunday-night treat for the Clemenses. Katy grumbled at the beer that had to be kept on tap for all the English servants, to say nothing of the weekly bottle of whiskey exacted by the cook. But Twain grumbled over the five weeks it took to find the English cook in the first place and over the taste of the simplest products of her cuisine. "English Toast!" an entry in his notebook exclaims. "Execrable!"

He even dreamed about food, and his notebook records a somnolent fancy of buying a pie, "a mush apple pie—hot." Huckleberry, another pie that appealed to him, was used by Katy to lure her master into breaking his habit of going without lunch. She ordered a pie every morning, she said, recalling a period in which Twain was depressed. "Then I'd get a quart of milk and put it on the ice, and have it all ready—the huckleberry pie and the cold milk—about one o'clock. He'd eat half the huckleberry pie, anyway, and drink all the milk."

Katy was not the only one who worried about Mark Twain's eating habits. In her own account of the family, Clara Clemens described an unsuccessful effort "to prevail on Father to return to the house at noon and eat his favorite 'dishes' cooked in the old Southern way. . . ." But Sam Clemens remained a stubborn individualist, and spasmodic culinary enthusiasms were not the least of his idiosyncrasies. Once he wrote to his wife: "I take only one meal a day just now and would keep this up if you permitted it. It consists of four boiled eggs and coffee. I stir in a *lot* of salt and then keep on dusting and stirring in black pepper till the eggs look dirty—then they're booming with fire and energy and you can taste them all the way down and even after they get there."

His disregard for food when he himself was not hungry caused much talk in the family on the occasion of the first visit of Rudyard Kipling. As an unsung young journalist writing about the United States for an Indian newspaper, Kipling had pursued Twain from his home in Elmira, New York, to his nearby summer farm, and back to his mother-in-law's house, where Kipling arrived just as the Clemens family was sitting down to lunch.

The trouble, as Katy Leary remembered it, "was that Kipling had heard the sound of dishes in the dining-room and knew it was lunch time and there was something to eat, and I suppose it made him hungry as a bear to hear them." If so, Kipling became so engrossed in talking to the American author that he seems to have forgotten the absence of food. "A big darkened drawing room," he wrote for his readers in India: "a huge chair; a man with eyes, a mane of grizzled hair, a brown mustache covering a mouth as delicate as a woman's, a strong, square hand shaking mine, and the slowest, calmest, levelest voice in the world. . . . I was smoking his cigar and hearing him talk—this man I had learned to love and admire fourteen thousand miles away. . . . Blessed is the man who finds no disillusion when he is brought face to face with a revered writer."

Mark Twain was deeply loved and extravagantly admired at home, but in the unfinished biography begun by his daughter Susy when she was only thirteen, he is not quite perfect. "Papa uses very strong language," the little girl wrote, "but I have an idea not nearly so strong as when he first maried mamma." Indeed his behavior at meals was such that his wife made a habit of reprimanding him for his misdemeanors in a way that his children called "dusting Papa off." During a season in Paris in which the Clemenses entertained frequently, the harassed father told his wife that she might dust him off after every dinner for a year and still not eliminate all his bad habits. The solution, he thought, lay in a system of signals and the use of colored cards as a family code.

"The children got a screen arranged so that they could be behind it during the dinner and listen for the signals and entertain themselves," Twain recalled. "At a hint from behind the screen, Livy would look down the table and say, in a voice full of interest, if not of counterfeited apprehension, 'What did you do with the blue card that was on the dressing table—?'

"That was enough. I knew what was happening—that I was talking the lady on my right to death and never paying any attention to the one on my left. . . . [The system] headed off crime after crime all through dinner, and I always came out at the end successful, triumphant, with large praises owing to me, and I got them on the spot."

Sam and Livy Clemens had come a long way to those dinners given in Paris, or those in London, or at any of their several homes in the United States. Describing their lack of culinary education on the day of their marriage in 1870, Mark Twain wrote that at about midnight they were left alone in their new quarters. "Then Ellen, the cook, came in to get orders for the morning's marketing—and neither of us knew whether beefsteak was sold by the barrel or by the yard." He was joking, of course, but it was true that neither Sam nor Livy knew much about housekeeping.

In spite of such beginnings, when the Clemenses built a house in Hartford, Connecticut, soon after their marriage, they swiftly became noted among the literati for their hospitality. The house itself was an oddity of geometrically patterned red and white bricks that had a balcony like a pilot-house and a porch like a Mississippi steamboat deck. Although newspapers gibed at the bizarre design, the Clemens home became a stopping place for traveling authors and publishers and was famous for dinner parties that were said to produce "an incomparable hilarity."

Over the library mantel Sam had set a brass plate inscribed with a line from Emerson: "The ornament of a house is the friends who frequent it." Sam so meant these words that he had ordered a guest room built on the ground floor, a revolutionary idea in those days. There were other precedent-breakers, among them the fact that all the rooms were free of the usual Victorian clutter because Sam liked to move as he talked, and he never freed himself of his compulsion to stride around the dining table between courses.

Bret Harte came more than once to drink Sam's whiskey, and frequent dinner guests included Charles Dudley Warner, Harriet Beecher Stowe, and Thomas Wentworth Higginson. William Dean Howells said Livy was a hostess "without a touch of weakness. . . . I suppose she had . . . her female fears of etiquette and conventions, but she did not let them hamper the wild and splendid generosity with which Clemens rebelled against the social stupidities and cruelties. . . ." Sam entertained so many people, and was wined and dined himself by so many others, that his daughter Jean said with enough inherited wit to make up for the irreverence: "Papa, the way things are going, pretty soon there won't be anybody left for you to get acquainted with but God."

Books poured from his pen; during the Hartford years Mark Twain created Tom Sawyer, Huck Finn, the Prince and the Pauper, and many other characters to delight his growing audience. Many friends shared in the birth of Twain's creations, whether he was at home or away, for it was his custom to give dinners, following which he would read his most recent manuscript. He described one such event at which "we had a gay time. . . . Shandy-gaff [beer and ginger ale] for the gentlemen & buttermilk & seltzer-lemonades for the ladies."

Living gaily was Mark Twain's nature, and so was living well. Yet, cosmopolitan as he became, he remained at heart the original of Tom Sawyer, the frontier boy whose great nostalgia was for the summer days he had spent on the Missouri farm of his Uncle John Quarles. Working on his autobiography at the age of sixty-two, he recalled the look of the dinner table and ticked off thirty-eight dishes that came from that farm kitchen—from roast pig to hot corn pone to peach cobbler. "Well," he wrote, "it makes me cry to think of them." When he wrote of the dinner given for him by Kaiser Wilhelm II it was not the royal menu in general that interested him; it was the kind of potatoes served, only because they reminded him of the midnight feasts in the Hannibal print shop. White-tie-and-tails did not change Sam Clemens, nor did the decades of what he called "banqueteering." As Mark Twain he was loved in every civilized part of the world, and to himself he seemed, as Bernard De Voto has put it, "a proof of the American Dream." So he was—and so he lived.

American Heritage Cookbook

9

Epicurean
Seductions

Long ago a British playwright set down a recipe that contrived to show how slowly-baked turtle doves could be the mystery ingredient in a love potion:

> *Take me a turtle dove*
> *And in an oven let her lie and bake*
> *So dry that you may powder of her make;*
> *Which, being put into a cup of wine,*
> *The wench that drink'st it will to love incline.*

In one court of love or another, scores of different foods—truffles, of course—have been believed to have aphrodisiac powers, but nothing works as well to heighten romance as the power of suggestion. Food and drink may sometimes prove useful allies, to be sure, but they need the wise impetus which belongs to an enchantress who knows the letter B is simple shorthand for bachelor, or the avuncular urgency of Brillat-Savarin. Although it was The Settlement Cook Book *that professed to have the right advice about "The Way to a Man's Heart," the path has its deviations, as attested here by Mimi Sheraton and John Steinbeck; and as for persuading "the wench . . . to love incline," well, there are surprises in James Laver's "Déjeuner de Rupture."*

B Is for Bachelors

M. F. K. FISHER

. . . And the wonderful dinners they pull out of their cupboards with such dining-room aplomb and kitchen chaos.

Their approach to gastronomy is basically sexual, since few of

them under seventy-nine will bother to produce a good meal unless it is for a pretty woman. Few of them at any age will con-
sciously ponder on the aphrodisiac qualities of the dishes they
serve forth, but subconsciously they use what tricks they have to
make their little banquets, whether intimate or merely convivial,
lead as subtly as possible to the hoped-for bedding down.

Soft lights, plenty of tipples (from champagne to straight rye),
and if possible a little music, are the timeworn props in any such
entertainment, on no matter what financial level the host is operating. Some men head for the back booth at the corner pub and play
the juke-box, with overtones of medium-rare steak and French-
fried potatoes. Others are forced to fall back on the soft-footed
alcoholic ministrations of a Filipino houseboy, muted Stan Kenton
on the super-Capeheart, and a little supper beginning with caviar
malossol on ice and ending with a soufflé au kirschwasser d'Alsace.

The bachelors I'm considering at this moment are at either end
of the gastronomical scale. They are the men between twenty-five
and fifty who if they have been married are temporarily out of it
and are therefore triply conscious of both their heaven-sent freedom and their domestic clumsiness. They are in the middle brack-
ets, financially if not emotionally. They have been around and
know the niceties or amenities or whatever they choose to call the
tricks of a well-set table and a well-poured glass, and yet they have
neither the tastes nor the pocketbooks to indulge in signing endless
chits at Mike Romanoff's or "21."

In other words, they like to give a little dinner now and again
in the far from circumspect intimacy of their apartments, which
more often than not consist of a studio-living-room with either a
disguised let-down bed or a tiny bedroom, a bath, and a stuffy
closet called the kitchen.

I have eaten many meals prepared and served in such surroundings. I am perhaps fortunate to be able to say that I have always
enjoyed them—and perhaps even more fortunate to be able to say
that I enjoyed them because of my acquired knowledge of the basic
rules of seduction. I assumed that I had been invited for either a
direct or an indirect approach. I judged as best I could which one
was being contemplated, let my host know of my own foreknowl-

edge, and then sat back to have as much pleasure as possible.

I almost always found that since my host knew I was aware of the situation, he was more relaxed and philosophical about its very improbable outcome and could listen to the phonograph records and savor his cautiously concocted Martini with more inner calm. And I almost always ate and drank well, finding that any man who knows that a woman will behave in her cups, whether of consommé double or of double Scotch, is resigned happily to a good dinner; in fact, given the choice between it and a rousing tumble in the hay, he will inevitably choose the first, being convinced that the latter can perforce be found elsewhere.

The drinks offered to me were the easy ones, dictated by my statements made early in the game (I never bothered to hint but always said plainly, in self-protection, that I liked very dry Gibsons with good ale to follow, or dry sherry with good wine: safe but happy, that was my motto). I was given some beautiful liquids: really old Scotch, Swiss Dézaley light as mountain water, proud vintage Burgundies, countless bottles of champagne, all good too, and what fine cognacs! Only once did a professional bachelor ever offer me a glass of sweet liqueur. I never saw him again, feeling that his perceptions were too dull for me to exhaust myself, if after even the short time needed to win my acceptance of his dinner invitation he had not guessed my tastes that far.

The dishes I have eaten at such tables-for-two range from home-grown snails in home-made butter to pompano flown in from the Gulf of Mexico with slivered macadamias from Maui— or is it Oahu? I have found that most bachelors like the exotic, at least culinarily speaking: they would rather fuss around with a complex recipe for Le Hochepot de Queue de Boeuf than with a simple one called Stewed Oxtail, even if both come from André Simon's *Concise Encyclopedia of Gastronomy.*

They are snobs in that they prefer to keep Escoffier on the front of the shelf and hide Mrs. Kander's *Settlement Cook Book.*

They are experts at the casual: they may quit the office early and make a murderous sacrifice of pay, but when you arrive the apartment is pleasantly odorous, glasses and a perfectly frosted shaker or a bottle await you. Your host looks not even faintly harried or stovebound. His upper lip is undewed and his eye is flatteringly wolfish.

Tact and honest common sense forbid any woman's penetrating with mistaken kindliness into the kitchen: motherliness is unthinkable in such a situation, and romance would wither on the culinary threshold and be buried forever beneath its confusion of used pots and spoons.

Instead the time has come for ancient and always interesting blandishments, of course in proper proportions. The Bachelor Spirit unfolds like a hungry sea of anemone. The possible object of his affections feels cozily desired. The drink is good. He pops discreetly in and out of his gastronomical workshop, where he brews his sly receipts, his digestive attacks upon the fortress of her virtue. She represses her natural curiosity, and if she is at all experienced in such wars she knows fairly well that she will have a patterned meal which has already been indicated by his ordering in restaurants. More often than not it will be some kind of chicken, elaborately disguised with everything from Australian pine-nuts to herbs grown by the landlady's daughter.

One highly expert bachelor-cook in my immediate circle swears by a recipe for breasts of young chicken, poached that morning or the night before, and covered with a dramatic and very lemony sauce made at the last minute in a chafing dish. This combines all the tricks of seeming nonchalance, carefully casual presentation, and attention-getting.

With it he serves chilled asparagus tips in his own version of vinaigrette sauce and little hot rolls. For dessert he has what is also his own version of riz à l'Impératrice, which he is convinced all women love because he himself secretly dotes on it—and it can be made the day before, though not too successfully.

This meal lends itself almost treacherously to the wiles of alcohol: anything from a light lager to a Moët et Chandon of a great year is beautiful with it, and can be well bolstered with the preprandial drinks which any bachelor doles out with at least one ear on the Shakespearean dictum that they may double desire and halve the pursuit thereof.

The most successful bachelor dinner I was ever plied with, or perhaps it would be more genteel to say served, was also thoroughly horrible.

Everything was carried out, as well as in, by a real expert, a man then married for the fifth time who had interspersed his connubial adventures with rich periods of technical celibacy. The cocktails were delicately suited to my own tastes rather than his, and I sipped a glass of Tio Pepe, properly chilled. The table, set in a candle-lit patio, was laid in the best sense of the word "nicely," with silver and china and Swedish glass which I had long admired. The wine was a last bottle of Chianti, " 'stra vecchio."

We ate thin strips of veal that had been dipped in an artful mixture of grated parmigiano and crumbs, with one of the bachelor's favorite tricks to accompany it, buttered thin noodles gratinés with extra-thin and almond-brown toasted noodles on top. There was a green salad.

The night was full of stars, and so seemed my eager host's brown eyes, and the whole thing was ghastly for two reasons: he had forgotten to take the weather into his menu planning, so that we were faced with a rich, hot, basically heavy meal on one of the worst summer nights in local history, and I was at the queasiest possible moment of pregnancy.

Of course the main mistake was in his trying to entertain a woman in that condition as if she were still seduceable and/or he still a bachelor: we had already been married several months.

An Alphabet for Gourmets

There was a young lady of Kent,
Who said that she knew what it meant
  When men asked her to dine,
  And served cocktails and wine;
She knew, oh she knew!—but she went!
—ANONYMOUS

THE FOOD OF LOVE

Many foods . . . have been claimed to be aphrodisiacs. Antiquity favored onions, though our more squeamish times would probably regard them as definitely inhibitory. The Elizabethans ascribed the power to so many articles of diet that one suspects that in that virile but undernourished age all anyone needed was a square meal. They set especial store by potatoes, eryngoes, and tobacco, and thought so well of prunes, in this respect, that they served them as free lunches in their brothels. Modern lore follows Casanova's prescription of oysters but places equal faith in raw eggs, which are thought to be great strengtheners of virility as well.

—BERGEN EVANS
The Natural History of Nonsense

A man for whom cooking is not a passion seldom prepares a meal except for a girl he is trying to make. His characteristic culinary defect is due to the self-centeredness of the masculine imagination; he tends to plan his meal in terms of what he imagines would seduce him if he were a woman.

—W. H. AUDEN

IN PRAISE OF COCOA, CUPID'S NIGHTCAP

Lines written upon hearing the startling news that cocoa is, in fact, a mild aphrodisiac.

STANLEY J. SHARPLESS

Half past nine—high time for supper;
"Cocoa, love?" "Of course, my dear."
Helen thinks it quite delicious,
John prefers it now to beer.
Knocking back the sepia potion,
Hubby winks, says, "Who's for bed?"
"Shan't be long," says Helen softly,

Cheeks a faintly flushing red.
For they've tumbled on the secret
Of a love that never wanes,
Rapt beneath the tumbled bedclothes,
Cocoa coursing through their veins.

Pepper with biting nettle-seed they bruise
With yellow pillitory wine infuse. . . .
Eat the white shallots sent from Megara
Or garden herbs that aphrodisiac are,
Or eggs, or honey on Hymettus flowing,
Or nuts upon the sharp-leaved pine trees growing.

—Ovid

BOUILLABAISSE FOR MEN

And chilly beauties, not a few,
Will do whate'er you wish,
Partaking, tête-à-tête with you,
Of this perfidious dish.

—Charles Monselet

WHAT ONE LEARNS FROM MEN
DACHINE RAINER

I always think of a man when I'm cooking, not of one man, but of one per recipe, and I think of him not in the ordinary way; that is, not in order to meander that well-traveled channel between his heart and his stomach. That impressed me as a route for a canal construction engineer and not for a cook—a helpless, female cook. It seems quixotic to fix oneself in a man's heart when one can secure him eternally in one's memory.

Every man is not an exceptional cook but every man I've come to know . . . well . . . has, in his book of tricks, at least one remarkable recipe. It is a slow process to cull this forth. Men seem content to permit their ladies, night after night, to wrestle with dinner when it is manifestly apparent—invariably to themselves, and most generally as a conversational gambit—that they could improve matters considerably. Consequently, it takes me a number of years to acquire a man's most splendid culinary performance by heart and by that time, not infrequently, I'm no longer interested in cooking it for him.

Thus I learned a superb spaghetti sauce from wandering around with an Italian street musician; lamb, red cabbage and string beans from a Greek philosopher; and a magnificent clam chowder from settling down, briefly, with a clam digger on Long Island.

Through my association with Mohib A——, a Mohammedan, a native of Assam province, India, I acquired (along with a stint in the Woman's Home of Detention on the not-too-preposterous charge of possessing illegal firearms) my most formidable recipe. Curry.

To make a great curry you have to establish a Zen kind of concentration. It will not do to work out your latest *Sturm und Drang* or think up a zany plot for a novel while preparing curry. That requires altogether another sort of dish.

For example, I make a psychologically-troubled soup. In it I ferociously pick and slice and chop up anything I find in the garden or the larder—vegetables and herbs and bits of flowers—and after the bones and onions brown and it all begins to boil and bubble, it comes to me that I'm stewing impertinent editors in my cauldron, and wayward children and miscreant husbands. However, a curry is indifferent to your literary and personal problems.

The Artists' & Writers' Cookbook

Report from Karen Geld, Screenwriter

When Gary asked me to marry him, I said, "I don't know, what are your views on takeout food?" He said he liked it, I said yes, and now it's nine years, one child, and lots of Chicken Delights later.

—Peg Bracken
The I Hate to Cook Almanac

Cupboard Love
HILARY HAYWOOD

My fragrant love, when I return,
Is ever at her stove,
Her hair is rich with garlic
And her breath with Eastern clove.

Fresh onion stains her pearly hands
And wets her loving eye.
When I weep too, she understands
I'll love her till I die.

Oh! pungent-aromatic wife,
Thank God that I will dine
Throughout our earthly wedded life
At such a board as thine!

"I Had Not Underestimated This Man"
MIMI SHERATON

Once there was a very special man whom I dated for almost a year. We had all kinds of things in common including an appreciation of food and a love of cooking. He had many perfect meals at my apartment and I had a number at his; he was beginning to walk around absent-mindedly humming strains of *Lohengrin.* My ears perked up considerably and I decided to pull out all the stops and invite him to a really gorgeous dinner with just the right amount of candlelight and music, and the kind of food he couldn't resist.

On the day of the dinner I shopped for food and flowers, a couple of serving pieces I needed, and exactly the right wine. I planned to have some of the coarse *pâté en terrine* that I knew he loved and purchased it from a small French charcuterie formerly on Ninth Avenue. I thought I'd follow this with his favorite soup, a petite marmite, and then go on to sautéed veal birds served with risotto and a crisp, raw zucchini salad. For dessert I bought some of the fresh goat cheese we both liked—a huge cube that I dipped in white wine and then coated with rosemary, to be eaten with ripe pears and the rest of our wine.

That, at least, was the plan, but it definitely wasn't my day. I was about to serve the pâté when I tasted it and found it was wildly salty and impossible to eat. I announced the fact, he tasted it, agreed, and we both decided to skip it, figuring there'd be enough to eat without it. I wanted to serve the soup in an old Limoges tureen which I had inherited from my mother, but as I poured the broth into it I heard a crack as sharp as pistol fire. By the time I found out what it was, the soup was running all over the counter, and as I picked up the tureen to save the remaining soup, the whole thing came apart in my hands, spilling over me and the kitchen floor and thereby ending the second course. Still, my guest, a man who really cared about his food, remained amiable. But as I was changing into dry clothes, the untended meat burned black as charcoal, and looked like some fossil unearthed from the ruins of Pompeii.

Dinner, in short, was ruined; in about twenty minutes the whole day's work had been wiped out. There was the risotto and the zucchini but that was hardly enough, and besides, the rice was beginning to get mushy and the squash was going limp. I was embarrassed beyond recall, and by this time my starved dinner guest had stopped humming the Wedding March and was switching instead to "Good Night, Ladies, We're Going to Leave You Now."

But I had not underestimated this man. He said we could go out to dinner, but the table looked so nice, the fire was just going well in the fireplace, and it was cold and rainy outside. He suggested that since I was so overwrought, I sit down, have one more sherry, and he would fix dinner. He said he would rustle up something on the condition that I stay out of the kitchen until he was through. There was rummaging through the grocery closet; the refrigerator door slammed a few times; I heard some chopping and, finally, the rattle of pots and pans. Then came the sounds of sizzling and bubbling, and in about twenty-five minutes he announced dinner. Out he came, this darling man, with a tray holding two huge soup bowls full of steaming, fragrant, thin spaghettini, over which he had poured an exquisitely aromatic sauce of nut-brown garlic cracklings and golden oil, flecked with freshly chopped parsley and lightly sprinkled with crushed peppers. He set down one bowl at each place, apologizing for the simplicity of the food, and poured each of us a glass of cool white Orvieto wine. The sauce (aglio e olio), and the spaghettini done perfectly *al dente* were just satisfying and soothing enough for my distraught state. We wound up with cheese, pears and more wine—and to this day I can't remember how the dishes got done.

Funny thing was, this man was so swept away by his own masculine ability that he proposed that very night out of sheer self-satisfaction. I accepted and he still prepares aglio e olio for me on occasion and kids about my fall from culinary grace.

The Seducer's Cookbook

A DECLARATION OF LOVE
WILLIAM MAKEPIECE THACKERAY

Her lovely name is Blanche, the veil of the maiden is white; the wreath of roses which she wears is white. I determined that my dinner should be as spotless as snow. At her accustomed hour, and instead of the rude *gigot à l'eau* which was ordinarily served at her too simple table, I sent her up a little *potage à la Reine—à la Reine Blanche* I called it—as white as her own tint—and confectioned with the most fragrant cream and almonds. I then offered up at her shrine a *filet de merlan à l'Agnes* and a delicate *plat,* I have designated as *Éperlan à la Sainte Theresa,* and of which my charming Miss partook with pleasure. I followed this by two little *entrées* of sweetbreads and chicken; and the only brown thing which I permitted myself in the entertainment was a little roast lamb, which I laid in a meadow of spinaches, surrounded with croustillons, representing sheep, and ornamented with daisies and other savage flowers. After this came my second service: a pudding *à la Reine Elizabeth* . . . a dish of opal-coloured plovers' eggs which I called *Nid de Tourtereaux à la Roucoule;* placing in the midst of them two of the most tender volatiles, billing each other, and confectioned with butter; a basket containing little *gâteaux* of apricots, which, I know, all young ladies adore, and a jelly of maraschin, bland, insinuating, intoxicating as the glance of beauty. This I designated *Ambroisie de Calypso à la Souveraine de mon Coeur.* And when the ice was brought in—an ice of *plombière* and cherries—how do you think I had shaped them. . . . In the form of two hearts united with an arrow, on which I had laid, before it entered, a bridal veil, in cut-paper, surmounted by a wreath of virginal orange-flowers. I stood at the door to watch the effect of this entry. It was but one cry of admiration. The three young ladies filled their glasses with the sparkling Ay, and carried me in a toast. I heard it—I heard Miss speak of me —I heard her say, "Tell Monsieur Mirobolant that we thank him —we admire him—we love him!"

Pendennis

LOVE AND ONIONS
GRAHAM GREENE

A whole week went by after the fumbling kiss in Maiden Lane before I rang Sarah up. She had mentioned at dinner that Henry didn't like the cinema and so she rarely went. They were showing a film of one of my books at Warner's and so, partly to show off, partly because I felt that kiss must somehow be followed up for courtesy's sake, partly too because I was still interested in the married life of a civil servant, I asked Sarah to come with me. . . .

The film was not a good film, and at moments it was accutely painful to see situations that had been so real to me twisted into the stock clichés of the screen. I wished I had gone to something else with Sarah. At first I had said to her, "That's not what I wrote, you know," but I couldn't keep on saying that. She touched me sympathetically with her hand, and from then on we sat there with our hands in the innocent embrace that children and lovers use. Suddenly and unexpectedly, for a few minutes only, the film came to life. I forgot that this was my story and that for once this was my dialogue, and was genuinely moved by a small scene in a cheap restaurant. The lover had ordered steak and onions, the girl hesitated for a moment to take the onions because her husband didn't like the smell; the lover was hurt and angry because he realized what was behind her hesitation, which brought to his mind the inevitable embrace on her return home. . . .

Afterwards—we were back at Rule's, and they had just fetched our steaks—she said, "There was one scene you did write."

"Yes."

"About the onions?"

"Yes." She helped me to them and then helped herself.

Is it possible to fall in love over a dish of onions? It seems improbable, and yet I could swear it was just then that I fell in love. It wasn't, of course, simply the onions; it was that sudden sense of an individual woman, of a frankness that was so often later to make me happy and miserable. I put my hand under the cloth and laid it on her knee, "It's a good steak"—and heard like poetry her reply, "It's the best I've ever eaten."

There was no pursuit and no seduction. We left half the good steak on our plates and a third of the bottle of claret and came into Maiden Lane with the same intention in both our minds. At exactly the same spot as before, by the doorway and the grill, we kissed. I said, "I'm in love."

"Me too."

The End of the Affair

The Haitian Peasant Declares His Love
EMILE ROUMER

High-yellow of my heart, with breasts like tangerines,
you taste better to me than eggplant stuffed with crab,
you are the tripe in my pepper-pot,
the dumpling in my peas, my tea of aromatic herbs.
You are the corned beef whose customhouse is my heart,
my mush with syrup that trickles down my throat.
You are a steaming dish, mushroom cooked with rice,
crisp potatoe fries, and little fish fried brown . . .
My hankering for love follows you wherever you go.
Your bum is a gorgeous basket brimming with fruits and meat.
— TRANSLATED FROM THE FRENCH BY JOHN PEALE BISHOP

Good for Married Men

Put a portion of cheese in silver paper. Wrap it up and put it over a fire. When the paper starts to glow the cheese is ready to eat and deliciously creamy. . . . This is good food which enhances sex for married men.

— MUHAMMAD SIDQI EFFENDI

Vegetable Vestments
JOYCE WADLER

I am on the phone with Robert Kushner, a twenty-three-year-old conceptual artist who makes clothes out of food, and we are having a discussion about what he will design for me.

"I'd love to make you something in asparagus," he says. "I could get very excited about that—asparagus is in season now, and I've never worked with it before."

"Okay," I say. "I've always liked asparagus."

A few days later I go over to his place on the Lower East Side of Manhattan, and Robert takes out of the refrigerator the halter he has made. "Cold, crisp, fresh, and beautiful," he says, holding it up for me to admire. "Though you can't really see the line till it's on."

The halter, mostly asparagus, has a radish inset and a scallion back, and Robert has made me a hard salami necklace to go with it. "I've only had two shows, so far," Robert says as I try the halter on and he adjusts the asparagus. "For my first show, in California, I used only fruits and vegetables. I designed banana skirts, strawberry shirts, celery necklaces. Then I invited the audience to eat the food off the models, and we all had a lot of fun.

"My second show, in New York, marked a major development in my work because I moved into cooked meats and cheese—I did Velveeta epaulets, my favorite work, in that show. Recently I whipped up some stuff for an entertainment at Fairleigh Dickinson, but it wasn't serious; they just wanted a few quick things the audience could have as appetizers before going to dinner."

Is this an expensive medium to work in?

"I couldn't really say," says Robert. "Like with this, a friend's mother gave me the scallions and the salami, and I sort of borrowed the asparagus from this restaurant that I manage. But I'll have to bring it back, because we're having asparagus soup tomorrow."

"Maybe we could have it for lunch ourselves?" I suggest, nibbling my necklace.

Ten minutes later, Robert is chopping my halter into a large wooden bowl, adding mushrooms and feta cheese and onions and a red wine vinegar dressing, and we sit down to eat while he explains his art form.

"Using food as subject matter creates a tension between food as food and food as ornamentation," he says. "It's kinetic sculpture, treating the body as sculptural form. There's the public sexual confrontation of eating someone's clothes. There's the absurdity of it. And, of course, I always try to make the food taste good.

"You know," he goes on, chewing a scallion, "you might really enjoy my next show. I'm going to have this costume made entirely of roast duck; duck mittens and duck slippers—*only*. Also a Jell-O dress. It will be part of a new concept where the models are wheeled out, and special assistants serve them. Maybe you'd like to be a model."

"I'll think about it," I say. "I've always liked Jell-O."

Harper's Magazine

LOVE SONG

A. P. HERBERT

On May Day, after oysters,
   They say that monk and nun
Run madly from their cloisters
   In search of love and fun:
They say some stuff called celery
   Is good for wedding-bellery:
      These aids may do
      For one or two,
         But I need none.

I need no oyster
   To be in love with you.
Nor, when I roister,
   Raw roots to chew;
I need not suffer hard-boiled eggs
To see that you have lovely legs.
  I need no rations
    Of Danish Blue,
  To improve my passions,
    And, as for you,
  To see you walk,
  To hear you talk,
    Gives me my clue.

I need no oysters
>To be in love with you.

They recommend red pepper
>With quantities of stout:
It may get hep men hepper,
>But I can do without.
They say that frangipani
Can make a man more manny,
>>But who requires
>>Such borrowed fires
>>When you're about?

I need no oysters
>*To be in love with you*
Nor at my roisters
>*Mussels for two:*
No radishes, I beg, and please
No curried prawns or Persian cheese!
>*I need no shellfish,*
>>*No hellebore,*
>*To make me elfish*
>>*Or even more;*
If you but blow
A kiss or so
>*I'm on the floor.*
I need no oysters
>To be in love with you.

"To Encourage the Customers"
JOHN STEINBECK

Old Guillermo Lopez died when his daughters were fairly well
grown, leaving them forty acres of rocky hillside and no money at
all. They lived in a whitewashed, clapboard shack with an out-
house, a well and a shed beside it. Practically nothing would grow

on the starved soil except tumbleweed and flowering sage, and, although the sisters toiled mightily over a little garden, they succeeded in producing very few vegetables. For a time, with grim martyrdom, they went hungry, but in the end the flesh conquered. They were too fat and too jolly to make martyrs of themselves over an unreligious matter like eating.

One day Rosa had an idea. "Are we not the best makers of tortillas in the valley?" she asked of her sister.

"We had that art from our mother," Maria responded piously.

"Then we are saved. We will make enchiladas, tortillas, tamales. We will sell them to the people of Las Pasturas del Cielo."

"Will those people buy, do you think?" Maria asked skeptically.

"Listen to this from me, Maria. In Monterey there are several places where tortillas, only one finger as good as ours, are sold. And those people who sell them are very rich. They have a new dress thrice a year. And do their tortillas compare with ours? I ask that of you, remembering our mother."

Maria's eyes brimmed with tears of emotion. "They do not," she declared passionately. "In the whole world there are none like those tortillas beaten by the sainted hands of our mother."

"Well, then, *adelante!*" said Rosa with finality. "If they are so good, the people will buy."

There followed a week of frenzied preparation in which the perspiring sisters scrubbed and decorated. When they had finished, their little house wore a new coat of whitewash inside and out. Geranium cuttings were planted by the doorstep, and the trash of years had been collected and burned. The front room of the house was transformed into a restaurant containing two tables which were covered with yellow oilcloth. A pine board on the fence next to the county road proclaimed: Tortillas, enchiladas, tamales and some other Spanish cooking, R. & M. Lopez.

Business did not come with a rush. Indeed very little came at all. The sisters sat at their own yellow tables and waited. They were childlike and jovial and not very clean. Sitting in the chairs they waited on fortune. But let a customer enter the shop, and they leaped instantly to attention. They laughed delightedly at everything their client said; they boasted of their ancestry and of the marvelous texture of their tortillas. They rolled their sleeves to the elbows to show the whiteness of their skin in passionate denial of their Indian blood. But very few customers came. The sisters began to find difficulties in their business. They could not make a quantity of their product, for it would spoil if it kept for long. Tamales require fresh meat. So it was that they began to set traps for birds and rabbits; sparrows, blackbirds and larks were kept in cages until they were needed for tamales. And still the business languished.

One morning Rosa confronted her sister. "You must harness old Lindo, Maria. There are no more corn husks." She placed a piece of silver in Maria's hand. "Buy only a few in Monterey," she said. "When the business is better we will buy very many." Maria obediently kissed her and started out toward the shed.

"And Maria—if there is any money left over, a sweet for you and for me—a big one."

When Maria drove back to the house that afternoon, she found her sister strangely quiet. The shrieks, the little squeals, the demands for every detail of the journey, which usually followed a reunion, were missing. Rosa sat in a chair at one of the tables, and on her face was a scowl of concentration.

Maria approached timidly. "I bought the husks very cheaply," she said. "And here, Rosa, here is the sweet. The biggest kind, and only four cents."

Rosa took the proffered candy bar and put one huge end of it in her mouth. She still scowled with thought. Maria settled herself nearby, smiling gently, quizzically, silently pleading for a share of her sister's burden. Rosa sat like a rock and sucked her candy bar. Suddenly she glared into Maria's eyes. "Today," she said solemnly, "today I gave myself to a customer."

Maria sobbed with excitement and interest.

"Do not make a mistake," Rosa continued. "I did not take money. The man had eaten three enchiladas—three!"

Maria broke into a thin, childish wail of nervousness.

"Be still," said Rosa. "What do you think I should do now? It is necessary to encourage our customers if we are to succeed. And he had three, Maria, three enchiladas! And he paid for them. Well? What do you think?"

Maria sniffed and clutched at a moral bravery in the face of her sister's argument. "I think, Rosa, I think our mother would be glad, and I think your own soul would be glad if you should ask forgiveness of the Mother Virgin and of Santa Rosa."

Rosa smiled broadly and took Maria in her arms. "That is what I did. Just as soon as he went away. He was hardly out of the house before I did that."

Maria tore herself away, and with streaming eyes went into her bedroom. Ten minutes she kneeled before the little Virgin on the wall. Then she arose and flung herself into Rosa's arms. "Rosa, my sister," she cried happily. "I think—I think I shall encourage the customers, too."

The Pastures of Heaven

After a perfect meal we are more susceptible to the ectasy of love than at any other time.

—Dr. Hans Balzli

INFLUENCE OF GOURMANDISM ON WEDDED HAPPINESS
JEAN ANTHELME BRILLAT-SAVARIN

Finally, when gourmandism is shared, it has the most marked influence on the happiness which can be found in marriage.

A married couple who enjoy the pleasures of the table have, at least once a day, a pleasant opportunity to be together; for even those who do not sleep in the same bed (and there are many such) at least eat at the same table; they have a subject of conversation which is ever new; they can talk not only of what they are eating, but also of what they have eaten, what they will eat, and what they have noticed at other tables; they can discuss fashionable dishes, new recipes, and so on and so on; and of course it is well known that intimate table talk [CHITCHAT] is full of its own charm.

Doubtless music too holds a strong attraction for those who love it; but it demands work and constant practice.

Moreover, it can be interrupted by a cold in the nose, or the music may be lost, the instruments out of tune; one of the musicians may have a headache, or feel lackadaisical.

On the other hand, a shared necessity summons a conjugal pair to the table, and the same thing keeps them there; they feel as a matter of course countless little wishes to please each other, and the way in which meals are enjoyed is very important to the happiness of life.

This observation, rather new in France, did not escape the English moralist Fielding, and he developed it by depicting, in his novel *Pamela,* the different ways two married couples might bring their day to a close.

The first husband is a nobleman, the older son, and for that reason possessor of all the family wealth.

The second is his younger brother, married to Pamela: he has been disinherited because of this union, and is living on half pay, in circumstances so straitened that they border on abject poverty.

The peer and his wife enter the dining room from opposite directions, and greet each other coldly in spite of not having been together at all during the day. They sit down to a magnificently appointed table, surrounded by gold-braided footmen, serve themselves in silence, and eat without pleasure. As soon as the servants have withdrawn, however, a kind of conversation begins between them: bitterness creeps into it; it becomes a quarrel, and they get up in fury, each one to go alone to his apartment, to meditate on the delights of widowhood.

The nobleman's brother, on the contrary, is welcomed with the tenderest warmth and the sweetest caresses as he comes to his modest dining room. He seats himself at a frugal table; but need that mean that the dishes served to him are not excellent? It is Pamela herself who has prepared them! They eat with joy, while they chat of their projects, of their day's happenings, of their affection. A half bottle of Madeira helps them to prolong both the meal and the companionship; soon the same bed welcomes them, and after the ecstasies of well-shared love, a sweet sleep makes them forget the present and dream of an even better future.

All praise then to gourmandism, as we thus present it to our readers, and for as long as it does not distract mankind from either his honest labors or his duties! Even as the excesses of Sardanapalus could not make women a thing of horror, so the excesses of Vitellius have not succeeded in forcing anyone to turn his back on a well-ordered banquet.

When gourmandism turns into gluttony, voracity, or perversion, it loses its name, its attributes, and all its meaning, and becomes fit subject either for the moralist who can preach upon it or the doctor who can cure it with his prescriptions.

Gourmandism as the Professor has discussed it in this Meditation has no true name except the French one, *la gourmandise;* it cannot be designated by the Latin word *gula,* any more than by the English *gluttony* or the German *lusternheit;* therefore I advise whoever is tempted to translate this instructive book to use the noun as I have, and simply to change the article, which is what everyone has done with *la coquetterie* and everything connected with it.

—Translated by M. F. K. Fisher
The Physiology of Taste

Love and Cooking . . . A Special Feeling

In later years I learned that love and cooking are the most important, the most basic, natural, and essential, as well as the most entertaining pastimes in the world. Without love and cooking there would be no babies, no inheritance taxes, and no crêpe suzettes. The course of affairs of the world has often been changed by a pretty woman and a good meal.

But don't think that because you can crack two eggs over a piece of bacon, you are a cook or that because you have a house full of children, you are a lover. Certainly not! because for love and cooking you must be born. There must be in your eyes, in your heart, and in your hands that special feeling, that special understanding and warmth, which can change night to day and rain to sunshine.

You may have learned to cook, you may possess a dozen cook books, and still you may not be a cook. You may have studied all the books on love and sex ever written . . . and still you may not be a lover, not be able to kindle the sublime fire that gives sense, soul, and fulfillment to our lives.

For love and cooking you must be born.

—EDWARD G. DANZIGER
Papa D: A Saga of Love and Cooking

In Holland when a Dutch lad goes courting on New Year's Day, he takes his sweetheart a pastry made in the form of her initials.

—ANONYMOUS

My First Love
HARRY GRAHAM

I recollect in early life,
I loved the local doctor's wife.

I ate an apple ev'ry day
To keep the doctor far away!
Alas! he was a jealous man
And grew suspicious of my plan.

He'd noticed sev'ral pips about
When taking my appendix out
(A circumstance that must arouse
Suspicion in the blindest spouse).

And though I squared the thing somehow,
I always eat bananas now!

The World We Laugh In

DÉJEUNER DE RUPTURE
JAMES LAVER

Holroyd and Lavigne were friends; that is, they came as near to friendship as two such different temperaments could. They often argued, in fact they always argued, and Holroyd was sometimes convinced that Lavigne was right. That never happened to Lavigne, whose opinions, being perfectly logical and founded upon an exact appreciation of human appetites, never varied. Perhaps it is enough to say that Lavigne was French.

Holroyd frequently differed from him on political questions, for that is the Englishman's way, but he had a profound respect for his knowledge of life, his infallible instinct for the art of living. For that also, when he contemplates a Frenchman, is the Englishman's way.

Now it happened that six months before this story opens, Holroyd had consulted Lavigne, as was his custom, on what seemed to him a particularly difficult and delicate matter, and Lavigne's advice had been so much to the point that Holroyd's respect for him was now even greater than it had been before. The question was simply this: what kind of meal, or series of meals, should be offered to Marguerite in order that she look upon Holroyd with a kinder eye, with an eye so kind (not to put too fine a point up on it) that Holroyd would have nothing further to desire of her except that such kindness should continue.

Lavigne had entered into the project with the mingled enthusiasms of the culinary expert and the *galant homme.* He had prepared a series of menus, he had gone round in person to various carefully selected restaurants and arranged with the chefs that the menus should be carried out. He had chosen the wines, not such wines, necessarily, as he would have chosen for himself or for a dinner party of men, but with the principal object in view: the softening of the heart of Marguerite. The dinners culminated in a particularly careful one at Holroyd's flat with everything so arranged that the services of a waiter could be dispensed with after the soup.

"The rest of the meal will be cold. Of course, you will make the coffee yourself?"

In the event, Holroyd had *not* made the coffee; no one had made it, but that did not invalidate the principle, and Holroyd's respect for Lavigne's judgment in these matters henceforth knew no bounds.

Lavigne, although his artistic conscience was satisfied, regretted, in one way, that he had been so successful, for he saw very little of Holroyd, who was busy elsewhere. It was therefore with pleasure that, returning one evening from his office, he found Holroyd on his doorstep, or what corresponds to a doorstep in modern flats.

"I want your help," said Holroyd, and the expression on his face told the Frenchman that the need was urgent. He opened the door quickly and led the way into his tiny sitting-room.

"Will you have something to drink?"

"Yes! A whisky and soda."

Lavigne made a face, but he kept whisky for his English friends and produced it now. Holroyd gulped it down quickly, but still said nothing of the purpose of his visit. Lavigne did not press him; he knew that, sooner or later, the whole story would come out. At last Holroyd said:

"I've got to end it."

"End what?"

"This Marguerite business."

"Why, may one ask?"

"I'm getting more deeply involved than I ever intended. Besides, I'm in love with someone else."

"I see," said Lavigne, "and you want me to arrange another series of menus, similar to the last, but not quite the same, of course. One must respect the personality of the woman, is it not? What is this new person like?"

Holroyd shook his head. "That's the difficult part," he admitted.

The Frenchman understood. "I see," he said, "you want me to undo the work I did for you six months ago. I am to arrange a graceful farewell. Is that it?"

"Yes," said Holroyd, and poured himself another whisky. "I want you to work out a little dinner—"

But the Frenchman interrupted him. "Not a dinner, *mon cher.*"

"Why not?"

"It must be a luncheon. *Un déjeuner de rupture.* Believe me, it is a regular institution in Paris, the *déjeuner de rupture.* Certain restaurants specialize in it, and once they are known, it makes everything easy. The lady understands from the start, and either does not come at all (in which case you have only one luncheon to pay for), or if she is a woman of the world, comes solely in order to see with what delicacy you will carry the matter off. One puts a little *cadeau* perhaps among the *petits fours,* and *voilà!*"

"Things are not quite so easy here," said Holroyd. "We have hotels that lend themselves to the preliminaries of divorce, but no restaurants that specialize in *déjeuners de rupture.*"

The Frenchman made a deprecatory gesture. "It takes many years," he said, "to emerge from the twilight of barbarism. The Latin Culture—"

"I know," cried Holroyd, "but let us stick to the point. Will you help me or won't you?"

"Of course I will help you. Only you must not rush me. These things need thought—and *finesse.*"

"I believe you," said Holroyd.

Lavigne walked up and down the room, and, as he walked, meditated aloud something after this fashion.

"The choice of a restaurant is, of course, all important—no music —quiet, with little alcoves—no, not alcoves—you must eat your meal out of hearing, but in full view of everybody; as she is English that will probably prevent her from making a scene, but if you handle things properly there will be no scene, anyhow. Some rather old-fashioned English place like—like Walters' might do—but no oysters—they are not really an aphrodisiac, but there is a legend— and legends are sometimes very powerful. Lobster, perhaps, cold lobster, with a simple mayonnaise, and after that—after that? A *ballotine de canard*—it is a kind of stuffed, boned duck...."

"You will drink a white wine—a rosé is too vinous and a generous burgundy or a good claret out of the question. *Entre-deux-mers* perhaps. It is thin and rather fruity; it quenches the thirst without uplifting the heart, and it is an excellent wine for luncheon."

Three days later Holroyd was back again.

"Eh bien?" asked Lavigne.

"It didn't work," replied Holroyd. "It didn't work at all. In fact she seems to be more in love with me than ever."

The Frenchman knitted his brows. "She must have the digestion of a horse," he said.

"I don't understand you."

"That rich duck after the lobster was calculated to make her feel very cross at the end of the meal."

"But it didn't," cried Holroyd. "It made me feel awful, but she loved it."

"I must see Marguerite," Lavigne said, with sudden resolution. "You must understand that while it is perfectly easy for me to arrange a dinner—such as I arranged for you a short while ago—without seeing Marguerite, for that was a matter of general principles merely, it is quite impossible for me to arrange a *déjeuner de rupture.* There the individual element enters. *Et comment!"* Lavigne tapped his chest.

"What do you propose, then?"

"You must invite me to lunch also."

"How will that help?"

"You will see. And it must be at one of the very best restaurants in London. I will order the meal myself beforehand, and you will have nothing to do but to pay the bill."

Holroyd agreed, although he could not see how luncheon for three could possibly be a *déjeuner de rupture,* and when the day came he presented himself at the restaurant in question. Lavigne was already there and Marguerite entered a few minutes later. The two strangers were introduced, and after a cocktail, which Lavigne, to Holroyd's astonishment, insisted on ordering, they sat down to table.

The lunch was excellent, and Holroyd noticed with amusement that everything was black-and-white, a kind of *demi-deuil: canapé de caviar,* with little dishes of white onions, *la sole blanche avec des truffes noires,* black cock with a *purée de pommes,* and *glace Helène,* the white mounds contrasting with the almost black hot chocolate sauce. But it did not seem to be depressing Marguerite. On the contrary she was enjoying herself immensely. Holroyd had never seen her in better form.

After lunch was over, Lavigne announced that he had an important engagement and left the other two together. He was awakened next morning by the telephone. It was Holroyd, who seemed to be really angry. Lavigne let him talk for some time; then he interrupted: "But my dear fellow," he said, "there was never any question that *that* was the *déjeuner de rupture*. Yesterday's lunch was merely to find out the character of Marguerite, and then to prescribe."

"Well, *what* do you prescribe?" Came Holroyd's voice down the telephone.

"This," said the Frenchman calmly. "You will take her to an A.B.C. in the rush hour and give her stuffed sheep's heart, and a cup of cocoa, and tell her quite seriously, that that is what you really like." He rang off.

He was not in the least surprised to find Holroyd once more on his doorstep when he arrived back from his office.

"Well," he said, "did it work?"

"Yes," replied Holroyd, miserably, "it did. Only too well."

"Only too well?"

"She's left me, for good. And now—now I wish she hadn't."

The Frenchman shrugged his shoulders despairingly. "Ah, my friend. It is necessary to know what one wants in life. It is not my fault if you change your mind."

His key was already in the lock, and Holroyd made as if to follow him into the apartment.

"You will forgive me," said Lavigne, "if I do not ask you in. I have someone coming to see me. *You* understand—"

Holroyd nodded, and turned away. Lavigne watched him safely out of the building and then entered his flat. In the little sitting-room in front of the fire a manservant was already laying a table for two.

"I want everything to be ready in an hour," Lavigne said.

"Bien, m'sieur."

"A quarter of an hour before you will put the champagne on ice. I want it *frappé*, not frozen."

"Bien, m'sieur."

"You will understand, of course, that I shall not want you after the soup. I will make the coffee myself."

"And the flowers, *m'sieur?"* He indicated the cardboard box which he had not yet untied.

"Ah, yes, the flowers. You will put the spray of orchids against the lady's plate, and in that bowl, in the middle of the table—the marguerites."

10

Consuming
Passions

PRODUIT
DU
PÉRIGORD

Consummate hunger isn't the lot of everyone, happily enough, and a passionate attitude toward food is a matter of degree even among many who feel it their due to be classified as "gourmets." The kind of persons gathered in the following pages are those who are eaters, unrestrained. The conclave would not be complete without A. J. Liebling learning to eat in Paris, or even the flamboyant populist of the 1930s, Huey Long, beating the drum for potlikker. Passions of this sort don't have to be inelegant, else why would Colette feel so vehemently about truffles and Nero Wolfe so imperious in his notion starlings may be seasoned in one way and one way only. No consideration of gusto at the table would be complete without the introduction of Dr. Johnson, nor can Joseph Mitchell's Old Mr. Flood be forgotten by any connoisseur of either prose or provender. Here is a gallery of gourmands— honest eaters, most of them.

THE VICARAGE MUTTON

Hot on Sunday,
Cold on Monday
Hashed on Tuesday,
Minced on Wednesday,
Curried on Thursday,
Broth on Friday,
Cottage pie Saturday.
— OLD ENGLISH JINGLE

LEARNING TO EAT

A. J. LIEBLING

The reference room where I pursued my own earnest researches as a feeder without the crippling handicap of affluence
was the Restaurant des Beaux-Arts, on the Rue Bonaparte, in
1926–27. I was a student, in a highly generalized way, at the
Sorbonne, taking targets of opportunity for study. Eating soon
developed into one of my major subjects. The franc was at
twenty-six to the dollar, and the researcher, if he had only a
certain sum—say, six francs—to spend, soon established for himself whether, for example, a half bottle of Tavel *supérieur,* at three
and a half francs, and braised beef heart and yellow turnips, at
two and a half, gave him more or less pleasure than a *contre-filet* of
beef, at five francs, and a half bottle of *ordinaire,* at one franc. He
might find that he liked the heart, with its strong, rich flavor and
odd texture, nearly half as well as the beef, and that since the
Tavel was overwhelmingly better than the cheap wine, he had
done well to order the first pair. Or he might find that he so
much preferred the generous, sanguine *contre-filet* that he could
accept the undistinguished *picrate* instead of the Tavel. As in a
bridge tournament, the learner played duplicate hands, making
the opposite choice of fare the next time the problem presented
itself. (It was seldom as simple as my example, of course, because
a meal usually included at least an hors d'oeuvre and a cheese,
and there was a complexity of each to choose from. The arrival,
in season, of fresh asparagus or venison further complicated matters. In the first case, the investigator had to decide what course
to omit in order to fit the asparagus in, and, in the second,
whether to forego all else in order to afford venison.) . . .

There is small likelihood that a rich man will frequent modest
restaurants even at the beginning of his gustatory career; he will
patronize restaurants, sometimes good, where the prices are high
and the repertory is limited to dishes for which it is conventionally
permissible to charge high prices. From this list, he will order the
dishes that in his limited experience he has already found agreeable. Later, when his habits are formed, he will distrust the origi-

nality that he has never been constrained to develop. A diet based chiefly on game birds and oysters becomes a habit as easily as a diet of jelly doughnuts and hamburgers. It is a better habit, of course, but restrictive just the same. Even in Paris, one can dine in the most costly restaurants for years without learning that there are fish other than sole, turbot, salmon (in season), trout, and the Mediterranean *rouget* and *loup de mer.* The fresh herring or sardine *sauce moutarde;* the *colin froid mayonnaise;* the conger eel *en matelote;* the small fresh-water fish of the Seine and the Marne, fried crisp and served *en buisson;* the whiting *en colère* (his tail in his mouth, as if contorted with anger) and even the skate and the *dorade*—all these, except by special and infrequent invitation, are out of the swim. (It is a standing tourist joke to say that the fishermen on the quays of the Seine never catch anything, but in fact they often take home the makings of a nice fish fry, especially in winter. In my hotel on the Square Louvois, I had a room waiter—a Czech naturalized in France—who used to catch hundreds of *goujons* and *ablettes* on his days off. He once brought a shoe box of them to my room to prove that Seine fishing was not pure whimsey.) All the fish I have mentioned have their habitats in humbler restaurants, the only place where the aspirant eater can become familiar with their honest fishy tastes and the decisive modes of accommodation that suit them. Personally, I like tastes that know their own minds. The reason that people who detest fish often tolerate sole is that sole doesn't taste very much like fish, and even this degree of resemblance disappears when it is submerged in the kind of sauce that patrons of Piedmontese restaurants in London and New York think characteristically French. People with the same apathy toward decided flavor relish "South African lobster" tails—frozen as long as the Siberian mammoth—because they don't taste lobstery. ("South African lobsters" are a kind of sea crayfish, or *langouste,* but that would be nothing against them if they were fresh.) They prefer processed cheese because it isn't cheesy, and synthetic vanilla because it isn't vanillary. They have made a triumph of the Delicious apple because it doesn't taste like an apple, and of the Golden Delicious because it doesn't taste like anything. . . .

The consistently rich man is also unlikely to make the acquaintance of meat dishes of robust taste—the hot *andouille* and *andouillette,* which are close-packed sausages of smoked tripe, and the *boudin,* or blood pudding, and all its relatives that figure in the pages of Rabelais and on the menus of the market restaurants. He will not meet the *civets,* or dark, winy stews of domestic rabbit and old turkey. A tough old turkey with plenty of character makes the best *civet,* and only in a *civet* is turkey good to eat. Young turkey, like young sheep, calf, spring chicken, and baby lobster, is a pale preliminary phase of its species. The pig, the pigeon, and the goat— as suckling, squab, and kid—are the only animals that are at their best to eat when immature. The first in later life becomes gross through indolence; the second and third grow muscular through overactivity. And the world of tripery is barred to the well-heeled, except for occasional exposure to an unexpurgated version of *tripes à la mode de Caen.* They have never seen *gras-double* (tripe cooked with vegetables, principally onions) or *pieds et paquets* (sheep's tripe and calves' feet with salt pork). . . .

Finally, to have done with our rich man, seldom does he see even the simple, well-pounded *bifsteck* or the *pot-au-feu* itself. . . . *Pot-au-feu* is so hard to find in chic restaurants nowadays that every Saturday evening there is a mass pilgrimage from the fashionable quarters to Chez Benoît, near the Châtelet—a small but not cheap restaurant that serves it once a week. . . .

A drastically poor man, naturally, has even less chance than a drastically rich one to educate himself gastronomically. For him eating becomes merely a matter of subsistence; he can exercise no choice. The chief attraction of the cheapest student restaurants in my time was advertised on their largest placards: *"Pain à discrétion"* ("All the Bread You Want"). They did not graduate discriminating eaters. During that invaluable year [in Paris], I met a keen observer who gave me a tip: "If you run across a restaurant where you often see priests eating with priests, or sporting girls with sporting girls, you may be confident that it is good. Those are two classes of people who like to eat well and get their money's worth. If you see a priest eating with a layman, though, don't be too sure about the parishioner, and the good Father won't worry about the price. And if the girl is with a man, you can't count on anything. It may be her kept man, in which case she won't care what she spends on him, or the man who is keeping her, in which case she won't care what he spends on her."

Between Meals

On Eating

Can you inform me of any other pleasure which can be enjoyed three times a day, and equally in old age as in youth?

—Charles Maurice Talleyrand Périgord

When Handel Dined with Handel

Handel, it will be remembered, once ordered a tavern dinner for two. He came at the time appointed, sat down at the board, and ordered the meal to be served. The landlord craved his honour's pardon, but thought his honour had expected company.

"I am the company," said Handel, and devoured the dinner for two with great enjoyment. Here, I confess, we have a tinge of Teutonic greediness and love of gross bulk, rather than delicacy, in food. But, at all events, the instance shows that the good and great composer of *Acis and Galatea,* of the most exquisite vocal music ever written, was a lover of good and great feasts.

—Arthur Machen

Memories of New England
WAVERLEY ROOT

I breakfast lightly now, but I thought nothing in New England, circa 1920, of starting the day, after a preliminary bout with oatmeal and milk, or perhaps buttered buckwheat cakes swimming in maple syrup, or chipped beef in cream, or fish cakes and ketchup, with a slab of steak accompanied by onions and German-fried potatoes, and topping the whole with apple pie. I was encouraged in these morning excesses by my father, who was the first to get up and took advantage of his early rising to create new breakfast dishes. I think he was the only one who took more than one bite of his chocolate griddle cakes with sliced bananas.

These solid breakfasts did not induce us to ease up for the rest of the day. We ate a great deal, but how could we help it? The food was irresistible. I have not tasted since, and shall probably never taste again, bread like that my mother made at home before baker's bread became as good as she thought it should be to justify her abandoning what was, after all, a pretty onerous task. I remember especially her graham bread; sweet corn bread, served hot and buttered at breakfast; broad toasted scones; and that marvel of New England culinary invention, blueberry bread. A large pail, milking size, with mixing bars activated by a rotating handle attached to its brim, was used for kneading the dough; it doubled for mixing mincemeat, filling the kitchen with the rich spicy fragrance of currants, seedless raisins, chopped apples, lemon and orange peel, cinnamon, mace, cloves, nutmeg, and all the other spices that gave life to the chopped beef and suet (it never occurred to anyone in our nondrinking family to put brandy in it). Another homemade mixture I recall with regret, for I have not met its equal since, is piccalilli. I don't remember exactly what went into it, except little green tomatoes and hot red peppers, finely chopped, but the result was sharp and piquant and put to shame the feeble imitations offered under the same name in restaurants. It was served, of course, with baked beans, also practically unrecognizable as the same dish when prepared in commercial eating places. All that went into the beans, if memory serves, was brown sugar, molasses, and a slab of salt pork. The dish was cooked in a great earthenware pot ever so slowly overnight and was served with steamed raisin-studded brown bread, the butter melting lusciously into its receptive surface.

New England boiled dinner! A simple rustic dish, but how delectable it was as it came steaming onto our table, heaped upon an enormous platter! And New England pot roast! And the delicious meat-loaf preparations! I remember especially one we called Vienna loaf—though I am sure Vienna had never heard of it—which came with a pinkish sauce that must have had tomato in it. And the desserts! Hasty pudding, a dish unknown in Europe; chocolate doughnuts, deep-fried in boiling lard and dusted with confectioners' sugar; apple dumplings with a thin lemon syrup, plus hard sauce; devil's food cake with chocolate sauce and whipped cream; and homemade ice cream, for the production of which we were especially blessed. My father, an electrical engineer, maintained a small machine shop in the cellar. One of the machines was an electrically powered ice-cream freezer. Thus we benefited from the smooth, even, mechanized mixing of the professional product, the enjoyment of high quality ingredients whose use would have been ruinous to a commercial establishment, and the careful attention possible only in small-scale operations. My mother made the basic custard the night before. The flavoring was added the next day; in season it was often fresh fruit from our own backyard. Raspberries grew along the rear fence; there was a small pear tree, a magnificent spreading plum tree whose blue fruit was most abundant, I seem to remember, every third year, and a rectangular grape arbor large enough so that we children could put a table under it and play house there. Fresh grape ice cream was our most luscious product, but plum and peach were splendid too. Alas, when the automobile era arrived, both the grape arbor and the plum tree were cut down to make room for a garage.

Our own produce also provided some of the raw materials for the abundant store of food in the preserve closet in our cellar, which was three times as large as my present kitchen. As each fruit came into season, we bought it in wholesale quantities—a whole crate, or two, or three, of cherries or currants, strawberries or raspberries. The kitchen turned into a steaming inferno populated chiefly by Mason jars. By the time winter set in, we were prepared to withstand a siege of several months. The thick plank shelves bent under the weight of fat jars of peas, green beans, sweet corn, succotash, tomatoes, lima beans, piccalilli, and relishes; crab apple jelly, apricot jelly, quince jelly, gooseberry preserves, strawberry jam, and raspberry jam (I don't seem to recall apple butter); peach halves, pear halves, plums (blue, red, or light green), cherries, strawberries, raspberries, and tart rhubarb.

"An Epicure's Memories of a New England Boyhood," Gourmet, July 1972

THE MARROWBONE DINNER
CAROL TRUAX

In London, it was Father's turn for fittings. Father could never cram himself into ready-made garments, and he wouldn't have done so if he could. His tailor in Bond Street kept his rather improbable measurements on file. After a fitting, Father would hurry off to Simpson's or the Savoy and order marrowbones, which would arrive, like Father, wrapped in fine linen. When I was taken to lunch at Simpson's, I always admired the tidy way each marrowbone was folded into its napkin.

Simpson's well-dressed marrowbones inspired Father. One afternoon he came triumphantly back to our suite at the Hotel Cecil.

"Look at this!"

Out of his pockets he produced a collection of silver instruments, long and narrow, with a blade at each end—one wider than the other—rounded and slightly scooped.

"What in the world, Father?"

"Marrow spoons," said Father.

"How do you use them?"

"I'll show you." Father acted it out. "Here I have a plate of marrowbones." I saw it clearly on the empty table. "Here's a piece of toast. Here is my marrow spoon." He brandished it. "Now watch."

Father was a treat to watch as he took the spoon in his enormous hand and loosened the imaginary marrow within the non-existent bone, using the long, narrow side of the implement. Then, deftly reversing the spoon, he pulled out the invisible core of marrow whole on the wider end and slipped it onto the fictitious piece of toast. It made my mouth water.

"Caroline, my dear," said my Father to my Mother, "we'll serve marrowbones at our very next dinner party, just as soon as we get home, now that we have the right spoons."

"That's all very well, my dear Charlie," said Mother, "but where are you going to get marrowbones? Besides, I'm sure Nora doesn't know how to cook them."

"Mr. Joseph will cut the bones as I direct," said Father confidently, "and anybody can cook them."

Back at home, Father planned his marrowbone dinner party with care.

"Cotuits on the half shell, roast Philadelphia capon—nothing too filling, then we'll have plenty of appetite left for the marrow-bone course."

When the day approached, he made a special trip to the butcher's to show Mr. Joseph exactly how to saw up the shank bones. At the table that night, Father sampled the oysters and the capon with unwonted moderation. He beamed as the swathed bones appeared and each guest helped himself. With a flourish, he picked up his marrow spoon and attacked his bone.

It was empty.

Father looked around at his guests. Their faces were puzzled.

Every bone was empty.

Father turned purple. He rose direfully, as if he was about to sentence some heinous malefactor. As he stalked from the room, Mother wailed after him:

"Please, dear! Remember! Nora's the best cook we ever had! I don't want to lose her!"

"You've lost her!" shouted Father, stamping down the back stairs.

At the foot of the stairs he composed himself and addressed the erring cook politely.

"You found the marrowbones troublesome to cook?"

"Well, not exactly, Your Honor. After I thought of using the ice pick and the pantry screwdriver, it was no bother to get rid of all that fat."

Father Was a Gourmet

"I Broke Off a Lump & Ate It Pure"

I wish I were Queen Victoria [she wrote to Vita Sackville-West].
Then I could thank you. From the *depths* of my *Broken* Widowed
heart. *Never* never NEVER have we had such a *rapturous* atounding
GLORIOUS—no, I can't get the hang of the style. All I can say is
that when we discovered the butter in the envelope box, we had
in the household—Louie that is—to look. That's a whole pound of
butter I said. Saying which, I broke off a lump & ate it pure. Then
in the glory of my heart I gave all our week's ration—which is
about the size of my thumb nail—to Louie—earned undying gratitude: then sat down & ate bread and butter. It would have been
desecration to have added jam. You've forgotten what butter tastes
like. So I'll tell you—it's something between dew & honey. Lord,
Vita!—your broken po, your wool; & then on top your butter!!!
Please congratulate the cows from me, & the dairymaid, & I would
like to suggest that the calf should be known in the future (if its
a man) as Leonard if a woman as Virginia.

Think of our lunch tomorrow! Bunny Garnett and Angelica are
coming: in the middle of the table I shall put the whole pat. And I
shall say: Eat as much as you like. I can't break off this rhapsody, for
its a year since I saw a pound. . . . Bombs fall near me—trifles; a
'plane shot down on the marsh—trifles; floods damned—no, nothing seems to make a wreath on the pedestal fitting your butter. . . .

Here L breaks in: if I'm writing to you, will I add his deepest
thanks for the
Butter.

V.

—Virginia Woolf to Vita Sackville-West

Beer and Rugged Individualism

I have an independent spirit. I think a Welsh rabbit and porter
with freedom of spirit better than ortolans and burgundy with
servility.

—James Boswell

"Get Yo' Hot, Baked Car'lina Yam"
RALPH ELLISON

. . . far down at the corner I saw an old man warming his hands against the sides of an odd-looking wagon, from which a stove pipe reeled off a thin spiral of smoke that drifted the odor of baking yams slowly to me, bringing a stab of swift nostalgia. I stopped as though struck by a shot, deeply inhaling, remembering, my mind surging back, back. At home we'd bake them in the hot coals of the fireplace, had carried them cold to school for lunch; munched them secretly, squeezing the sweet pulp from the soft peel as we hid from the teacher behind the largest book, the *World's Geography.* Yes, and we'd loved them candied, or baked in a cobbler, deep-fat fried in a pocket of dough, or roasted with pork and glazed with the well-browned fat; had chewed them raw—yams and years ago. More yams than years ago, though the time seemed endlessly expanded, stretched thin as the spiraling smoke beyond all recall.

I moved again. "Get yo' hot, baked Car'lina yam," he called. At the corner the old man, wrapped in an army overcoat, his feet covered with gunny sacks, his head in a knitted cap, was puttering with a stack of paper bags. I saw a crude sign on the side of the wagon proclaiming YAMS, as I walked flush into the warmth thrown by the coals that glowed in the grate underneath.

"How much are your yams?" I said, suddenly hungry.

"They ten cents and they sweet," he said, his voice quavering with age. "These ain't none of them binding ones neither. These here is real, sweet, yaller yams. How many?"

"One," I said. "If they're that good, one should be enough."

He gave me a searching glance. There was a tear in the corner of his eye. He chuckled and opened the door of the improvised oven, reaching gingerly with his gloved hand. The yams, some bubbling with syrup, lay on a wire rack above the glowing coals that leaped to low blue flames when struck by the draft of air. The flash of warmth set my face aglow as he removed one of the yams and shut the door.

"Here you are, suh," he said, starting to put the yam into a bag.

"Never mind the bag, I'm going to eat it. Here . . ."

"Thanks." He took the dime. "If that ain't a sweet one, I'll give you another one free of charge."

I knew that it was sweet before I broke it; bubbles of brown syrup had burst the skin.

"Go ahead and break it," the old man said. "Break it and I'll give you some butter since you gon' eat it right here. Lots of folks takes 'em home. They got their own butter at home."

I broke it, seeing the sugary pulp steaming in the cold.

"Hold it over here," he said. He took a crock from a rack on the side of the wagon. "Right here."

I held it, watching him pour a spoonful of melted butter over the yam and the butter seeping in.

"Thanks."

"You welcome. And I'll tell you something."

"What's that?" I said.

"If that ain't the best eating you had in a long time, I give you your money back."

"You don't have to convince me," I said. "I can look at it and see it's good."

"You right, but everything what looks good ain't necessarily good," he said. "But these is."

I took a bite, finding it as sweet and hot as any I'd ever had, and was overcome with such a surge of homesickness that I turned away to keep my control. I walked along, munching the yam, just as suddenly overcome by an immense feeling of freedom—simply because I was eating while walking along the street. It was exhilarating. I no longer had to worry about who saw me or about what was proper. To hell with all that, and as sweet as the yam actually was, it became like nectar with the thought . . . to hell with being ashamed of what you liked. No more of that for me. I am what I am! I wolfed down the yam and ran back to the old man and handed him twenty cents. "Give me two more," I said.

"Sho, all you want, long as I got 'em. I can see you a serious yam eater, young fellow. You eating them right away?"

"As soon as you give them to me," I said.

"You want 'em buttered?"

"Please."

"Sho, that way you can get the most out of 'em. Yessuh," he said, handing over the yams, "I can see you one of these old-fashioned yam eaters."

"They're my birthmark," I said. "I yam what I am!"

Invisible Man

"It Is Not the Enjoyment of Eating They Aim At"

As the Makololo [people of the Zambezi Valley] have great abundance of cattle, and the chief is expected to feed all who accompany him, he either selects an ox or two of his own . . . or is presented by the head-men of the villages he visits with as many as he needs. . . . The animals are killed by a thrust of a small javelin in the region of the heart, the wound being purposely small in order to avoid any loss of blood, which, with the internal parts, are the perquisites of the men who perform the work of the butcher; hence all are eager to render service in that line. Each tribe has its own way of cutting up and distributing an animal. Among the Makololo the hump and ribs belong to the chief. . . . After the oxen are cut up, the different joints are placed before Sekeletu [the chief], and he apportions them among the gentlemen of the party. The whole is rapidly divided . . . cut into long strips, and so many of these are thrown into the fires at once that they are nearly put out. Half broiled and burning hot, the meat is quickly handed round; everyone gets a mouthful, but no one except the chief has time to masticate. It is not the enjoyment of eating they aim at, but to get as much food into the stomach as possible during the short time.

—Dr. David Livingstone
Travels and Researches in South Africa

Ah! some folks boast of quail on toast
  Because they think it's tony;
But I'm content to owe my rent
  And live on abalone.
—GEORGE STERLING

"EASY AS A BOILED EGG"

A favorite dessert in my household is Ice Cream Pie. I always make it in a cookie crumb crust. Nothing but ice cream softened sufficiently to press into the baked crumb pie shell. Then the pie is returned to the freezer to wait until wanted. Jellies, fruit sauces or even maple syrup marbled through the ice cream creates all kinds of interesting variations. This dessert is handsome enough to serve at a formal dinner, and as easy to make as a boiled egg.
—ELLA EATON KELLOGG

"NEVER AGAIN IN THIS WORLD ANYTHING SO GOOD"

After the soup, we had what I do not hesitate to call the very best beefsteak I ever ate in my life. . . . As I write about it now, a week after I have eaten it, the old, rich, sweet, piquant, juicy taste comes smacking on my lips again; and I feel something of that exquisite sensation I then had. I am ashamed of the delight which the eating of that piece of meat caused me. G—— and I had quarreled about the soup; but when we began on the steak, we looked at each other, and loved each other. We did not speak,— our hearts were too full for that; but we took a bit, and laid down our forks, and looked at one another, and understood each other. There were no two individuals on this wide earth,—no two lovers billing in the shade,—no mother clasping baby to her heart, more supremely happy than we. Every now and then, we had a glass of honest, firm, generous Burgundy, that nobly supported the meat.

As you may fancy, we did not leave a single morsel of the steak; but when it was done, we put bits of bread into the silver dish, and wistfully sopped up the gravy. I suppose I shall never in this world taste anything so good again.

—WILLIAM MAKEPEACE THACKERAY
Memorials of Gourmandizing

ULTIMATE GOURMET EXPERIENCE?

There are times when born hollandaise heads, as well as nouveaux turbot freaks and *recherché* escargotphiles alike, crave the *saignant* abundance of a New York steak. Atavists and adventurists, we willingly suffer the insolence of the stockyard: sawdust and surliness, the cigar-tangy din, the meaningless reservation. And the isolation of non-chic: no sign of Eugenia or Truman or the astigmatic EYE of *Women's Wear.* Only the ubiquitous electrical-appliance supplier from the Middle West with his tourmaline-stoled helpmate and our naïf New York brother, the man whose idea of the ultimate gourmet experience is a great slab of crusty sirloin, a bowl of home fries, cheesecake, and a double Dewar's on the rocks.

—GAEL GREENE
Bite, A New York Restaurant Strategy

PART OF A PAEAN
WILLIAM MAKEPEACE THACKERAY

A street there is in Paris famous,
  For which no rhyme our language yields,
Rue Neuve des Petits Champs its name is—
  The New Street of the Little Fields.
And here's an inn, not rich and splendid,
  But still in comfortable ease;

The which I oft in youth attended,
　　To eat a bowl of Bouillabaisse.

This Bouillabaisse a noble dish is—
　　A sort of soup, or broth, or brew,
Or hotchpotch of all sorts of fishes,
　　That Greenwich never could outdo:
Green herbs, red peppers, mussels, saffron,
　　Soles, onion, garlic, roach, and dace:
All these you eat at Terre's tavern
　　In that one dish of Bouillabaisse.

Indeed, a rich and savory stew 'tis;
　　And true philosophers, methinks,
Who love all sorts of natural beauties,
　　Should love good victuals and good drinks.
And Cordelier or Benedictine
　　Might gladly, sure, his lot embrace,
Nor find a fast day too afflicting,
　　Which served him up a Bouillabaisse.

The Ballad of Bouillabaisse

THE EFFICACY OF HOPPIN' JOHN
CARSON McCULLERS

They stopped off a few minutes to get on with the dinner. F. Jasmine ate with her elbows on the table and her bare heels hooked on the rungs of the chair. She and Berenice sat opposite each other, and John Henry faced the window. Now hopping-john was F. Jasmine's very favorite food. She had always warned them to wave a plate of rice and peas before her nose when she was in her coffin, to make certain there was no mistake; for if a breath of life was left in her, she would sit up and eat, but if she smelled the hopping-john, and did not stir, then they could just nail down the coffin and be certain she was truly dead. Now Berenice had chosen for her death-test a piece of fried fresh-water trout, and for John Henry it was divinity fudge. But though F. Jasmine loved the hopping-john the very best, the others also liked it well enough, and all three of them enjoyed the dinner that day: the ham knuckle, the hopping-john, cornbread, hot baked sweet potatoes, and the buttermilk. And as they ate, they carried on the conversation. . . .

"Tell me. Is it just us who call this hopping-john? Or is it known by that name through all the country? It seems a strange name somehow."

"Well, I have heard it called various things," said Berenice.

"What?"

"Well, I have heard it called peas and rice. Or rice and peas and pot-liquor. Or hopping-john. You can vary and take your pick."

"But I'm not talking about this town," F. Jasmine said. "I mean in other places. I mean through all the world. I wonder what the French call it."

"Oh," said Berenice. "Well, you ask me a question I cannot answer."

A Member of the Wedding

MY LIFE IN RICE
UPTON SINCLAIR

. . . Call me a Hindu, call me a Jap, call me a Chinaman, call me anything you please—rice is the food for me. Just think of it: I, who for forty years had been accustomed to saying that I was never more than twenty-four hours ahead of a headache, have not had a headache for seven years; and I am quietly confident that I shall never have another as long as I live—or as long as rice is grown in the Central California delta or imported from the Orient.

Seven years and a half works out at two thousand, five hundred and fifty-five days, plus half a day which is finishing as I write this. At three meals a day, that is eight thousand, six hundred and sixty-five. Twice in that period I recall having taken a visitor out to a hotel for lunch so that reduced the total. All the rest of the meals have been cooked by me, served by me, and eaten by me. . . .

I have what is called a sweet tooth, and all my meals are dessert and nothing else. I am writing this paragraph after supper, and that supper was as follows, all of it in one aluminum bowl: Two Japanese persimmons, dead ripe, each as big as my fist; two lumps of cold boiled brown rice, as big as the persimmons; one heaping teaspoon of dried milk powder; one teaspoon of corn oil; as much lecithin as you could put on a penny; and, poured over the mixture, a glass of pineapple juice, fresh out of the icebox. With this I eat half a dozen pieces of well-washed celery, and take one all-purpose vitamin pill. If I am still hungry, I eat a couple of dates or a graham cracker or a teaspoon of chocolate-milk powder.

Of course the fruit varies with the season. I am writing from California in January and it is persimmons, ripe bananas, and winter pears; it will be peaches, berries and grapes, then figs and melons. I may open a can of fruit once a month. I never drink water, and one large can of pineapple juice does me for a day. (I no longer play tennis; instead I take care of flowers and shrubs.) Because a doctor worried me with the idea that I was not getting enough protein, I added a little packet of gelatine to my noon meal —which I call lunch since I could not dignify it with the term dinner.

The only disadvantage of this diet is that you can't get it in a restaurant or in any other person's home. But since I have to choose between sociability with headaches and solitude without, I have chosen the latter. To prepare meals and clear up afterwards takes less than half an hour of my time, and I am happy not to have a stranger in the house.

. . . so I conclude: I am 83, am 5 feet 7, and keep my weight at 130 to 135.

The Artists' & Writers' Cookbook

FISH IS THE ONLY GRUB
JOSEPH MITCHELL

A tough Scotch-Irishman I know, Mr. Hugh G. Flood, a retired house-wrecking contractor, aged ninety-three, often tells people that he is dead set and determined to live until the afternoon of July 27, 1965, when he will be a hundred and fifteen years old. "I don't ask much here below," he says. "I just want to hit a hundred and fifteen. That'll hold me." Mr. Flood is small and wizened. His eyes are watchful and icy-blue, and his face is red, bony, and clean-shaven. He is old-fashioned in appearance. As a rule, he wears a high, stiff collar, a candy-striped shirt, a serge suit, and a derby. A silver watch-chain hangs across his vest. He keeps a flower in his lapel. When I am in the Fulton Fish Market neighborhood, I always drop into the Hartford House, a drowsy waterfront hotel at 309 Pearl Street, where he has a room, to see if he is still alive. . . .

To Mr. Flood, the flesh of finfish and shellfish is not only good to eat, it is an elixir. "When I get through tearing a lobster apart, one of those tender West Coast octopuses," he says, "I feel like I had a drink from the fountain of youth." He eats with relish every kind of seafood, including sea-urchin eggs, blowfish tails, winkles, ink squids, and barn-door skates. He especially likes an ancient Boston breakfast dish—fried cod tongues, cheeks, and sounds, sounds being the gelatinous air bladders along the cod's backbone. The more unusual a dish, the better he likes it. It makes him feel superior to eat something that most people would edge away from. He insists, however, on the plainest of cooking . . . Consequently, he takes most of his meals in Sloppy Louie Morino's, a busy bee on South Street frequented almost entirely by wholesale fishmongers from Fulton Market, which is across the street. Customarily, when Mr. Flood is ready for lunch, he goes to the stall of one of the big wholesalers, a friend of his, and browses among the bins for half an hour or so. Finally he picks out a fish, or an eel, or a crab, or the wing of a skate, or whatever looks best that day, buys it, carries it unwrapped to Louie's, and tells the chef precisely how he wants it cooked. Mr.

Flood and the chef, a surly old Genoese, are close friends. "I've made quite a study of fish cooks," Mr. Flood says, "and I've decided that old Italians are best. Then comes old colored men, then old mean Yankees, and then old drunk Irishmen. They have to be old; it takes almost a lifetime to learn how to do a thing simply. Even the stove has to be old. If the cook is an awful drunk, so much the better. I don't think a teetotaler could cook a fish. If he was a mean teetotaler, he might."

Mr. Flood's attitude toward seafood is not altogether mystical. "Fish," he says, "is the only grub left that the scientists haven't been able to get their hands on and improve. The flounder you eat today hasn't got any more damned vitamins in it than the flounder your great-great-granddaddy ate, and it tastes the same. Everything else has been improved *and* improved *and* improved to such an extent it ain't fit to eat. Consider the egg. When I was a boy on Staten Island, hens ate grit and grasshoppers and scraps from the table and whatever they could scratch out of the ground and a platter of scrambled eggs was a delight. Then the scientists developed a special egg-laying mash made of old corncobs and sterilized buttermilk, and nowadays you order scrambled eggs and you get a platter of yellow glue, Grade A. Consider the apple. Years ago you could enjoy an apple. Then the scientists took hold and invented chemical fertilizers especially for apple trees, and apples go big and red and shiny and beautiful and absolutely tasteless. As for vegetables, vegetables have been improved until they're downright poisonous. Two-thirds of the population has the stomach jumps, and no wonder. . . ."

Old Mr. Flood

A Traveling Salesman's Supper
JOHN KENDRICK BANGS

For his supper this fellow ordered fried eggs, bacon, "a little of that steak," baked beans, German fried potatoes, kippered herring, milk toast, cereal and cream, preserved peaches, hot biscuit, sponge cake, and a cup of coffee. After the commissariat had responded faithfully, an old friend came in and sat next to the traveling man. "Well, Tommy, how's things?" he asked. "Business is all right," said Tommy, "but I ain't feelin' well myself. My stummick don't seem just right. I guess I been workin' too hard." "You'd ought to eat milk toast," said the new arrival. "Yes," said Tommy, "I've ordered some." At this point the waitress came up for the newcomer's order. Among other things he ordered buckwheat cakes. "Gee!" cried Tommy; "I didn't know there was buckwheats. Bring me a stack of 'em, too, Jennie."

From Pillar to Post

A CONFISHION

The fact is I simply adore fish,
    But I don't know a perch from a pike;
And I can't tell a cray from a crawfish
    They look and they taste so alike.

—WILLIAM COLE

A—APPLE PIE

WALTER DE LA MARE

Little Pollie Pillikins
Peeped into the kitchen,
"H'm," says she, "Ho," says she,
    "Nobody there!"
Only little meeny mice,
Minikin and miching
On the big broad flagstones, empty and bare.

Greedy Pollie Pillikins
Crept into the pantry,
There stood an Apple Pasty,
   Sugar white as snow.
Off the shelf she toppled it,
Quick and quiet and canty,
And the meeny mice they watched her
   On her tip-tap-toe.

" 'Thief, Pollie Pillikins!"
Crouching in the shadows there,
Flickering in the candle-shining,
   Fee, fo, fum!
Munching up the pastry,
Crunching up the apples,
"Thief!" squeaked the smallest mouse,
   "Pollie, spare a crumb!"

Collected Poems

THOUGHTS OF LOVED ONES

While Eating Christmas Dinner in a Restaurant Far from Home and Mother

MARGARET FISHBACK

Will lightning strike me if I take
Some mushrooms and a juicy steak
Instead of turkey? Probably
If I can keep the family
From hearing how depraved I am
The gods won't give a tinker's damn
About my Christmas bill of fare.
I'll have the steak and have it rare.
But Mother . . . she must never know
That I have sunk to depths so low.

One to a Customer

"I REFUSE EVERYTHING EXCEPT FOOD AND DRINK
OSCAR WILDE

JACK: How you can sit there, calmly eating muffins, when we are in this horrible trouble, I can't make out. You seem to be perfectly heartless.

ALGERNON: Well, I can't eat muffins in an agitated manner. The butter would probably get on my cuffs. One should always eat muffins quite calmly. It is the only way to eat them.

JACK: I say it's perfectly heartless your eating muffins at all, under the circumstances.

ALGERNON: When I am in trouble, eating is the only thing that consoles me. Indeed, when I am in really great trouble, as anyone who knows me intimately will tell you, I refuse everything except food and drink. At the present moment I am eating muffins because I am unhappy. Besides, I am particularly fond of muffins. [*Rising.*]

JACK [*Rising*]: Well, that is no reason why you should eat them all in that greedy way. [*Takes muffins from ALGERNON.*]

ALGERNON [*Offering tea-cake*]: I wish you would have a tea-cake instead. I don't like tea-cake.

JACK: Good heavens! I suppose a man may eat his own muffins in his own garden.

ALGERNON: But you just said it was perfectly heartless to eat muffins.

JACK: I said it was perfectly heartless of you, under the circumstances. That is a very different thing.

ALGERNON: That may be. But the muffins are the same. [*He seizes the muffin dish from JACK.*]

JACK: Algy, I wish to goodness you would go.

ALGERNON: You can't possibly ask me to go without having some dinner. It's absurd. I never go without my dinner. No one ever does, except vegetarians and people like that. . . .

The Importance of Being Earnest

Diplomatic Chop Suey

F. T. CHENG

Most Westerners, except Continental people and those who have tasted Chinese delicacies in the East or in a place like China Town in New York or San Francisco, think that the best dish the Chinese cuisine can offer is what is known as "Chop Suey," which, though it can be very tasty and appetizing, is far from being a Chinese delicacy and is hardly known as such in China. It is only a made-up dish specially prepared for American customers by pioneer Chinese restaurants early set up in the United States. It consists of slices of several kinds of vegetables, such as bamboo shoot, mushroom, onion, bean sprouts, celery, cabbage, tomato, and water chestnut, cooked together with fillets of meat or chicken. . . . However, it is so popular in America and England that some Chinese restaurants in these countries sell nothing but "Chop Suey."

In connection with this dish there is a story which may now be told. . . . Ernest Bevin, former British Foreign Secretary, dined several times at the Chinese Embassy and, every time, was given, partly, Chinese food. One evening he was asked whether he had ever had Chinese food before, and he answered "yes," adding that he often went to Chinese restaurants before he took office. Hearing this, I naturally asked him what dish he liked best and his answer was "No. 8." This sounded like a conundrum. Therefore I followed up my question with a series of queries like "Animal? Mineral? Vegetable?" In other words, I asked him whether it was meat, poultry or sea food, and his replies were a successive "No." Then I said, "I know it now!" He dined at the Embassy a few weeks later and "No. 8" prominently figured in the menu. After he had tasted it, I asked him whether it was right, and his answer was "Quite right, but you have improved it!" This was, in fact, "Chop Suey." As "No. 8" became so well known afterwards as a gastronomic choice of the Foreign Secretary, it always formed an item on the menu in subsequent "diplomatic" dinners during my term of office.

Musings of a Chinese Gourmet

What is patriotism but the love of good things we ate in our childhood?

—Lin Yutang

Dining with the Sun King
ALEXANDRE DUMAS PÈRE

The king, then, was seated alone at a small separate table, which, like the desk of a president, overlooked the adjoining tables. Although we say a small table, we must not omit to add that this small table was yet the largest one there. Moreover, it was the one on which were placed the greatest number and variety of dishes, —consisting of fish, game, meat, vegetables, and preserves. The king was young and vigorous, very fond of hunting, addicted to all violent exercises of the body, and possessed, besides, like all the members of the Bourbon family, a rapid digestion and an appetite speedily renewed. Louis XIV was a formidable table companion. He delighted to criticize his cooks; but when he honoured them by praise and commendation, the honour was overwhelming. The king began by eating several kinds of soup, either mixed together or taken separately. He intermingled, or rather he isolated, the soups with glasses of old wine. He ate quickly and somewhat greedily.

Porthos, who from the beginning had out of respect been waiting for a jab of D'Artagnan's elbow, seeing the king make such rapid progress, turned to the musketeer and said in a low tone, "It seems as if one might go on now; his Majesty is very encouraging in the example he sets. Look!"—"The king eats," said D'Artagnan, "but he talks at the same time. Try to manage matters in such a manner that if he should happen to address a remark to you, he would not find you with your mouth full, for that would be very awkward."—"The best way, in that case," said Porthos, "is to eat no supper at all. And yet, I am very hungry, I admit; and everything looks and smells most inviting, as if appealing to all my senses at once."

"Don't for a moment think of not eating," said D'Artagnan; "that would put his majesty out terribly. The king has a habit of saying that he who works well eats well, and he does not like to have people eat daintily at his table."—"But how can I avoid having my mouth full if I eat?" said Porthos.

"All you have to do," replied the captain of the musketeers, "is simply to swallow what you have in it, whenever the king does you the honour to address a remark to you."—"Very good," said Porthos; and from that moment he began to eat with a well-bred enthusiasm.

The king occasionally looked at the different persons who were at table with him, and as a connoisseur would appreciate the different dispositions of his guest. "M. du Vallon!" he said. Porthos was enjoyinga ragoût of hare, and swallowed half the back. His name pronounced in such a manner made him start, and by a vigorous effort of his gullet he absorbed the whole mouthful. "Sire," replied Porthos, in a stifled voice, but sufficiently intelligible, nevertheless.

"Let that leg of lamb be handed to M. du Vallon," said the king. "Do you like browned meats, M. du Vallon?"—"Sire, I like everything," replied Porthos. D'Artagnan whispered, "Everything your Majesty sends me." Porthos repeated, "Everything your Majesty sends me,"—an observation which the king apparently received with great satisfaction.

"People who eat well work well," replied the king, delighted to have opposite him a guest of Porthos's capacity. Porthos received the dish of lamb and put a portion of it on his plate. "Well?" said the king.—"Exquisite," said Porthos, calmly.—"Have you as good mutton in your part of the country, M. du Vallon?" continued the king. "Sire," said Porthos, "I believe that from my own province, as everywhere else, the best of everything is sent to Paris for your Majesty's use; but, on the other hand, I do not eat mutton in the same way your Majesty does."

"Ah! and how do you eat it?"—"Generally, I have a lamb dressed quite whole."—"Quite whole?"—"Yes, Sire."—"In what manner, then?"—"In this, Sire: my cook, who is a German, first stuffs the lamb in question with small sausages which he procures from Strasbourg, forcemeat-balls which he procures from Troyes, and larks which he procures from Pithiviers; by some means or other, with which I am not acquainted, he bones the lamb as we would bone a fowl, leaving the skin on, however, which forms a brown crust all over the animal. When it is cut in beautiful slices, in the same way that one would cut an enormous sausage, a rose-coloured gravy issues forth, which is as agreeable to the eye as it is exquisite to the palate"; and Porthos finished by smacking his lips.

The king opened his eyes with delight, and, while cutting some of the *faisan en daube*, which was handed to him, he said: "That is a dish I should very much like to taste, M. du Vallon. Is it possible? —a whole lamb!"—"Yes, Sire."—"Pass these pheasants to M. du Vallon; I perceive that he is a connoisseur." The order was obeyed. Then, continuing the conversation, he said, "And do you not find the lamb too fat?"—"No, Sire; the fat falls down at the same time that the gravy does, and swims on the surface; then the servant who carves removes the fat with a silver spoon, which I have had made expressly for that purpose."

"Where do you reside?" inquired the king.—"At Pierrefonds, Sire."—"At Pierrefonds; where is that, M. du Vallon,—near Belle-Isle?"—"Oh, no, Sire; Pierrefonds is in the Soissonais."—"I thought that you alluded to the mutton on account of the salt marshes."—"No, Sire; I have marshes which are not salt, it is true, but which are not less valuable on that account."

The king had now arrived at the *entrées*, but without losing sight of Porthos, who continued to play his part in his best manner. "You have an excellent appetite, M. du Vallon," said the king, "and you make an admirable table companion."—"Ah, Sire, if your Majesty were ever to pay a visit to Pierrefonds, we would both of us eat our lamb together; for your appetite is not an indifferent one, by any means."

D'Artagnan gave Porthos a severe kick under the table, which made Porthos colour up. "At your Majesty's present happy age," said Porthos, in order to repair the mistake he had made, "I was in the musketeers, and nothing could ever satisfy me then. Your Majesty has an excellent appetite, as I have already had the honour of mentioning, but you select what you eat with too much refinement to be called a great eater."

The king seemed charmed at his guest's politeness. "Will you try some of these creams?" he said to Porthos.—"Sire, your Majesty treats me with far too much kindness to prevent me from speaking the whole truth."—"Pray do so, M. du Vallon."—"Well, Sire, with regard to sweet dishes, I recognize only pastry, and even that should be rather solid; all these frothy substances swell my stomach, and occupy a space which seems to me too precious to be so badly tenanted."—"Ah, Messieurs," said the king, indicating Porthos by a gesture, "here is indeed a perfect model of gastronomy. It was in such a manner that our fathers, who so well knew what good living was, used to eat; while we," added his Majesty, "can do nothing but trifle with our food;" and as he spoke he took a fresh plate of chicken, with ham, while Porthos attacked a ragoût of partridges and land-rails.

The cup-bearer filled his Majesty's glass to the brim. "Give M. du Vallon some of my wine," said the king. This was one of the greatest honours of the royal table. D'Artagnan pressed his friend's knee. "If you can only manage to swallow half of that boar's head I see yonder," said he to Porthos, "I shall believe that you will be a duke and a peer within the next twelvemonth."—"Presently," said Porthos phlegmatically: "I shall come to it by and by."

The Vicomte de Bragelonne

CALL IT PREFERENCE
BERGEN EVANS

The average man regards his own diet as sensible and all deviations from it as finicky or loathsome. When the normal American, for instance, reads that Mexicans eat fried worms, that Indians eat dogs and monkeys, that Africans eat grasshoppers, and that the Chinese and many Europeans eat coagulated blood, he simply retches and thanks God for the good old U.S.A. where wholesome food comes in bright cans and crisp boxes. As for the delicacies of antiquity—Heliogabalus' combs and wattles of cocks, Maecenas' asses' flesh, and Trimalchio's "dugs of a pregnant sow"—it is probably just as well for his digestion that he never even heard of them.

Yet among his own simple viands are several that other people would regard with abhorrence. A third of mankind would rather die than touch his morning bacon. Biologically considered, his glass of milk is grossly indecent, and, even among those who accept milk as edible, millions prefer the milk of horses. His juicy steak would be an abomination to hundreds of millions, and many more would gladly exchange it, as a mere piece of muscle, for the liver, stomach, or heart of the same animal.

The fairly limited numbers of foods that most people commonly permit themselves is still further limited, in practice, by the widespread belief that certain foods that are good in themselves are bad when mixed. Cucumbers and ice cream were formerly thought to give the eater cholera, possibly because of some false analogy between their coldness and the subnormal temperature that characterizes that disease. Pickles-and-milk and fish-and-celery were, and by many still are, regarded as dangerous combinations. A whole cult gravitates around the delusion that proteins and starches should not be eaten at the same meal, despite the fact that there is some protein in all food and that milk, nature's basic food, contains proteins and carbohydrates.

The Natural History of Nonsense

THE POTLIKKER OF HUEY LONG
T. HARRY WILLIAMS

Potlikker is the juice that remains in the pot after certain vegetables and their greens are boiled. Huey began to extol the concoction in 1930, and in the following year he talked so much about it that he received national attention. Potlikker was good for gallbladder trouble or almost any other human ailment and would help women trim down their figures, he proclaimed. He revealed to the public his own recipe for preparing it. Mocking his critics, he called his creation "potlikker a le dictator" and described it as "the noblest dish the mind of man has yet conceived." Take some turnips, cut up into pieces, and some turnip greens, he advised, and place in a pot with a half pound of salt fat pork, for seasoning, on the top; add water and boil until the vegetables are tender; then remove and place the potlikker in a bowl and the greens and pork in a dish. Next came the eating, which had to be done in a certain way or the food could not be appreciated. There should be plenty of "cornpone"—patties made of corn meal, hot water and salt— "cooked in a greasy skillet" until "hard enough to knock down a yearling." The diner must hold the cornpone in the left hand and a soup spoon in the right, take a sip of the soup, and then dunk the cornpone in the juice and bite a piece. The real potlikker devotee always dunked, Huey insisted; he never committed the crudity of crumbling the pone in the soup.

Huey's description of the ceremonial consumption of potlikker delighted newspapermen all over the country. In the first grim years of the depression they welcomed any item that promised relief from the drab daily record of lengthening unemployment. Julian Harris, the witty and cultured editor of the influential Atlanta *Constitution,* devoted a lead editorial to Huey's recipe. The governor of Louisiana might know how to prepare potlikker, Harris said, but he certainly did not know how to eat it: anybody who appreciated this delectable dish crumbled the cornpone. Huey, matching Harris's mock seriousness, fired off a telegram to the editor, defending his recipe. Harris retaliated with a charge that Huey crumbled in private. Huey replied in a letter addressed to Harris as the editor of the Potlikker and Cornpone Department. He had been resentful at first, he said, but had concluded that Harris was honest at heart though "ignorant of the finer arts of the subject." But, continued Huey, Harris had gone beyond the limits of respectable journalism with the charge that he crumbled privately. He had merely crumbled before a few friends to demonstrate the faults of the technique.

The dunking-versus-crumbling controversy ballooned into national proportions. People all over the country lined up on one side or the other or pronounced on the merits of potlikker as a food,

showing a familiarity with it that must have surprised Southerners. Dr. W. A. Evans, who wrote a widely syndicated newspaper
column, "Health Hints," said that he did not like Huey Long but
for once Long was right: potlikker was a good food, rich in vitamins. Emily Post, arbiter of taste, was asked her opinion on the
relative merits of dunking and crumbling, but she refused to take
a stand. Governor Franklin D. Roosevelt of New York, forging to
the front as a Democratic presidential possibility, rushed uninvited
into the argument. Roosevelt, who had a farm in Georgia and
considered himself an adopted son of the state, wrote a public
letter to Julian Harris, whom he addressed, copying Huey's saluta-
tion, as editor of the Potlikker and Cornpone Department. He was
"deeply stirred by the great controversy," Roosevelt said, and was
gratified that the North was at last learning about this fine Southern dish. He suggested referring the dunking-crumbling issue to
the platform committee of the 1932 Democratic national conven-
tion. But he did not mind stating his own preference. "I must admit
that I crumble mine," said Roosevelt. . . . The controversy was,
Huey said, the "only delightful pastime" he had had since becoming governor.

Huey Long

"You Eat Too Quickly"

Brillat-Savarin has himself reported what one of his friends said
to him,—"You have but one fault: you eat too quickly." That,
however, is a great fault in a gourmet, and it is a fault which is
much too common in England. Napoleon lost the two great battles
of Borodino and Leipsic through indigestion brought on by his
habit of eating too fast. Let the frivolous pause and think of this
—the chance of losing an empire through unseemly disregard of
the dinner-table.

—E. S. Dallas

THE FOOD OF MONTEZUMA

I have heard it said that they were wont to cook for him the flesh of young boys, but as he had such a variety of dishes, made of so many things, we could not succeed in seeing if they were of human flesh or of other things, for they daily cooked fowls, turkeys, pheasants, native partridges, quail, tame and wild ducks, venison, wild boar, reed birds, pigeons, hares and rabbits, and many sorts of birds and other things which are bred in this country, and they are so numerous that I cannot finish naming them in a hurry; so we had no insight into it, but I know for certain that after our Captain censured the sacrifice of human beings, and the eating of their flesh, he ordered that such food should not be prepared for him thenceforth.

—BERNAL DIAZ DEL CASTILLO
The Discovery and Conquest of Mexico

GEORGE BERNARD SHAW, VEGETARIAN WITH A SWEET TOOTH

Mr. Shaw was very particular about the calories in his food. These had to be most carefully worked out. The calories in each dish had to be weighed and the total for the meal had to be right. The reason for this was his concern not to put on any weight. He was, as you know, a very tall man—over six foot in height—with a fine, slender figure, and this he was resolved to retain. He stood on the scales every morning to make sure there was not a fraction of an ounce of difference in his weight from one day to the next. He retained his figure to the end. His health was perfect. He never suffered from indigestion. . . .

[However,] I don't know how it is he didn't get sick, popping so many spoonfuls of honey into his tummy. I knew he was very fond of sweet things. I always used honey instead of sugar when I made his dessert. I even put some honey or sugar into his soup. With his dish of raw vegetables he always had sweet chutney. And

I rarely saw him—between meals mind you—without a large chunk of cake heavily coated with sugar icing in his hand. One day, as he walked into the street to say goodbye to Greer Garson, who always came to see him when she was over from Hollywood, I saw him munching at the same time on an enormous piece of cake covered with marzipan and thick icing.

—ALICE LADEN
The George Bernard Shaw Vegetarian Cook Book

TRUFFLE-DAY

Once a year at home we had truffle-day. But that could only take place if the bank account allowed, for Colette used to say: "If I can't have too many truffles, I'll do without truffles," and she declared they should be eaten like potatoes. We waited until, with the coming of the frost, Périgord should send the finest of its mushrooms. It appears that cleaning them is an art and Colette would not entrust the responsibility for this to anyone else. You put half a bottle of dry champagne in a black stew-pan, with some bits of bacon fat lightly browned, salt and pepper. When this mixture boils you throw in the truffles. A divine and slightly suspect odour, like everything that smells really good, floats through the house. Under no pretext must the truffles leave the stew-pan, the scented sauce is served separately, hot in port glasses, and anyone who does not declare himself ready to leave Paradise or Hell for such a treat is not worthy to be born again.

—MAURICE GOUDEKET
Close to Colette

"NO MAN ATE MORE HEARTILY THAN JOHNSON"
JAMES BOSWELL

The cheering sound of, "Dinner is upon the table," dissolved his reverie and we all sat down without any symptom of ill humour. . . . Mr. Wilkes [a notorious Boswell crony whose behavior Johnson had publicly castigated] placed himself next to Dr. Johnson, and behaved to him with so much attention and politeness, that he gained upon him insensibly. No man ate more heartily than Johnson, or loved better what was nice and delicate. Mr. Wilkes was very assiduous in helping him to some fine veal. "Pray give me leave, Sir:—It is better here—A little of the brown—Some fat, Sir—A little of the stuffing—Some gravy—Let me have the pleasure of giving you some butter—Allow me to recommend a squeeze of this orange;—or the lemon, perhaps, may have more zest."—"Sir, Sir, I am obligated to you, Sir," cried Johnson, bowing and turning his head to him with a look for some time of "surly virtue," but, in a short while, of complacency.

Life of Johnson

Receipt for Winter Salad
SYDNEY SMITH

Two large potatoes, passed through kitchen sieve
Unwonted softness to the salad give;
Of mordent mustard, add a single spoon,
Distrust the condiment which bites so soon;
But deem it not, thou man of herbs, a fault,
To add a double quantity of salt;
Three times the spoon with oil of Lucca crown,
And once with vinegar, procured from town;
True flavour needs it, and your poet begs
The pounded yellow of two well-boiled eggs;
Let onion atoms lurk within the bowl,
And, scarce suspected, animate the whole;
And lastly, in the flavoured compound toss
A magic teaspoon of anchovy sauce;
Then, though green turtle fail, though venison's tough,
And ham and turkey are not boiled enough,
Serenely full, the epicure may say—
"Fate cannot harm me—I have dined to-day."

NINETEENTH-CENTURY AMERICAN APPETITES
FRANCES TROLLOPE

The ordinary mode of living is abundant, but not delicate. They consume an extraordinary quantity of bacon. Ham and beefsteaks appear morning, noon, and night. In eating, they mix things together with the strangest incongruity imaginable. I have seen eggs and oysters eaten together; the sempiternal ham with apple-sauce; beef-steak with stewed peaches; and salt fish with onions. The bread is everywhere excellent, but they rarely enjoy it themselves, as they insist upon eating horrible half-baked hot rolls both morning and evening. The butter is tolerable; but they have seldom such cream as every little dairy produces in England; in fact, the cows are very roughly kept, compared with ours. Common vegetables are abundant and very fine. I never saw sea-kale, or cauliflowers, and either from the want of summer rain, or the want of care, the harvest of green vegetables is much sooner over than with us. They eat the Indian corn in a great variety of forms; sometimes it is dressed green, and eaten like peas; sometimes it is broken to pieces when dry, boiled plain, and brought to table like rice; this dish is called hominy. The flour of it is made into at least a dozen different sorts of cakes; but in my opinion all bad. This flour, mixed in the proportion of one-third, with fine wheat, makes by far the best bread I ever tasted.

I never saw a turbot, salmon, or fresh cod; but the rock and shad are excellent. There is a great want of skill in the composition of sauces; not only with fish, but with every thing. They use very few made dishes, and I never saw any that would be approved by our savants. They have an excellent wild duck, called the Canvass Back, which, if delicately served, would surpass the black cock; but the game is very inferior to ours; they have no hares, and I never saw a pheasant. They seldom indulge in second courses, with all their ingenious temptations to the eating a second dinner; but almost every table has its dessert (invariably pronounced desart) which is placed on the table before the cloth is removed, and consists of pastry, preserved fruits, and creams. They are "extravagantly fond," to use their own phrase, of puddings, pies, and all kinds of "sweets," particularly the ladies; but are by no means such connoisseurs in soups and ragoûts as the gastronomes of Europe. Almost every one drinks water at table, and by a strange contradiction, in the country where hard drinking is more prevalent than in any other, there is less wine taken at dinner; ladies rarely exceed one glass, and the great majority of females never take any. In fact, the hard drinking, so universally acknowledged, does not take place at jovial dinners, but, to speak plain English, in solitary dram-drinking. Coffee is not served immediately after dinner, but makes part of the serious matter of tea-drinking, which comes some hours later.

Domestic Manners of the Americans

Anyone who does not enjoy a Churchillian girth is guilty of insufficient living.

—THE OLD CURMUDGEON (ROGERS C. M. WHITTAKER)

AN INSATIABLE APPETITE FOR HAMBURGERS
CHARLES KURALT

It is truly said that America is an infinite and various country. The infinity shows up on our speedometer. As for the variety, well, we have found, for example, that at lunchtime on the road, we have our choice—of all kinds of hamburgers.

Americans ate forty billion hamburgers in the last year, give or take a few hundred million, and on the road you tend to eat more than your share. You can find your way across this country using burger joints the way a navigator uses stars. . . . We have munched bridge burgers in the shadow of the Brooklyn Bridge and Cable Car burgers hard by the Golden Gate, Dixie burgers in the sunny South and Yankee Doodle burgers in the North. The Civil War must be over—they taste exactly alike. . . .

We had a Capitol burger—guess where. And, so help us, in the inner courtyard of the Pentagon, a Penta burger. . . . We have also consumed burgers from the grills of guys named Oliver, Buddy, Murray, Chuck, Ben, and Juan. It begins to get you after a while. In Tulsa we took note of a machine that turns out twelve burgers a minute, complete with a machine that mustards and catsups a burger in a tenth of a second.

We've had king burgers, queen burgers, mini burgers, maxi burgers, tuna burgers, Smithfield burgers, bacon burgers, wine burgers, heavenly burgers, and yum burgers. Yum. Yum. In Independence, Kansas, we lunched on poppa burgers, momma burgers, and little teeny baby burgers.

The Acropolis of burger joints is probably the Hippo in San Francisco, home of the nude burger, strip burger, hamburger de luxe, bippie burger, Italian burger, Joe's burger, mushroom burger, Bronx burger, Terry burger, Russian burger, Tahitian burger, onion burger, taco burger, smorgasburger, continental burger, French burger, and so on, ad infinitum, to hundreds of strains and mutations.

But this is not merely a local phenomenon. The smell of fried onions is abroad in the land, and if the French chefs among us will avert their eyes, we will finish reciting our menu of the last few weeks on the highways of America. We've had grabba burgers, kinga burgers, lotta burgers, castle burgers, country burgers, bronco burgers. Broadway burgers, broiled burgers, beefnut burgers, bell burgers, plus burgers, prime burgers, flame burgers, lunch burgers, top burgers, Plaza burgers, tasty burgers, dude burgers, char burgers, tall boy burgers, golden burgers, 747 burgers, whiz burgers, nifty burgers, and thing burgers.

One day in the desert I had a vision that the last ding dong of doom had sounded, that the land was empty and that the last American had left only one small monument to mark his passing. [In that mirage the single structure left in the world was a gloriously garish hamburger stand.]

Honoré de Balzac, Gourmand

While I contented myself with a soup and a wing of a chicken, Balzac devoured before my eyes a hundred Ostend oysters, a dozen *pré salé* cutlets, a duck with turnips, a brace of roast partridges, a *sole Normande,* without counting the hors-d'oeuvre, side dishes, and more than a dozen Doyenné pears; the whole of it washed down with delicate wines of the most renowned vintages; everything gulped down without mercy.

—M. Werdet

The Not-to-Be-Trifled-With Palate of Nero Wolfe
REX STOUT

Each year around the middle of May, by arrangement, a farmer who lives up near Brewster shoots eighteen or twenty starlings, puts them in a bag, and gets in his car and drives to New York. It is understood that they are to be delivered to our door within two hours after they are winged. Fritz dresses them and sprinkles them with salt, and, at the proper moment, brushes them with melted butter, wraps them in sage leaves, grills them, and arranges them on a platter of hot polenta, which is thick porridge of fine-ground yellow corn meal with butter, grated cheese, and salt and pepper. It is an expensive meal and a happy one, and Wolfe looks forward to it, but that day he put on an exhibition. When the platter was brought in, steaming, and placed before him, he sniffed, ducked his head, and sniffed again, and straightened to look up at Fritz.

"The sage?"

"No, sir."

"What do you mean, no, sir?"

"I thought you might like it once in a style I have suggested, with saffron and tarragon. Much fresh tarragon, with just a touch of saffron, which is the way. . . ."

"Remove it."

Fritz went rigid and his lips tightened.

"You did not consult me," Wolfe said coldly. "To find that without warning one of my favorite dishes has been radically altered is an unpleasant shock. It may possibly be edible, but I am in no humor to risk it. Please dispose of it and bring me four coddled eggs and a piece of toast."

Nero Wolfe Cookbook

What a Friend We Have in Cheeses!
WILLIAM COLE

What a friend we have in cheeses!
For no food more subtly pleases,
Nor plays so grand a gastronomic part;
Cheese imported—not domestic—
For we all get indigestic
From the pasteurizer's Kraft and sodden art.

No poem we shall ever see is
Quite as lovely as a Brie is,
For "the queen of cheese" is what they call the Brie;
If you pay sufficient money
You will get one nice and runny,
And you'll understand what foods these morsels be!

How we covet all the skills it
Takes in making Chèvre or Tilsit,
But if getting basic Pot Cheese is your aim,
Take some simple curds and wheys, a
Bit of rennet—Lo! you've Kaese!
(Which is what in German, is a cheese's name.)

Good lasagna, it's a-gotta
Mozzarella and Ricotta
And a lot of freshly grated Parmesan;
With the latter *any* pasta
Will be eaten up much faster,
For with Parmesan an added charm is on.

Ask Ignacio Silone
What he thinks of Provolone,

And the very word will set his eyes aflame;
Then go ask the bounteous Gina
Her reaction to Fontina—
If you'll raise your eyes you'll see she feels the same.

A Pont-l'Évêque *au point!* What ho!
How our juices all will flow!
But don't touch a Pont-l'Évêque beyond that stage,
For what you'll have, you'll surely find
Is just an over-fragrant rind—
There's no benefit to this fromage from age.

Claret, dear, not Coca-Cola,
When you're having Gorgonzola—
Be particular to serve the proper wines;
Likewise pick a Beaune, not Coke for
Pointing up a Bleu or Roquefort—
Bless the products of the bovines and the vines!

Ave Gouda! Ave Boursault!
Ave Oka even more so!
Ave Neufchâtel, *Saluto* Port-Salut!
And another thing with cheeses—
Every allied prospect pleases—
Ah cheese blintzes! Ah! Welsh rabbit! Ah fondue!

And we all know that "Say cheese" is
How a cameraman unfreezes
A subject in a stiff, or shy, or dour way;
There's no other food so useful,
So bring on a whole cabooseful
Of the stuff of life! The cheeses of the gourmet!
. . . And Be Merry!

"I Sing of Champagne and Rum Raisin"

Ice cream unleashes the uninhibited eight-year-old's sensual
greed that lurks within the best of us. I do not celebrate the Spartan
scoop of vanilla the incurably constricted grownup suffers to cap

a pedestrian dinner. I sing of great gobs of mellow mint chip slopping onto your wrist as your tongue flicks out to gather the sprinkles. I sing of champagne and rum raisin and two spoons in bed on New Year's Eve. I sing of the do-it-yourself sundae freak-out with a discriminating collector's hoard of *haute* toppings—wet walnuts, hot fudge, homemade peach conserve, Nesselrode, marrons, and brandied cherry—whisk-whipped ice cream, a rainbow of sprinkles and crystals and crisp toasted almonds, inspiring a madness that lifts masks, shatters false dignity, and bridges all generation gaps. . . . In these harsh and uncertain times, as the establishment cracks and institutions crumble, it is no wonder we reach out to ice cream. It is a link to innocence and security, healing, soothing, wholesome. . . .

—GAEL GREENE
Bite, A New York Restaurant Strategy

11

"A New Creation Glows!"

New things—whether or not a glowing creation of Shakespeare —arouse curiosity. More, when the newness has worn off and the thing becomes commonplace, as in the case of cleverly contrived dishes whose origin has been forgotten, interest develops in who it was who invented whatever it is that—in the course of epicurean debate—may be in question. It is therefore pleasant to know that Marie Ritz, whose husband transformed the caravansary world, has left her own account of the evolution of Melba toast, and that Louis Diat can take us back to his boyhood for the inspiration of his cold leek and potato soup which was, for a time at least, an almost necessary addition to summer menus. And it is cheering to have a similar childhood memory in Julia Child's dissertation on the true Caesar salad. Woody Allen's account of the invention of the sandwich may be tongue-in-cheek (sorry), but the word about Ben Wenberg and lobster is as serious as the identity of Suzette is open to argument. There are fistfuls of stories about various English monarchs knighting a loin of beef, yet none of the whimsey about "Sir Loin" is as jaunty as Mark Twain in the process of creating "Barometer Soup."

AMERICAN FIRSTS

JEFFERSON WILLIAMSON

A long list could be made of American culinary creations. It would include such concoctions as clam and fish chowder, pumpkin pie, hominy, Saratoga chips, chicken à la King, Philadelphia pepper pot, succotash, porterhouse steaks, Virginia's sweet-potato pie, catchup, and an endless variety of tomato preparations, including tomato soup; Indian pudding, flapjacks, Graham bread, cinnamon buns, Parker House rolls, corn fritters and other corn dishes, including corn on the cob; chocolate pie, the candied yams of Dixie—these and a wide variety of others. Delmonico's, that celebrated cradle of American epicureanism, was the birthplace of several dishes that continue to tickle the palate of the world. Founded just one hundred years ago [in 1827] by an Italian-Swiss pastry-cook, Delmonico's unquestionably did more than any other institution to change and elevate the standards of American cookery. Its style and menu were imitated everywhere. Before the Civil War it was practically the only restaurant whose cuisine could outdo that of the first-class hotels.

The American Hotel

"Madame Melba Had to Wait"

I remember one of those afternoons, at tea-time, I complained about the toast in Escoffier's hearing. "Toast is never thin enough to suit me," I said. "Can't you do something about it?"

As usual Escoffier and Ritz took such a remark with absolute seriousness. They discussed the problem of thin toast. "Why not," said Ritz, "toast thin slices of bread once, then cut it through again, and again toast it?" And with Escoffier he retired to the kitchens to see if it could not be done. The result was Escoffier's justly famous *Toast Melba*. When they brought out on the lawn a plate full of the thin, crisp, curled wafers, Escoffier said, "Behold! A new dish, and it is called *Toast Marie.*" But as I ate it I tried to think up another name. Marie was far too anonymous to suit me.

During that year Melba had returned from America very ill. She was staying at the Savoy where she was a much-indulged invalid. I had heard Escoffier discuss her regime. Dry toast figured on it . . . "Call it *Toast Melba,*" I said.

And so it was done. I was the first to taste *Toast Melba;* Madame Melba herself had to wait until the following day!

—Marie Louise Ritz
Ritz, Host to the World

How Crème Vichyssoise Evolved

Even as a boy of eight, I can remember now distinctly how strongly I was drawn toward cooking. I used to watch my mother and my grandmother, both excellent cooks, as they went busily about our kitchen . . . and one day, I was permitted to try my hand at making soup. It must have been fairly successful, for, from that time, it was my privilege to make the soup, which constituted the country breakfast for our family. But it was a loved privilege even though it meant my rising at five o'clock. While the soup was simmering, I was busy usually with my books preparing my school home work. . . .

I recall clearly the boyish pride I felt when my first dish was set on the table. It was Potato Paysanne. . . . Another dish which has since become well-known throughout this country had its origin also in my mother's kitchen. She used to make a hot soup of leeks and potatoes which was liked very much by her children. But in summer when the soup seemed to be too hot, we asked for milk with which to cool it. Many years later, it was this memory which gave me the inspiration to make the soup which I have named Crème Vichyssoise. Of course I could not forget its recipe.

—Chef Louis Diat
Cooking à la Ritz

Musings Upon Caesar and His Salad
JULIA CHILD

One of my early remembrances of restaurant life was going to Tijuana in 1925 or 1926 with my parents, who were wildly excited that they should finally lunch at Caesar's restaurant. Tijuana, just south of the Mexican border from San Diego, was flourishing then, in the prohibition era. People came down from the Los Angeles area in droves to eat in the restaurants; they drank forbidden beer and cocktails as they toured the bars of the town; they strolled in the flowered patio of Agua Caliente listening to the marimba band,

and they gambled wickedly at the casino. Word spread about Tijuana and the good life, and about Caesar Cardini's restaurant, and about his salad.

My parents, of course, ordered the salad. Caesar himself rolled the big cart up to the table, tossed the romaine in a great wooden bowl, and I wish I could say I remember his every move, but I don't. The only thing I see again clearly is the eggs. I can see him break two eggs over that romaine and roll them in, the greens going all creamy as the eggs flowed over them. Two eggs in a salad? Two one-minute coddled eggs? And garlic-flavored croutons, and grated Parmesan cheese? It was a sensation of a salad from coast to coast, and there were even rumblings of its success in Europe.

How could a mere salad cause such emotion? But, one remembers, that was way back in 1924, when Caesar Cardini invented it, and it was only in the early twenties that refrigerated transcontinental transportation came into being. Before then, when produce was out of season in the rest of the country, there was no greenery to be had. . . . It is a very simple salad, really, and its beauty rests entirely in the excellence of its ingredients—the best and freshest of everything, from romaine to oil, eggs, lemons, croutons, garlic, and cheese.

Julia Child's Kitchen

"That's What I Call an Oyster Cocktail"

Even the bewhiskered sourdoughs of California's Argonaut days have a few first rate receipts to their credit. The oyster cocktail originated in San Francisco in the 1860s and was, so tradition says, invented by a miner who came back from the diggings loaded with nuggets. He dropped in to a restaurant and ordered a big meal. "How long will it take you to get it ready?" he asked. "About fifteen minutes," said the waiter. "All right," said the miner; "but bring me a plate of California raws right away, and some catchup and horseradish and a whisky cocktail." After drinking the cocktail he put the oysters into the goblet, salted and peppered them, poured in two spoonfuls of vinegar and one of Worcestershire sauce, and added a pinch of horseradish. On top of this he filled the goblet with catsup and stirred the mixture. The restaurant-keeper looked on with interest. "What sort of a mess do you call that, pardner?" he inquired. "That?" said the miner; "oh, that's what I call an oyster cocktail; they're good. You'd better try one." Next day a sign appeared on the bar-room mirror: "Oyster Cocktail! Four Bits per Glass." And within a week every joint on the Barbary Coast was serving oyster cocktails. It was not long before the cocktails were admitted to the menu cards of the best hotels and cafés of San Francisco.

—JEFFERSON WILLIAMSON
The American Hotel

"THE FIRST OF THE MODERN BREAKFAST FOODS"

I invented the first ready-cooked flaked cereal food. I prescribed zweiback for an old lady, and she broke her false teeth on it. She demanded that I pay ten dollars for her . . . teeth. I began to think that we ought to have a ready-cooked food which would not break people's teeth.

One night about three o'clock I was awakened by a phone call from a patient, and as I went back to bed I remembered that I had been having a most important dream. Before I went to sleep again I gathered up the threads of my dream, and I found I had been dreaming of a way to make flaked foods.

The next morning I boiled some wheat, and while it was soft, I ran it through a machine Mrs. Kellogg had for rolling dough out thin. This made the wheat into thin films, and I scraped it off with a case knife, and baked it in the oven.

That was the first of the modern breakfast foods. Later, I invented nearly sixty other foods to meet purely dietetic needs.

—DR. JOHN HARVEY KELLOGG

A Fowl à la Marengo

On the evening of the battle the first consul [Napoleon] was very hungry after the agitation of the day, and a fowl was ordered with all expedition. The fowl was procured, but there was no butter at hand, and unluckily none could be found in the neighbourhood. There was oil in abundance, however; and the cook having poured a certain quantity into his skillet, put in the fowl, with a clove of garlic and other seasoning, with a little white wine, the best the country afforded; he then garnished it with mushrooms, and served it up hot. This dish proved the second conquest of the day, as the first consul found it most agreeable to his palate, and expressed his satisfaction. Ever since, a fowl à la Marengo is a favourite dish with all lovers of good cheer.

—ISABELLA BEETON
The Book of Household Management

How a Lobster Got Its Name
ROBERT COURTINE

Despite all the claims of the culinary chauvinists, *homard à l'armoricaine* does not exist. *Homard à l'américaine* is the correct name of the dish.

It is an argument that went on for a long time though.

The supporters of *homard à l'armoricaine* put forward as their arguments the French "style" of the dish and the fact that the lobster is a Breton, or Armorican, product. The confusion arose, they explained, from an error in the transcription of a menu: "given a hasty pen, *armoricaine* can quickly become *américaine.*"

Too true. But it happened the other way around, when a copyist, faced with someone else's bad writing—or handicapped by a slight hardness of hearing—turned *américaine* into *armoricaine.*

And in support of that statement there is the fact that no menu from any important restaurant, either in Paris or elsewhere, has ever been found with *armoricaine* antedating *américaine*. No, the latter has always preceded the former.

But in fact the origin of the dish was settled quite clearly a score or so years ago in a letter from an Old Parisian gentleman to the noted gastronome Curnonsky in which he wrote: "As you so rightly say, the *homard à l'américaine* was created in Paris, and naturally enough by a Frenchman: Peters, born in Sète and in fact christened Pierre Fraisse. I knew Peters in about 1900 when he was seventy-eight, living quietly with his wife on the rue Germain Pilon. One evening when he was in a reminiscing mood he told me the story of that famous lobster dish."

From Pierre Fraisse's reminiscences and what was already known of him it is clear that this Frenchman from the South of France in fact began his career in the United States. Then, having returned to Paris, he took premises on the Passage des Princes and found Peter's Restaurant around 1860. . . .

And it was in the same restaurant that a party of Americans appeared late one evening, in a hurry, when there was almost nothing left except for some live lobsters awaiting next day's *court-bouillon*. Seized by inspiration, while the soup was being served, Fraisse created his new lobster dish.

The customers found it delicious.

"What is the name of this exquisite dish?"

And recalling that he had run a Café Américain in Chicago, that his present restaurant had an anglicized name, and that his customers were from over the Atlantic, Pierre Fraisse replied: "It's called *homard à l'américaine.*"

To be truthful, the recipe is more Mediterranean than anything else, both in its conception and its ingredients. It recalls the crawfish *à la provençale* with which Escoffier launched his career, in Nice, at the restaurant Favre, in 1869. But that in no way implies that Fraisse was copying. Great minds do think alike, even in cooking.

The Hundred Glories of French Cooking

BAROMETER SOUP

I knew, by my scientific reading, that either thermometers or
barometers ought to be boiled, to make them accurate; I did not
know which it was, so I boiled both. There was still no result.
. . . I hunted up another barometer; it was new and perfect. I boiled
it half an hour in a pot of bean soup which the cooks were making.
The result was unexpected: the instrument was not affected at all,
but there was such a strong barometer taste to the soup that the
head cook, who was a most conscientious person, changed its
name in the bill of fare. The dish was so greatly liked by all, that
I ordered the cook to have barometer soup every day.

—MARK TWAIN
A Tramp Abroad

THREE FROM ANTOINE'S
HERMANN B. DEUTSCH

From the time when Antoine Alciatore, the founder, brought to
New Orleans the secret Collinet recipe for *Pommes Soufflées,* and that
of his own creation, *Filet de Boeuf Robespierre,* new dishes have been
presented in the historic dining rooms at Antoine's in New Orleans. Antoine himself created here the *Dinde Talleyrand*—the turkey roasted with herbs which brought the establishment its first
fame. Alas, this dish can never more be served. When he left New
Orleans that he might die and be buried in his native Provence, he
took with him all his private papers, among which may have been
the recipe for this dish, whose secret he did not confide even to his
sons, who were mere youths at the time. He had created this dish
as a tribute to the land of his adoption, for the strutting *Dinde* was
not only native to the Western world, but had been the national
emblem of prosperity and bounteous living since the time of the
Pilgrim's first harvest in the early 1600's.

Soufflée potatoes, which were likewise introduced to the western hemisphere by Antoine Alciatore, were the result of a king's

tardiness. In the year 1837 the French government of Citizen-King Louis Philippe prepared to celebrate with a great banquet the first run of France's first railroad, a short line from Paris to St. Germain en Laye. Louis Philippe was very fond of French-fried potatoes in their original thin, crisp form. Collinet, the chef who was to prepare the feast, knew this. But the chamber of deputies refused to let the King ride from Paris to St. Germain in the dangerous, newfangled steam cars, decreeing that he must make the journey by carriage. The train arrived on time, but the carriage of Louis Philippe did not, and Collinet was on the verge of despair, for he had already begun the preparation of the fried potatoes. As a last expedient he removed them from the pot of boiling lard where they had begun to brown, and laid them aside until the King should arrive. As soon as His Citizen-Majesty's post-horses came prancing to the new railway station, he re-immersed the potatoes in the boiling lard. Imagine his astonishment when they puffed out into crisp and crunchy little hollow, finger-shaped balloons, a bit like empty sausage skins. The King was delighted, and personally complimented Mr. Collinet upon his achievement. One of the very few close friends to whom Collinet confided the secret was young Antoine Alciatore, chef of the Hotel de Noailles in Marseilles, who in the following year emigrated to the United States to seek his fortune. When he found his first restaurant in New Orleans he introduced, among other things, *Pommes Souflées* just as they are served you at Antoine's today.

Oysters Rockefeller—or if you prefer the original name, *Huitres en Coquille à la Rockefeller*—constitute what is the most famous of the Antoine dishes. They are the creation of Jules Alciatore, son of Antoine and father of Roy. . . . By the time Jules took over the reins in 1887, New Orleans had become much more Americanized than the city to which Antoine, his father, had come as an *emigré* in 1840, and calls for *Escargots Bourguignonne* were not as frequent, by any means, as the calls for oysters from Lac Barre, Quatre Bayous and Bayou Cook. Therefore, thought Jules, why not prepare oysters with the *sauce Bourguignonne?* And why not make certain changes in the *sauce Bourguignonne* which, after all, belonged with the *escargot* but not with the *huitre?* Thus Jules' blending of new ingredients and the basic sauce for snails resulted in a new oyster dressing so rich that it was given the name which, in those years, stood for the richest man in the world. It also resulted in a dish perhaps more widely imitated than any in the world. The recipe was not to be lost like that for *Dinde Talleyrand,* but its secret has been so zealously guarded that the original Oysters Rockefeller of Antoine's has never been duplicated. It can only be simulated.

New Orleans Item, April 4, 1940

Ben Wenberg and His Lobster

Ben Wenberg was a sea captain engaged in the fruit trade between Cuba and New York. When on shore, he bivouacked at Delmonico's. . . . One day in 1876, home from a cruise, he entered the café at Madison Square and announced that he had brought back a new way to cook lobster. Calling for a blazer (a chafing dish with spirit lamp), he demonstrated his discovery by cooking the dish beside his table, and invited Charles Delmonico ("Old Charley") to taste. Charles said, "Delicious!" and forthwith entered the dish on the restaurant menu, naming it in honor of its inventor, or at least its introducer to New York, *Lobster à la Wenberg.* It caught the public fancy and became a standby of the after-theater suppers that were in vogue, and Wenberg preened himself upon having perpetuated his name to the remotest posterity.

Unfortunately, he and "Charley" had a falling out. The cause is not known, but the consequence was devastating to Wenberg's expectations of gastronomic immortality. Charles erased the dish from the menu; but since patrons kept calling for it, he was forced to compromise. By typographical sleight-of-hand, he reversed the spelling of "Wen" to "New," and *Lobster à la Newberg* was born.

—Lately Thomas
Delmonico's, A Century of Splendor

YES, BUT CAN THE STEAM ENGINE DO THIS?
WOODY ALLEN

I was leafing through a magazine while waiting for Joseph K., my beagle, to emerge from his regular Tuesday fifty-minute hour with a Park Avenue therapist—a Jungian veterinarian who, for fifty dollars per session, labors valiantly to convince him that jowls are not a social drawback—when I came across a sentence at the bottom of the page that caught my eye like an overdraft notice. It was just another item in one of those boiler-plate specials with a title like "Historagrams" or "Betcha Didn't Know," but its magnitude shook me with the power of the opening strains of Beethoven's Ninth. "The sandwich," it read, "was invented by the Earl of Sandwich." Stunned by the news, I read it again and broke into an involuntary tremble. My mind whirled as it began to conjure with the immense dreams, the hopes and obstacles, that must have gone into the invention of the first sandwich. My eyes became moist as I looked out the window at the shimmering towers of the city, and I experienced a sense of eternity, marvelling at man's ineradicable place in the universe. Man the inventor! Da Vinci's notebooks loomed before me—brave blueprints for the highest aspirations of the human race. I thought of Aristotle, Dante, Shakespeare. The First Folio. Newton. Handel's *Messiah*. Monet. Impressionism. Edison. Cubism. Stravinsky. $E = mc^2$ . . .

Holding firmly to a mental picture of the first sandwich lying encased at the British Museum, I spent the ensuing three months working up a brief biography of its great inventor, his nibs the Earl. Though my grasp of history is a bit shaky, and though my capacity for romanticizing easily dwarfs that of the average acid-head, I hope I have captured at least the essence of this unprecedented genius, and that these sparse notes will inspire a true historian to take it from there.

1718: Birth of the Earl of Sandwich to upper-class parents. Father is delighted at being appointed chief farrier to His Majesty the King—a position he will enjoy for several years, until he discovers he is a blacksmith and resigns embittered. Mother is a simple *Hausfrau* of German extraction, whose uneventful menu consists essentially of lard and gruel, although she does show some flair for culinary imagination in her ability to concoct a passable sillabub.

1725–35: Attends school, where he is taught horseback riding and Latin. At school he comes in contact with cold cuts for the first time and displays unusual interest in thinly sliced strips of roast beef and ham. By graduation this has become an obsession, and although his paper on "The Analysis and Attendant Phenomena of Snacks" arouses interest among the faculty, his classmates regard him as odd.

1736: Enters Cambridge University, at his parents' behest, to pursue studies in rhetoric and metaphysics, but displays little enthusiasm for either. In constant revolt against everything academic, he is charged with stealing loaves of bread and performing unnatural experiments with them. Accusations of heresy result in his expulsion.

1738: Disowned, he sets out for the Scandinavian countries, where he spends three years in intensive research on cheese. He is much taken with the many varieties of sardines he encounters and writes in his notebook, "I am convinced that there is an enduring reality, beyond anything man has yet attained, in the juxtaposition of foodstuffs. Simplify, simplify." Upon his return to England, he meets Nell Smallbore, a greengrocer's daughter, and they marry. She is to teach him all he will ever know about lettuce.

1741: Living in the country on a small inheritance, he works day and night, often skimping on meals to save money for food. His first completed work—a slice of bread, a slice of bread on top of that, and a slice of turkey on top of both—fails miserably. Bitterly disappointed, he returns to his studio and begins again.

1745: After four years of frenzied labor, he is convinced he is on the threshold of success. He exhibits before his peers two slices of turkey with a slice of bread in the middle. His work is rejected by all but David Hume, who senses the imminence of something great and encourages him. Heartened by the philosopher's friendship, he returns to work with renewed vigor.

1747: Destitute, he can no longer afford to work in roast beef or turkey and switches to ham, which is cheaper.

1750: In the spring, he exhibits and demonstrates three consecutive slices of ham stacked on one another; this arouses some interest, mostly in intellectual circles, but the general public remains unmoved. Three slices of bread on top of one another add to his reputation, and while a mature style is not yet evident, he is sent for by Voltaire.

1751: Journeys to France, where the dramatist-philosopher has achieved some interesting results with bread and mayonnaise. The two men become friendly and begin a correspondence that is to end abruptly when Voltaire runs out of stamps.

1758: His growing acceptance by opinion-makers wins him a commission by the Queen to fix "something special" for a luncheon with the Spanish ambassador. He works day and night, tearing up hundreds of blueprints, but finally—4:17 A.M., April 27, 1758 —he creates a work consisting of several strips of ham enclosed, top and bottom, by two slices of rye bread. In a burst of inspiration, he garnishes the work with mustard. It is an immediate sensation, and he is commissioned to prepare all Saturday luncheons for the remainder of the year.

1760: He follows one success with another, creating "sandwiches," as they are called in his honor, out of roast beef, chicken, tongue, and nearly every conceivable cold cut. Not content to repeat tried formulas, he seeks out new ideas and devises the combination sandwich, for which he receives the Order of the Garter.

1769: Living on a country estate, he is visited by the greatest men of his century; Haydn, Kant, Rousseau, and Ben Franklin stop at his home, some enjoying his remarkable creations at table, others ordering to go.

1778: Though aging physically he still strives for new forms and writes in his diary, "I work long into the cold nights and am toasting everything now in an effort to keep warm." Later that year, his open hot roast-beef sandwich creates a scandal with its frankness.

1783: To celebrate his sixty-fifth birthday, he invents the hamburger and tours the great capitals of the world personally, making burgers at concert halls before large and appreciative audiences. In

Germany, Goethe suggests serving them on buns—an idea that delights the Earl, and of the author of *Faust* he says, "This Goethe, he is some fellow." The remark delights Goethe, although the following year they break intellectually over the concept of rare, medium, and well done.

1790: At a retrospective exhibition of his works in London, he is suddenly taken ill with chest pains and is thought to be dying, but recovers sufficiently to supervise the construction of a hero sandwich by a group of talented followers. Its unveiling in Italy causes a riot, and it remains misunderstood by all but a few critics.

1792: He develops genu varum, which he fails to treat in time, and succumbs in his sleep. He is laid to rest in Westminster Abbey, and thousands mourn his passing. At his funeral, the great German poet Hölderlin sums up his achievements with undisguised reverence: "He freed mankind from the hot lunch. We owe him so much."

Getting Even

Billings Equestrian Banquet 1903

12

Gastronomic Extravaganzas

Was the world ready, even in the affluent autumn of 1975, for a dinner tab for two in the amount of $4,000? The matter is still debated warily in winy moments here and there. Was the world ever ready for a white-dinner on horseback indoors at an elegant Manhattan watering place? I doubt it. Still, enormous appetites are legendary, and history is salted and peppered with accounts of professional eaters like Hungry Sam of the Susquehanna Valley. In the middle of the nineteenth century, Blackwood's Magazine paid tribute to the renowned Dando, who had earned his living eating oysters, with an epitaph in rather undisciplined verse. Dando's gustatory powers, it was reported by an unnamed poet, had been inherited from

> *A Mayor of Colchester who, it was said,*
> *Married a mermaid and sometimes would eat*
> *Half his own weight of oysters in a day.*

Every man to his own taste, as the saying goes. In the 1970s a self-styled "worm farmer" in the Middle West began merchandising earthworms as an exotic food, which he compared to the escargots of Burgundy, with or without garlic.

JUST A QUIET DINNER FOR TWO
CRAIG CLAIBORNE

If one were offered dinner for two at any price, to be eaten in any restaurant anywhere in the world, what would the choice be? And in these days of ever-higher prices, what would the cost be?

By submitting the highest bid on Channel 13's fund-raising

auction last June, we found ourselves in a position earlier this week to answer these questions. The place: Chez Denis in Paris. The cost: $4,000.

Our winning bid was $300.

One factor in the selection of the restaurant should be noted quickly: The donor of the dinner that Channel 13 auctioned was American Express, which set forth as its only condition the requirement that the establishment be one that accepts its credit card.

In turn, when American Express ultimately learned what we had done, its reaction went from mild astonishment to being cheerful about the outcome. "Four thousand—was that francs or dollars?" asked Iris Burkat, a company official, at one point.

At any rate, the selection of the restaurant dominated our fantasies for weeks as in our minds, we dined on a hundred meals or more. At times we were in Paris, then in Alsace. We considered Rome, Tokyo and Hong Kong, Copenhagen and Stockholm, Brussels and London.

The consideration of restaurants competed with thoughts of the greatest of champagnes and still wines, visions of caviar and foie gras, dreams of elaborate desserts. Perhaps we would choose nothing but vodka or champagne with caviar followed by foie gras with Château d'Yquem—but no, any old millionaire could do that.

In addition to excluding those that did not recognize the credit card of the donor, we dismissed from our potential list of restaurants several celebrated places, simply, perhaps, because of their celebrity.

In time we considered Chez Denis, which is a great favorite among several food writers (Henri Gault, Christian Millau and Waverley Root among them), but is nonetheless not well known. It is a tiny place on the Rue Gustave Flaubert, not far from the Arc de Triomphe.

We visited Chez Denis in a party of three to reconnoiter. It was not hard to go incognito, for we suspect that the proprietor, Denis Lahana, does not credit any Americans with even the most elementary knowledge of French wine and food.

The investigatory dinner was sumptuous. There was a chiffonade of lobster (a salad of cold lobster, cubed foie gras, a touch of cognac and, we suspect, cayenne, and a tarragon mayonnaise flavored with tomato, tossed with lettuce).

In addition, there was fresh foie gras with aspic, braised sweetbreads with a light truffle sauce, roast quail and those delectable tiny birds from the Landes region of France, ortolans. There was also a great personal favorite, andouillettes served with an outstanding sorrel sauce. The wine was a fine Pommard.

After dinner, we asked Mr. Denis, offhandedly, how much he would charge for the most lavish dinner for two that he and his chef could prepare. He spoke in terms of $2,000 to $3,000.

We told him that we were about to celebrate a birthday and that money was no obstacle in ordering the finest dinner in Europe. Mr. Denis, with little hesitation, pulled up a chair and sat down. He took us seriously.

We asked him to consider the matter at his convenience and write to us with his proposal. When he did, his letter stated:

"In accordance with your demand, I propose to organize for you a prestigious dinner. In the land of my birth, the region of Bordeaux, one speaks of a repas des vins, a meal during the course of which a number of wines of great prestige are served, generally nine wines.

"I am suggesting nine such wines, to be served in the course of a dinner à la Française in the classic tradition. To dine properly in this style, many dishes are offered and served to the guests, chosen with the sole thought that each dish be on the same high level as the wines and those most likely to give pleasure as the wines are tasted."

He suggested a dinner of thirty-one dishes that would start with an hors d'oeuvre and go on to three "services," the first consisting of soups, savory, an assortment of substantial main dishes, and ices or sherbets to clear the palate.

This would be followed by the second service: hot roasts or baked dishes, vegetables, cold, light, meaty dishes in aspic and desserts.

And then the third service: decorated confections, petits fours and fruits.

The youngest wine would be a six-year-old white burgundy, the oldest a 140-year-old madeira.

Mr. Denis set a price of $4,000. This, we must hasten to add, included service and taxes. We accepted.

The proprietor suggested that the meal be served to four persons —all for the same price—because the food had to be prepared in a certain quantity and would be enough to serve as many as 10 persons, while the wines were enough for four.

We declined, because the rules set by American Express called for dinner for two. The dinner party would be made up of me and my colleague, Pierre Franey. Anything left over, we knew, would not go to waste.

Mr. Denis noted that it was not required that all foods be sampled and that the quantity of the food served would depend on the guest's appetite.

And so, we sat down to our $4,000 dinner.

The hors d'oeuvre was presented: fresh Beluga caviar in crystal, enclosed in shaved ice, with toast. The wine was a superb 1966 Champagne Comtesse Marie de France.

Then came the first service, which started with three soups. There was consommé Denis, an inordinately good, rich, full-bodied, clear consommé of wild duck with shreds of fine crêpes and herbs. It was clarified with raw duck and duck bones and then lightly thickened as many classic soups are, with fine tapioca.

The second soup (still of the first service) was a crème Andalouse, an outstanding cream of tomato soup with shreds of sweet pimento and fines herbes, including fresh chives and chervil.

The first two soups were superb but the third, cold germiny (a cream of sorrel), seemed bland and anticlimactic. One spoonful of that sufficed.

The only wine served at this point was a touch of champagne. The soups having been disposed of, we moved on to a spectacularly delicate parfait of sweetbreads, an equally compelling mousse of quail in a small tarte, and a somewhat salty, almost abrasive but highly complementary tarte of Italian ham, mushrooms and a border of truffles.

There followed another curious but oddly appealing dish, a

classic chartreuse of partridge, the pieces of roasted game nested in a bed of cooked cabbage and baked in a mosaic pattern, intricately styled, of carrot and turnip cut into fancy shapes.

And a tender rare-roasted fillet of Limousin beef with a rich truffle sauce.

The wine with the meat and game was a 1928 Château Mouton Rothschild. It was ageless and beautiful.

The first service finally ended with sherbets in three flavors—raspberry, orange and lemon. The purpose of this was to revive the palate for the second service, and it did. We were two hours into the meal and going at the food, it seemed, at a devilish pace.

The second service included the ortolans en brochette, an element of the dinner to be anticipated with a relish almost equal to that of the caviar or the foie gras.

The wine was a 1918 Château Latour, and it was perhaps the best bordeaux we had ever known. It was very much alive, with the least trace of tannin.

The next segment of the first service included a fascinating dish that the proprietor said he had created, Belon oysters broiled quickly in the shell and served with a pure beurre blanc, the creamy, lightly thickened butter sauce.

Also in this segment were a lobster in a creamy, cardinal-red sauce that was heavily laden with chopped truffles and, after that, another startling but excellent dish, a sort of Provençale pie made with red mullet and baked with tomato, black olives and herbs, including fennel or anise seed, rosemary, sage and thyme.

The accompanying wine was a 1969 Montrachet Baron Thénard, which was extraordinary (to our taste, all first-rate Montrachet whites are extraordinary).

The final part of the first service consisted of what was termed filets et sots l'y laissent de poulard de Bresse, sauce suprême aux cèpes (the so-called "fillet" strips of chicken plus the "oysters" found in the afterbackbone of chicken blended in a cream sauce containing sliced wild mushrooms).

The ortolans, which dine on berries through their brief lives, are cooked whole, with the head on, and without cleaning except for removing the feathers. They are as fat as butter and an absolute joy to bite into because of the succulence of the flesh. Even the bones, except for the tiny leg bones, are chewed and swallowed. There is one bird to one bite.

The second service also included fillets of wild duck en salmis in a rich brown game sauce. The final dish in this segment was a rognonade de veau, or roasted boned loin of veal wrapped in puff pastry with fresh black truffles about the size of golf balls.

The vegetables served were pommes Anna—the potatoes cut into small rounds and baked in butter—and a purée rachel, a purée of artichokes.

Then came the cold meat delicacies. There was butter-rich fresh foie gras in clear aspic, breast meat of woodcocks that was cooked until rare and served with a natural chaudfroid, another aspic and cold pheasant with fresh hazelnuts.

The wines for this segment consisted of a 1974 Château Lafite-Rothschild, a 1961 Château Petrus, and the most magnificent wine of the evening, a 1929 Romanée Conti.

The dinner drew near an end with three sweets—a cold glazed charlotte with strawberries, an île flottante and poires alma. The wine for the sweets was a beautiful unctuous 1928 Château d'Yquem, which was quite sweet and yet "dry."

The last service consisted of the pastry confections and fruits, served with an 1835 madeira. With coffee came a choice of a 100-year-old calvados or an hors d'âge cognac.

And for the $4,000, logic asks if it was a perfect meal in all respects?

The answer is no.

The crystal was Baccarat and the silver was family sterling, but the presentation of the dishes, particularly the cold dishes such as the sweetbread parfait and quail mousse tarte, was mundane.

The foods were elegant to look at, but the over-all display was undistinguished, if not to say shabby.

The chartreuse of pheasant, which can be displayed stunningly, was presented on a most ordinary dish.

The food itself was generally exemplary, although there were regrettable lapses there, too. The lobster in the gratin was chewy and even the sauce could not compensate for that. The oysters, of necessity, had to be cooked as briefly as possible to prevent toughening, but the beurre blanc should have been very hot. The dish was almost lukewarm when it reached the table, and so was the chartreuse of pheasant.

We've spent many hours reckoning the cost of the meal and find that we cannot break it down. We have decided this: We feel we could not have made a better choice, given the circumstance of time and place.

Mr. Denis declined to apply a cost to each of the wines, explaining that they contributed greatly to the total cost of the meal because it was necessary to open three bottles of the 1918 Latour in order to find one in proper condition.

Over all, it was an unforgettable evening and we have high praise for Claude Mornay, the 37-year-old genius behind the meal.

We reminded ourselves of one thing during the course of that evening: If you were Henry VIII, Lucullus, Gargantua and Bacchus, all rolled into one, you cannot possibly sustain, start to finish, a state of ecstasy while dining on a series of thirty-one dishes.

Wines, illusion or not, became increasingly interesting, although we were laudably sober at the end of the meal.

The New York Times, November 14, 1975

FRANCS AND BEANS

RUSSELL BAKER

As chance would have it, the very evening Craig Claiborne ate his historic $4,000 dinner for two with 31 dishes and nine wines in Paris, a Lucullan repast for one was prepared and consumed in New York by this correspondent, no slouch himself when it comes to titillating the palate.

Mr. Claiborne won his meal in a television fund-raising auction and had it professionally prepared. Mine was created from spur-of-the-moment inspiration, necessitated when I discovered a note on the stove saying, "Am eating out with Dora and Imogene—make dinner for yourself." It was from the person who regularly does the cooking at my house and, though disconcerted at first, I quickly rose to the challenge.

The meal opened with a 1975 Diet Pepsi served in a disposable bottle. Although its bouquet was negligible, its distinct metallic aftertaste evoked memories of tin cans one had licked experimentally in the first flush of childhood's curiosity.

To create the balance of tastes so cherished by the epicurean palate, I followed with a *paté de fruites de nuts of Georgia,* prepared according to my own recipe. A half-inch layer of creamy-style peanut butter is troweled onto a graham cracker, then half a banana is crudely diced and pressed firmly into the peanut butter and cemented in place as it were by a second graham cracker.

The accompanying drink was cold milk served in a wide-brimmed jelly glass. This is essential to proper consumption of the paté, since the entire confection must be dipped into the milk to soften it for eating. In making the presentation to the mouth, one must beware lest the milk-soaked portion of the sandwich fall onto the necktie. Thus, seasoned gourmandisers follow the old maxim of the Breton chefs and "bring the mouth to the jelly glass."

At this point in the meal, the stomach was ready for serious eating, and I prepared beans with bacon grease, a dish I perfected in 1937 while developing my *cuisine du dépression.*

The dish is started by placing a pan over a very high flame until it becomes dangerously hot. A can of Heinz's pork and beans is then emptied into the pan and allowed to char until it reaches the consistency of hardening concrete. Three strips of bacon are fried to crisps, and when the beans have formed huge dense clots firmly welded to the pan, the bacon grease is poured in and stirred vigorously with a large screw driver.

This not only adds flavor but also loosens some of the beans from the side of the pan. Leaving the flame high, I stirred in a three-day-old spaghetti sauce found in the refrigerator, added a sprinkle of chili powder, a large dollop of Major Grey's chutney and a tablespoon of bicarbonate of soda to make the whole dish rise.

Beans with bacon grease is always eaten from the pan with a tablespoon while standing over the kitchen sink. The pan must be thrown away immediately. The correct drink with this dish is a straight shot of room-temperature gin. I had a Gilbey's, 1975, which was superb.

For the meat course, I had fried bologna *à la Nutley, Nouveau Jersey*. Six slices of A&P bologna were placed in an ungreased frying pan over maximum heat and held down by a long fork until the entire house filled with smoke. The bologna was turned, fried the same length of time on the other side, then served on air-filled white bread with thick lashings of mayonnaise.

The correct drink for fried bologna *à la Nutley, Nouveau Jersey* is a 1927 Nehi Cola, but since my cellar, alas, had none, I had to make do with a second shot of Gilbey's 1975.

The cheese course was deliciously simple—a single slice of Kraft's individually wrapped yellow sandwich cheese, which was flavored by vigorous rubbing over the bottom of the frying pan to soak up the rich bologna juices. Wine being absolutely *de rigueur* with cheese, I chose a 1974 Muscatel, flavored with a maraschino cherry, and afterwards cleared my palate with three pickled martini onions.

It was time for the fruit. I chose a Del Monte tinned pear, which, regrettably, slipped from the spoon and fell on the floor, necessitating its being blotted with a paper towel to remove cat hairs. To compensate for the resulting loss of pear syrup, I dipped it lightly in hot-dog relish which created a unique flavor.

With the pear I drank two shots of Gilbey's 1975 and one shot of Wolfschmidt vodka (non-vintage), the Gilbey's having been exhausted.

At last it was time for the dish the entire meal had been building toward—dessert. With a paring knife, I ripped into a fresh package of Oreos, produced a bowl of My-T-Fine chocolate pudding which had been coagulating in the refrigerator for days and, using a potato masher, crushed a dozen Oreos into the pudding. It was immense.

Between mouthfuls, I sipped a tall, bubbling tumbler of cool Bromo-Seltzer, and finished with six ounces of Maalox. It couldn't have been better.

The New York Times, November 16, 1975

"Gargantua Could Not Have Devoured More Food Than I"

ARTHUR RUBINSTEIN

After a restful summer spent partly in Deauville and a few weeks in Venice, I returned to my home in Montmartre where François helped me with the transformation of the primitive washing place into an elegant modern bathroom. I was preparing my autumn season of concerts. Richard Ordynski arrived in town and told me that he and an important group of Polish actors had been engaged by the Paramount cinema to dub into Polish a very successful picture of this company. "I have a wonderful idea, Arthur," he said. "We have a free day next week and it would be wonderful if you gave a luncheon to our actors whom you admire so much." It was true, there were three or four men and women among them who were my favorites of the Polish stage. I called François for a consultation. "Do you think it possible to have twelve persons for lunch in this place?"

"Certainly, sir," he said. "It is still warm and I could set up a large table in the garden."

"Well, then," I said to Richard, "invite them in my name on that free day, but not before two o'clock because I have to order the luncheon from different places in town and it usually takes time for it to be delivered and prepared."

For two days before the lunch, I was busy ordering a sumptuous meal; lobsters from Prunier, ducks from Larue, and the then-famous raspberry tart from Edouard, rue Donou. I took care also of the wine, vodka and cognac. François had to get the table, chairs and all we needed from a caterer, including the coffee.

I was looking forward to my first party in my home and to having as my guests the actors I admired so much. On the day of the luncheon, at nine o'clock I received a call from the Baronne Germaine de Rothschild. "Cher Arthur, I hope you did not forget the luncheon today at twelve thirty. Please don't be late because Edouard has to be at the Banque de France early." I almost fainted. I had completely forgotten I had accepted this invitation about two weeks earlier. I saw no way out of it, so I answered with an assumed cheerfulness, "Certainly, chère Germaine, I shall be on time." I dressed in a hurry, saw the man arranging the table and chairs in the garden and ordered François to take care of the flowers, to remind the different places to deliver the things on time, and, leaving at noon for the rue Saint Florentin, I said, "Have everything ready for two o'clock, but if I am not back on time, tell Mr. Ordynski that I had telephoned and was held up at a bank, and that I would be back any minute."

This was a day to be remembered! Gargantua, Rabelais's creation, could not have devoured more food than I did. Edouard de Rothschild was not only a great gourmet but a gourmand as well. His menus were famous for having the finest food in town and there was always a lavish assortment of it. He liked my company because I appreciated this and for my stories which amused him. It began with a saumon fumé: "Il n'est pas salé. Vous le trouverez excellent," said the Baron. Then came the perdreaux rôtis sur canapé with a very original salad made of celery, apple, and truffles finely cut up with a delicious sauce I cannot describe. After this dish from heaven came the plateau of cheeses. The Baron picked a big piece of one special one and forced me to eat it, praising it in a way that did not admit refusal. The last course was a parfait des glaces—it was full inside with powdered chocolate, a specialty of their table which I couldn't refuse, even on my death-bed. As it was getting late for both the Baron and myself, I succeeded in doing without coffee. It was almost two o'clock and I dashed home in a taxi and found my guests with a nervous Ordynski in the garden. I received a hungry welcome. François whispered, "Everything is in order, sir." I put the two lovely ladies next to me and the Lucullan feast—the first for them, the second for me—started off with gorgeous fresh lobsters, with well-cared-for mayonnaise with the right amount of pepper, to the great satisfaction of my guests. A few sips of vodka helped to loosen the tongues of the great actors, and every new course was received with an ovation. The bottles of wine were emptied in no time and the cognac gave the final touch to this culinary orgy. I may assure my readers that I didn't leave the table hungry. To this day I lose my appetite when I think of it.

My Happy Life

A Full Dress Feast in Marrakesh
John Gunther

Nothing in gastronomy is more exotically enticing than an Arab *diffa* or banquet. We went to several. First Hassan and Sadek [sons of the Pasha] gave us a "simple" lunch as a kind of dress rehearsal, so that we could learn in privacy what to expect and how to comport ourselves. Then General Guillaume, the French High Commissioner, drove us one day to a town called Demnat, where he was bestowing a decoration on a venerable caid. This was a full dress feast. At the gates of the city armed horsemen on white chargers fired their muskets in salute, and pranced in fierce display. We were given ceremonial offerings of dates and milk, and heard for the first time the most extraordinary sound that North Africa provides—the high sibilant whistle, which is almost a whinny, a neigh, made by the long files of women from the town, who line the castle walls, and, as they begin to oscillate in a slow rhythmic dance, let loose this penetrating horselike chant.

Guests at a Moorish meal sit on cushions or low divans, with a large white napkin laid over their knees. You may use this, but not too conspicupusly, to clean the lips, but not the fingers. You may hold bread in your left hand—bread is in large soft chunks—but otherwise the left hand is not supposed to touch food, because of a Moslem custom having to do with bodily cleanliness. Except in special cases there are no knives, forks, spoons, plates, or other impediments. The tablecloth is put on the floor, to catch crumbs. You eat with your right hand, taking everything from a common dish, and if you are a purist you use only the thumb and first two fingers. These fingers are not supposed to touch the mouth. To lick the fingers, no matter how greasy they may become, is bad form; but I have seen it done. These procedures are simple enough with some types of food, but not all. *Couscous* is difficult. Or try picking up a blazingly hot fried egg with three fingers and get it into your mouth without touching the lips or spilling. Unskilled people use wads of bread as a cleanser. Bones and similar debris are tossed on the floor or table.

First—at a typical feast—a servant arrives with a copper kettle, or pitcher with a thin spout, and pours water into a bowl over the hands of each guest. (At the conclusion of the meal, this ceremony takes place again, and soap is provided.) Next comes mint tea, thick and sticky. Then *plat* after *plat* arrives; each makes a separate course. Then, as in a Chinese meal properly served, you reach over to the common dishes, which all share, and choose a morsel to your taste. Women of the household are never present at a *diffa*. Each dish, if anything is left, is passed on down to the women, who are waiting in a different part of the castle or dwelling. When the wives and concubines have finished, it goes on in turn to male servants, then to female servants, and finally to retainers, hangers-on, or slaves.

It was interesting to watch French people of the most impeccable refinement, who might have been characters out of Marcel Proust, eat Moorish meals. They ate with their fingers with the most obvious gusto and relish; in fact they seemed to be possessed by a mad glee while tearing a hot slippery chicken apart with their bare hands. I offered the remark at one dinner that eating without implements was a simple enough indication of a suppressed tendency to revert to childhood, and a lady replied that, indeed, in the Faubourg St. Germain where she was brought up she had been strictly forbidden ever to touch food with her hands, had always yearned to do so, and now took a special and perverse joy in doing it.

But let me proceed to our dinner *chez* the Pasha. Twenty bearded retainers, looking like a line of owls, saluted our arrival at the palace. We entered a small room with maroon-striped settees, green curtains, and a flaming yellow carpet—Moslems love clashing colors—and with arched windows and a valuted ceiling. One guest this evening was a celebrated French official, the Préfet of Casablanca; another was a barefooted, white-robed Arab octogenarian, the Caid of Mogador. A cold wind whipped through the doors and windows, which are usually kept open at ceremonies of this kind. (At luncheon birds may fly in and out.) The Glaoui [Hadj Thami, pasha], who had been sitting alone on a hassock, rose to greet us. He wore Arab dress (and carried a poniard) except for Argyle socks and a bright red necktie. At once we moved across a courtyard filled with orange trees to another division of the palace, where an American-style bar was functioning. Of course the Glaoui and the Caid did not drink the cocktails that were offered, which were a brilliant pink in color. Dinner was announced by a major-domo who entered abruptly and twitched the Glaoui's elbow, in the peculiar informal manner of Moorish servants. We went outdoors again, crossed another courtyard, and emerged finally into a room big enough to seat two hundred. The chief colors here were pink, lettuce-green, white, and purple. The Pasha, with a chortle of satisfaction, slid out of his slippers unobtrusively, climbed gaily over a hassock, sat down on a divan, and invited us to sit around him. This is what we ate:

First, a pale green soup composed of almonds, peas, and bits of white fish. (This was a concession to the uncouth West. We were even allowed plates and spoons. Moors know full well that existence is impossible to a Frenchman unless dinner begins with soup.)

Second, a whole roast lamb, served naked and intact. This, the staple course at an elaborate Moorish meal, is known as a *mechoui*. With infinite dexterity the Glaoui broke into the hot crackling skin, and seized from underneath specially tender morsels, which he passed on with his fingers to my wife. Often a lively competition occurs among guests to get the meat deepest down, from the ribs, where it is particularly fat and tender. This procedure may sound gross, but it is not. Nobody tears off big chunks of flesh. People eat slivers and delicate strips. Sometimes at a big *diffa* the course following this is *another* whole roasted lamb, prepared with some sort of sauce to differentiate it from the first.

Third, a *pastilla*. This *plat*, which takes a full forty-eight hours to prepare, is the pride of a good Moorish cook. It is a pie, almost three feet in diameter, the crust of which is an inordinately fine, milky *mille-feuilles*, on which a design is made with powdered sugar. Underneath, as a bold guest dents the crust, and usually burns his fingers doing so, will be found a miscellany of shrimp, tripe, sweetbreads, olives, liver, *cervelles*, mussels, and fried eggs. It is a veritable treasure nest, and delicious beyond speech.

After this we had four more main courses in sober succession—squabs with a sauce like none other I have ever tasted before or since, a kind of hot, liquid and milky hollandaise; a covey of whole roast chickens, stuffed with olives and swimming in a lemon dressing; a ragout of lamb, onions, eggplant, and hard-boiled eggs; and a second, different ragout—slices of lamb laid tenderly atop a bed of peas and almonds. Then came a dish of strangely shaped pretzels seasoned with molasses, the equivalent of the sherbet still served occasionally at formal dinners in the West; it is sweet, and a refresher before what is to come.

Couscous is next. This, the basic food of Morocco for rich and poor alike, is made of semolina. The mound of grain may contain anything else from cool-skinned grapes to chunks of mutton; that of the Pasha came with turnips, carrots, and hazelnuts. *Couscous,* like rice in Japan, is always served toward the end of the meal so that you can fill up if you are still hungry, and it is bad manners to take too much. It is hard to manage with the fingers, since it is almost as dry as sand. The Glaoui is one of the world's foremost manipulators of *couscous* balls. We watched him fascinated. He picks up a handful of the hot grain, tosses this in his palm without touching it with the fingers, and gently bounces it in the hollow of his hand until by some miracle it forms a cohesive ball; this he then pops into his mouth, catching it on the fly. It was like watching a man with one hand make and eat golf balls.

At last came a cake made of frozen figs and tangerines. The Pasha picked up his napkin, and with a flourish dropped it on the tablecloth; this is the conventional gesture to indicate that the meal, any meal, is over. During all this we of the West drank champagne. The old Caid, who never said a word during dinner, sipped lemonade steadily with a peculiar hissing gurgle. Finally—the end is the beginning—we had mint tea again, the universal drink of North Africa, which is supposed to be an aphrodisiac.

Inside Africa

DISSERTATION ON ROAST BUFFALO
GEORGE FREDERICK RUXTON

Whether it is that the meat itself—which, by the way, is certainly the most delicious of flesh—is most easy of digestion, or whether the digestive organs of hunters are "ostrichified" by the severity of exercise and the bracing, wholesome climate of the mountains and plains, it is a fact that most prodigious quantities of fat cow may be swallowed with the greatest impunity, and not the slightest inconvenience ever follows the mammoth feasts of the gourmands of the Far West. The powers of the Canadian *voyageurs* [as trappers of French extraction were called] and hunters in the consumption of meat strike the greenhorn with wonder and astonishment, and are only equalled by the gastronomical capabilities exhibited by Indian dogs, both following the same plan in their epicurean gorgings.

On slaughtering a fat [buffalo] cow, the hunter carefully lays by, as a titbit for himself, the "boudins" and medullary intestine, which are prepared by being inverted and partially cleaned (this, however, is not thought indispensable). The *depouillé,* or fleece, the short and delicious hump-rib and "tender loin," are then carefully stowed away and with these the rough edge of the appetite is removed. But *the* course is, par excellence, the sundry yards of "boudin," which, lightly browned over the embers of the fire, slide down the well-lubricated throat of the hungry mountaineer, yard after yard, disappearing in quick succession.

I once saw two Canadians commence at either end of such a coil of grease, the mass lying between them on a dirty apishamore [saddle pad] like the coil of a huge snake. As yard after yard glided glibly down their throats, and the serpent on the saddlecloth was dwindling from an anaconda to a moderate-sized rattlesnake, it became a great point with each of the feasters to hurry his operation, so as to gain a march upon his neighbour, and improve the opportunity by swallowing more than his just proportion; each, at the same time, exhorting the other, whatever he did, to feed fair, and every now and then, overcome by the unblushing attempts of his partner to bolt a vigorous mouthful, would suddenly jerk back his head, drawing out at the same moment, by the retreating motion, several yards of boudin from his neighbour's mouth and stomach—for the greasy viand required no mastication, and was bolted whole—and, snapping up himself the ravished portions, greedily swallowed them; to be in turn again withdrawn and subjected to a similar process by the other.

Ruxton of the Rockies

DINING WITH A KALMUCK PRINCE AT ASTRACHAN

After the *Te Deum,* bless me, if he didn't give me a very good luncheon, the pièce de résistance of which was fillet of horse. If you see Geoffroy Saint-Hilaire, tell him I agree with him that, compared with horse, mutton is no better than veal. I say "veal" because I believe it to be the meat you most hold in contempt. After the feast there was a race of one hundred and fifty horses, ridden by young Kalmucks of both sexes, at which four of the Princess's ladies-in-waiting were present. . . . We went back to the other side of the Volga and watched a display of hawking, falcons against swans. That, together with the dresses of the Prince, the Princess, and the ladies-in-waiting, had a medieval look which would have delighted you, champion of the modern though you are. Then we sat down to table again. We started with foal soup which needed only a raven to be as good as our suppers at Sainte-Assise. The rest, apart from brawn made from horse's head, was just a variant of ordinary bourgeois cooking. Meanwhile, out in the courtyard, three hundred Kalmucks were being regaled with raw horseflesh minced with onions, and two cows and ten sheep roasted. . . .

Would you believe it, I have eaten raw horseflesh with little onions, and found it excellent? I can't say the same of mare's-milk brandy. Ugh! We went to bed late, after taking tea in the Princess's tent. . . . Next morning, we were each of us brought, *in bed,* a great bowl of camel's milk. I drank mine with a prayer for protection to the Buddha. . . .

—ALEXANDRE DUMAS PÈRE TO ALEXANDER DUMAS FILS

Pennsylvania's Mighty Eater
CARL CARMER

Nobody will let you forget Hungry Sam Miller . . . though he's been dead for more than fifteen years. Sam put on eating shows at farmer's picnics all the way from Wilkes-Barre to Harrisburg. Hungry Sam first made a splurge in his own neck of the woods around the time of the Spanish-American War when he demonstrated that he could consume more at one sitting than any big eater anybody else had ever heard of. He was no little surprised, moreover, to discover that by so doing he would not only be fed free, but paid a substantial bonus if he would dine before an audience. For a score of years then, without self-consciousness, he devoured incredible amounts of hearty food at community get-togethers before crowds of envious and enthusiastic onlookers.

During World War I, Sam patriotically gave up his remunerative specialty in order to conserve food, but he returned to it on Armistice Day when, before a cheering crowd of happy Susquehanna farmers, he put away two whole chickens as appetizers and topped them off with a dessert of 153 waffles.

Practical jokers used to hire Sam to show up whenever the pious ladies of one of the river towns advertised a church supper with the offer of "all you can eat for 50 cents," and he was said never to have failed eating them into a deficit.

At one farmers' picnic, he ate an eighteen-pound ham; at another, forty-eight ten-inch pies—the first thirty-eight in twenty-nine minutes—and, at a third, he downed a large bunch of bananas. Later, he astounded the valley by appearing at a country fair and betting hundreds of dollars that he could eat a bale of hay. He went home affluent after he had burned the hay and devoured the ashes.

Occasionally, when business was slow, Sam would stimulate it by walking into a restaurant and ordering at his own expense a meal that would more than satisfy a dozen men. Word of this would get about town and hundreds would crowd about to watch the champion eat. When he had finished his meal, spectators would bet him considerable sums that he could not eat more. He never lost a wager. He immortalized one eating place by gobbling down 144 of its fried eggs. At another, he ate a hundred eggs raw, shells and all.

Saloonkeepers along the river fronts used to offer the gastronomic celebrity money for professional appearances and he sometimes obliged, but he confined his drinking to an occasional glass of beer, and his heart never seemed to be in his eating when it was done in a place where the sale of liquor was the major interest. The best he ever did at a bar was a mere ten loaves of bread. . . .

Sam died in his eightieth year. He was never troubled by indigestion—not even in his last illness.

The Susquehanna

THE NEIGHS HAVE IT

In 1900 occurred (at Sherry's not at Delmonico's) what was perhaps the most inane feat of sheer showing-off ever perpetrated by an American plutocrat. This was the "horseback dinner" given by a man named C. K. G. Billings (otherwise unrenowned) to thirty-six horsey friends in celebration of the opening of his $200,000 stable for thoroughbreds in what is now Fort Tryon Park. Sherry's ballroom was ruralized for the occasion by a backdrop of rustic scenery, interspersed with potted palms. Real sod overlaid the dancing floor. The guests, in white ties and boiled shirts, perched precariously on hacks hired from a livery stable and pecked at the viands placed on trays attached to the pommels of their saddles. The horses dined, too, more at ease, out of troughs filled with selected oats; while the waiters, in riding boots and hunting pink, doubled as grooms of the chamber, sweeping up the droppings from this Centaur banquet in between popping champagne corks. The egregious Billings made his splash; and his name is embalmed in time's balsam, like a beetle in amber, for the derision of centuries to come.

—LATELY THOMAS
Delmonico's, A Century of Splendor

Diamond Jim Brady and Lillian Russell
WAVERLEY ROOT AND RICHARD DE ROCHEMONT

In the Waldorf's formal Palm Garden or its adventurous Roof Garden, open to the sky, Oscar again had occasion to serve his idolized Lillian Russell and Diamond Jim Brady. They also remained customers of Delmonico, but as a matter of fact the archetype of a new sort of restaurant which was now springing up, Rector's, in the hail-fellow-well-met vein, was more in accord with their life-style. Also, though neither of the pair was hard up for money, and though Rector's was not exactly cheap, it was still cheaper than Delmonico, no negligible detail when one ate as much as they did. "Jim Brady is the best twenty-five customers we have," George Rector said, and he considered his custom so valuable that when Brady remarked regretfully that Sole Marguery could only be had in the Paris restaurant which had created it and had given it its name, Rector took his son out of college and sent him to Paris to take a job in the Marguery's kitchen and burglarize the recipe—or at least that is the story which was told at the time. It goes on to report that after several months of espionage, the Rector scion succeeded, and when the first American-made Sole Marguery was plunked down before Diamond Jim, he devoured nine orders of it one after the other before going on to the next course.

This represented no record for Brady. A normal dinner for him, according to Rector, began with two or three dozen Lynnhaven oysters, six-inch giants rushed up from Maryland expressly for him. Then came half a dozen crabs, two bowls of green turtle soup, and, in Rector's words, "a deluge of lobsters," a term which he redefined more precisely, on request, as meaning six or seven. This whetted the appetite for a double portion of terrapin, two canvasback ducks, a large sirloin steak with appropriate vegetables, and, when a tray of French pastry was presented for dessert, its entire contents. That Brady was only a glutton, not a gourmet, seems evident from the fact that he did not drink wine, the almost irreplaceable accompaniment for this sort of food, nor, for that matter, even beer. He accompanied each enormous repast with several large glasses of his favorite drink, freshly squeezed orange juice or, alternatively, lemon soda pop. After such a meal, lingering at the table for after-dinner talk, he would dip from time to time into a box of chocolates placed handily near his plate by the knowing waiters who served him. The correct amount to tamp down such a meal was about two pounds.

For most persons, a dinner of these dimensions would have required the next twenty-four hours for its absorption; Brady ate six meals a day. Breakfast consisted of pancakes, hominy, eggs, cornbread, muffins, steak, chops and fried potatoes, washed down with a gallon of orange juice. At half past eleven he ate two or three dozen shellfish to stave off the pangs of hunger until lunch, an hour later—oysters and clams again (he was a great guzzler of seafood), deviled crabs, a couple of lobsters, roast beef, salad, and two or three wedges of different kinds of pie. With orange juice. Tea was slight: shellfish again, accompanied, for a change, by lemon sole. Dinner has already been described. If he could rise from the table afterwards he might go to the theatre, an appetite-provoking exercise, which had to be followed by supper—the traditional hot bird and cold bottle, except that in Brady's case this meant *several* game birds, and the bottles held orange juice or lemon soda. Though Brady himself drank so badly, as a host he treated his guests better. More than five hundred bottles of champagne were consumed at a dinner for fifty which he gave at the Hoffman House, Oscar Tschirky's first place of employment, in honor of his racehorse, Gold Heels, which had just proved itself to be aptly named by winning a large purse. On this occasion, Brady's guests tied on the feedbags at 4 P.M., and did not finish eating until nine the next morning—seventeen hours of stalwart stuffing . . .

It is easier to understand Brady's gluttony than that of his most constant dinner companion, Lillian Russell (real name, Helen Louise Leonard), the popular music hall and operetta singer, who shattered all conceptions of feminine delicacy by eating dish for dish with him; she remained nevertheless for thirty-five years the idol of American males, including Oscar of the Waldorf, running through five husbands and nobody knows how many lovers. She shared with Diamond Jim a passion for corn on the cob lashed with great gobs of melting fresh farm butter, a dish never included in thinning diets; and indeed neither of them was thin. America's dream girl weighed more than two hundred pounds; but the nineteenth century liked its women ample. As for Brady, when he died in 1917 at the age of fifty-six (from digestive troubles), his stomach was found to be six times normal size.

Eating in America

ACKNOWLEDGMENTS

Among numerous debts incurred in gathering material for this book, I owe a special one to Robert Lescher for friendship, sage advice, and a generous gift of time. I am also grateful to Alexis Bespaloff for sympathetic help. In addition, acknowledgments are due to the following:

American Heritage Publishing Co., Inc.:
"The Indomitable Fannie Farmer" from "Fannie Farmer" by Russell Lynes, and the "Mark Twain" piece by Evan Jones reprinted from *The American Heritage Cookbook and Illustrated History of American Eating and Drinking.* Copyright © 1964 by American Heritage Publishing Company, Inc.

The Artists' & Writers' Cookbook, Inc.:
"Some Thoughts on Guests for Dinner" from "Ratatouille Rowayton" by Kay Boyle, "My Life in Rice" by Upton Sinclair, and "Southern Fried Chicken" by William Styron from *The Artists' & Writers' Cookbook* edited by Beryl Barr and Barbara Turner Sachs. Copyright © 1961 by William H. Ryan. Reprinted by permission.

Atheneum Publishers, Inc.:
From *Delights and Prejudices* by James Beard. Copyright © 1964 by James Beard. From *Simple French Food* by Richard Olney. Copyright © 1974 by Richard Olney. Reprinted by permission of Atheneum Publishers.

John F. Blair, Publisher:
From *Papa D: A Saga of Love and Cooking* by Edward G. Danziger. Copyright © 1967 by John F. Blair, Publisher. Reprinted by permission.

Peg Bracken:
From *The I Hate to Cook Almanac, A Book of Days* by Peg Bracken. Copyright © 1976 by Peg Bracken.

Mrs. W. A. Bradley:
From *Cesar Ritz, Host to the World* by Marie Louise Ritz. Reprinted by permission of Mrs. W. A. Bradley.

Art Buchwald:
From *Is It Safe to Drink the Water?* by Art Buchwald. Copyright © 1962 by Art Buchwald. Reprinted by permission of the author.

Elizabeth B. Carmer:
From *The Susquehanna* by Carl Carmer. Copyright 1955 by Carl Carmer. Reprinted by permission of Elizabeth B. Carmer.

Chilton Book Co.:
From *Memoirs and Menus, the Confessions of a Culinary Snob* by Georges Spunt. Copyright © 1967 by Georges Spunt. Reprinted by permission.

CBS Inc.:
"An Insatiable Appetite for Hamburgers" by Charles Kuralt, CBS Evening News. © 1970 CBS Inc. All Rights Reserved. Reprinted by permission.

William Cole:
"What a Friend We Have in Cheeses!" and "A Confishion" by William Cole, from . . . *And Be Merry!* edited by William Cole. Copyright 1972 by William Cole. Reprinted by permission of the author.

Constable & Company Limited:
From *Tables of Content* by André Simon. Reprinted by permission.

Curtis Brown, Ltd.:
From *How Green Was My Valley* by Richard Llewellyn. Copyright 1940, renewed 1968 by Richard Llewellyn. Reprinted by permission of Curtis Brown, Ltd.

Delacorte Press:
"Dinty Moore's" from *Talking Woman* by Shana Alexander. Copyright © 1976 by Shana Alexander and used by permission of the publisher, Delacorte Press.

Doubleday & Company, Inc.:
Excerpted from *Metternich and the Dutchess* by Dorothy Gies McGuigan. Copyright © 1975 by Dorothy Gies McGuigan. Excerpted from *Tolstoy* by Henri Troyat. Copyright © 1967 by Doubleday & Company, Inc. Reprinted by permission of Doubleday & Company, Inc.

Doubleday & Company, Inc., and Vallentine, Mitchell & Co. Ltd.:
Excerpted from *Anne Frank: The Diary of a Young Girl* by Anne Frank. Copyright 1952 by Otto H. Frank. Reprinted by permission of Doubleday & Company, Inc., and Vallentine, Mitchell & Co. Ltd.

E. P. Dutton & Company, Inc.:
"Thoughts of Loved Ones" from *One to a Customer* by Margaret Fishback. Copyright, 1937, by E. P. Dutton & Company, Inc. Renewal, ©, 1965 by Margaret Fishback Antolini. Reprinted by permission of E. P. Dutton.

Faber and Faber, Ltd.:
From "Introduction" by W. H. Auden to *The Art of Eating* by M. F. K. Fisher. All rights reserved by Faber and Faber, Ltd., 1958; from *Three Rivers of France* by Freda White. Copyright © 1972 by Faber and Faber, Ltd. Reprinted by permission of the publisher.

Farrar, Straus & Giroux, Inc:
From *The Hundred Glories of French Cooking* by Robert Courtine, translated from the French by Derek Coltman. Copyright © 1971 by Robert Courtine. This translation copyright © 1973 by Farrar, Straus & Giroux, Inc. From *Oranges* by John McPhee. Copyright © 1966, 1967 by John McPhee. This selection originally appeared in *The New Yorker*. Reprinted by permission of Farrar, Straus & Giroux, Inc. "Le Poisson au Coup de Pied" ("The Kicked Fish") by Colette. Translated from the French by Paul Schmidt. Translation Copyright © 1979 by Colette de Jouvenel. Reprinted with the permission of Farrar, Straus & Giroux, Inc., and Mme. Colette de Jouvenel.

Marshall Fishwick:
"Dinner with Mr. Jefferson" by Marshall Fishwick from the *Ford Times*. Copyright © 1975 by Marshall Fishwick. Reprinted by permission of the author.

Mme. Sanda Goudeket:
From *Close to Colette* by Maurice Goudeket. Reprinted by permission of Laurent Goudeket.

Gourmet Magazine:
From "Remembering William Faulkner" by Anthony West. Copyright © 1969 by *Gourmet* Magazine. Reprinted by permission.

Geoffrey Grigson:
From *Notes from an Odd Country* by Geoffrey Grigson. Copyright © 1970 by Geoffrey Grigson. Reprinted by permission of the author.

Harcourt Brace Jovanovich, Inc.
From *Pearl's Kitchen* by Pearl Bailey. Reprinted by permission of Harcourt Brace Jovanovich, Inc.

Harcourt Brace Jovanovich, Inc., and A. M. Heath & Company Ltd.:
From *Down and Out in Paris and London* by George Orwell. Copyright 1933 by George Orwell; copyright 1961 by Sonia Pitt-Rivers. Published in England by Martin Secker & Warburg Ltd. Reprinted by permission of Harcourt Brace Jovanovich, Inc., A. M. Heath & Company Ltd. and Mrs. Sonia Brownwell Orwell.

Harcourt Brace Jovanovich, Inc., and The Hogarth Press Ltd.:
From *Virginia Woolf: A Biography* by Quentin Bell. Copyright © 1972 by Quentin Bell. Reprinted by permission of Harcourt Brace Jovanovich, Inc., and The Hogarth Press Ltd.

Harper & Row, Publishers, Inc.:
From *Party of One* by Clifton Fadiman. (World Publishing Co.) Copyright © 1955 by Clifton Fadiman. Abridgment of "The Great Carême . . . He Built a Better Cream Puff" from *The Good Life . . . or What's Left of It* by Phyllis and Fred Feldkamp. Copyright © 1972 by Phyllis and Fred Feldkamp. From *Only in America* by Harry Golden. (World Publishing Co.) Copyright © 1958 by Harry Golden. From *Inside Africa* by John Gunther. Copyright © 1953, 1954, 1955 by John Gunther. Abridged from "Relleno de Guavino" from *Recipes from the Regional Cooks of Mexico* by Diana Kennedy. Copyright © 1978 by Diana Kennedy. From "Introduction" by André Maurois to *Cooking with a French Touch* by Gerald Maurois. Copyright, 1950, 1951 by Gerald Maurois. From *The Alice B. Toklas Cook Book* by Alice B. Toklas. Copyright 1954 by Alice B. Toklas. "The Gourmet" from *People and Other Aggravations* by Judith Viorst. Copyright © 1970 by Judith Viorst. Reprinted by permission of Harper & Row, Publishers, Inc.

Harper's Magazine:
"Asparagus Tops" by Joyce Wadler. Copyright © 1973 by *Harper's Magazine*. All rights reserved. Reprinted from the July 1973 issue by special permission.

David Higham Associates Limited:
From *French Provincial Cooking* by Elizabeth David. Copyright © 1960, 1962 by Elizabeth David. Reprinted by permission of David Higham Associates Limited.

Holt, Rinehart and Winston:
From *The Art of Cuisine* by Henri de Toulouse-Lautrec and Maurice Joyant. Introduction by M. G. Dortu and Ph. Huisman. Translated by Margery Weiner. Copyright © 1966 by Edita, Lausanne. Copyright © 1966 by Holt, Rinehart and Winston and Michael Joseph. Reprinted by permission of Holt, Rinehart and Winston, Publishers.

Houghton Mifflin Company:
From *The Member of the Wedding* by Carson McCullers. Copyright © renewed 1974 by Florial V. Lasky. From *The Story of My Boyhood and Youth* by John Muir. Copyright renewed 1940 by Wanda Muir Hanna. From *The Great Railway Bazaar* by Paul Theroux. Copyright © 1975 by Paul Theroux. From *Delmonico's: A Century of Splendor* by Lately Thomas. Copyright © 1967 by Houghton Mifflin Company. Reprinted by permission of Houghton Mifflin Company.

Hutchinson Publishing Group Limited:
From *Musings of a Chinese Gourmet* by Dr. F. T. Cheng. Reprinted by permission of Hutchinson Publishing Group Limited.

International Creative Management:
From "Caviar" from *La Bonne Table* by Ludwig Bemelmans. Copyright © 1960 by Ludwig Bemelmans. Reprinted by permission of International Creative Management.

The International Wine & Food Society, 104 Pall Mall, London, England:
"Snails" by Dr. G. C. Williamson, "Dejeuner de Rupture" by James Laver, and "Feeding on the Train" by Maurice Healy, all from *Wine & Food,* published quarterly by the Society. Reprinted by permission of the Journal Committee.

Madhur Jaffrey:
"A Picnic in the Himalayas" by Madhur Jaffrey. Originally appeared in *Gourmet* Magazine, October, 1974. Reprinted by permission of the author.

Russell Jones:
"My Fill of Caviar" from *A Journey to Astrakhan* by Russell Jones. Reprinted by permission of the author.

Alfred A. Knopf, Inc.:
From *Simca's Cuisine* by Simone Beck in collaboration with Patricia Simon. Copyright © 1972 by Simone Beck and Patricia Simon. From *The Windward Road: Adventures of a Naturalist on Remote Caribbean Shores* by Archie Carr. Copyright © 1955 by Archie Carr. From *Death Comes for the Archbishop* by Willa Cather. Copyright 1927 by Willa Cather and renewed 1955 by The Executors of the Estate of Willa Cather. From "Musings Upon Caesar and His Salad" from *Julia Child's Kitchen* by Julia Child. Copyright © 1975 by Julia Child. "Baking Off" from *Crazy Salad: Some Things About Women* by Nora Ephron. Copyright © 1973 by Nora Ephron. From *The Natural History of Nonsense* by Bergen Evans. Copyright 1946, © 1958 by Bergen Evans. From *The Mushroom Feast* by Jane Grigson. Copyright © 1975 by Jane Grigson. From "Introduction" to *The Classic Italian Cookbook* by Marcella Hazan. Copyright © 1973 by Marcella Hazan and Victor Hazan. From *Home from the Hill* by William Humphrey. Copyright © 1957 by William Humphrey. From *Remembered Laughter: The Life of Noel Coward* by Cole Lesley. Copyright © 1976 by Cole Lesley. From *The Taste of Country Cooking* by Edna Lewis. Copyright © 1976 by Edna Lewis. Excerpt from "The Baltimore of the Eighties." Copyright 1939 by Alfred A. Knopf, Inc. and renewed 1967 by August Mencken and Mercantile Safe Deposit and Trust Company. Reprinted from *The Vintage Mencken* by H. L. Mencken, gathered by Alistair Cooke. From *The Bathtub Hoax and Other Blasts and Bravos from the Chicago Tribune* by H. L. Mencken, edited by Robert McHugh. Copyright © 1958 by Alfred A. Knopf, Inc. From *A Book of Middle Eastern Food* by Claudia Roden. Copyright © 1968, 1972 by Claudia Roden. From *My Young Years* by Arthur Rubinstein. Copyright © 1973 by Aniela Rubinstein, Eva Rubinstein Coffin, Alina Anna Rubinstein & John Arthur Rubinstein. From *My Happy Life* by Arthur Rubinstein. Copyright © 1979 by Aniela Rubinstein, Eva Rubinstein Coffin, Alina Anna Rubinstein & John Arthur Rubinstein. From *Table Topics* by Julian Street, edited by A. I. M. S. Street. Copyright © 1959 by A. I. M. S. Street. From *Huey Long* by T. Harry Williams. Copyright © 1969 by Alfred A. Knopf, Inc. From *Buchanan Dying* by John Updike. Copyright © 1974 by John Updike. Reprinted by permission of Alfred A. Knopf, Inc.

Alfred A. Knopf, Inc., and Hamish Hamilton Ltd.
From *Purely for Pleasure* by Margaret Lane. Copyright © 1966, 1967 by Margaret Lane. Reprinted by permission of Alfred A. Knopf, Inc. and Hamish Hamilton Ltd.

Alfred A. Knopf, Inc., and Hutchinson Publishing Group Limited:
From *Borstal Boy* by Brendan Behan. Copyright © 1958, 1959 by Brendan Behan. Reprinted by permission of Alfred A. Knopf, Inc. and Hutchinson Publishing Group Limited.

Robert Lescher Literary Agency:
From *Sam Ward: King of the Lobby* by Lately Thomas. Copyright © 1965 by Houghton Mifflin Company. Reprinted by permission of the Robert Lescher Literary Agency.

J. P. Lippincott Company:
From *Cooking à la Ritz* by Louis Diat. Copyright 1941 by Louis Diat. Copyright renewed 1969 by Mrs. Louis Diat. Reprinted by permission of J. P. Lippincott Company.

Dear, However Did You Think Up This Delicious Salad?" from *The Primrose Path* by Ogden Nash. Copyright 1935 by Ogden Nash. Reprinted by permission of Little, Brown and Co.

Little, Brown and Company in association with The Atlantic Monthly Press:
"The Catalina Restaurant in the Bayous" from *Grand and Private Pleasures* by Caskie Stinnett. Copyright © 1977 by Caskie Stinnett. Reprinted by permission of Little, Brown and Co. in association with The Atlantic Monthly Press.

Little, Brown and Company and A. D. Peters Co. Ltd:
From *Hornblower and the Hotspur* by C. S. Forester. Copyright © 1962 by C. S. Forester. Reprinted by permission of Little, Brown and Co. and A. D. Peters & Co. Ltd.

The Sterling Lord Agency, Inc.
From *Early Havoc* by June Havoc. Copyright © 1959 by June Havoc. Reprinted by permission of The Sterling Lord Agency, Inc.

David McKay Company, Inc.:
From *Stalking the Blue-Eyed Scallop* by Euell Gibbons. Copyright © 1964 by Euell Gibbons. From *Don't Just Stand There!* by Inez Robb. Copyright © 1962 by Inez Robb. Reprinted by permission of the David McKay Company, Inc.

Macmillan Publishing Co., Inc.
Excerpts from "B Is for Bachelors" and "P Is for Peas" (in *An Alphabet for Gourmets*) from *The Art of Eating* by M. F. K. Fisher. Copyright 1948, 1949 by M. F. K. Fisher. Copyrights renewed. Copyright 1954 by M. F. K. Fisher. Reprinted with permission of Macmillan Publishing Co., Inc.

Faith McNulty:
From "Brooklyn's Famous Chop House" by John McNulty, *Holiday* Magazine, March 1957 issue. Reprinted by permission of Faith McNulty.

Marshall Editions Ltd.:
From "Madame Point, Restaurant de la Pyramide, Vienne" from *Great Chiefs of France* by Anthony Blake and Quentin Crewe. Copyright © 1978 by Marshall Editions Ltd., London. Published in the United States by Harry N. Abrams, Inc., New York. Reprinted by permission.

William Morrow & Company, Inc.
From *Eating in America* by Waverley Root and Richard de Rochemont. Copyright © 1976 by Waverley Root and Richard de Rochemont. From *First Catch Your Eland* by Laurence Van der Post. Copyright © 1977 by Laurence Van der Post. Reprinted by permission of William Morrow & Company, Inc.

New Directions Publishing Corporation:
"The Peasant Declares His Love" by Emile Roumer, translated by John Peale Bishop from *Anthology of Contemporary Latin-American Poetry*, edited by Dudley Fitts. Copyright 1942 by New Directions Publishing Corporation. Reprinted by permission of New Directions.

New Statesman:
"Cupboard Love" by Hilary Haywood, "In Praise of Cocoa: Cupid's Nightcap" by Stanley J. Sharpless, "Dejeuner Sur L'Herbe" by Xico. Copyright © 1969 by New Statesman, London. Reprinted by permission.

The New York Times Company:
"Francs and Beans" by Russell Baker. © 1976 by The New York Times Company. "Birthday 1961" by Paul Child. © 1976 by The New York Times Company. "Just a Quiet Dinner for Two" by Craig Claiborne. © 1975 by The New York Times Company. "Caress the Perch . . ." by Israel Shenker. © 1973 by The New York Times Company. Reprinted by permission.

W. W. Norton & Company, Inc.
Excerpts reprinted from *Bite, A New York Restaurant Strategy* by Gael Greene. Copyright ©

ACKNOWLEDGMENTS   383

W. W. Norton & Company, Inc.
Excerpts reprinted from *Bite, A New York Restaurant Strategy* by Gael Greene. Copyright ©
1971, 1970, 1969, 1968 by Gael Greene. Reprinted by permission of W. W. Norton &
Company, Inc.

Harold Ober Associates Incorporated:
From *Father Was a Gourmet* by Carol Truax. Copyright © 1960, 1961, 1962, 1963, 1965 by
Carol Truax. Reprinted by permission of Harold Ober Associates Incorporated.

Peter Owen Ltd., Publishers:
From *Recollections of Virginia Woolf,* Edited by Joan Russell Noble. Published by Peter Owen,
London. Reprinted by permission.

Pantheon Books:
From *The Oysters of Locmariaquer* by Eleanor Clark. Copyright © 1963, 1964 by Eleanor Clark.
Reprinted by permission of Pantheon Books, a Division of Random House, Inc.

Prentice-Hall, Inc.:
From *Tales of the Table* by Barbara Norman. © 1972 by Barbara Norman. Published by
Prentice-Hall, Inc., Englewood Cliffs, New Jersey 07632.

G. P. Putnam's Sons:
From *Alone* by Richard E. Byrd. Copyright 1938 by Richard E. Byrd, renewed 1966 by Marie
A. Byrd. Reprinted by permission of G. P. Putnam's Sons.

Dachine Rainer:
Extract from "Curry" by Dachine Rainer. Copyright 1961 by Dachine Rainer. From *The
Artists' & Writers' Cookbook.* Contact Editions, Sausalito, California. Reprinted by permission
of Dachine Rainer.

Random House, Inc.:
"Yes, But Can the Steam Engine Do This?" from *Getting Even* by Woody Allen. Copyright
© 1966 by Woody Allen. This story originally appeared in *The New Yorker.* From *Invisible Man*
by Ralph Ellison. Copyright 1952 by Ralph Ellison. From *Italian Family Cooking* by Edward
Giobbi. Copyright © 1971 by Edward Giobbi. From *Iberia* by James A. Michener. Copyright
© 1968 by Random House, Inc. From *Remembrance of Things Past* by Marcel Proust, translated
by C. K. Scott-Moncrieff. Copyright 1934 and renewed 1962 by Random House, Inc.
"Living High on the No-Frills Flight" by Calvin Trillin, as it appeared in *Travel & Leisure.*
A different version appears in *Alice, Let's Eat: Further Adventures of a Happy Eater* by Calvin
Trillin. Copyright © 1978 by Calvin Trillin. Reprinted by permission of Random House,
Inc.

Cyril Ray:
"The Man Who Came to Dinner" by Cyril Ray, which appeared in the July 16, 1961, issue
of *The Observer* and in *The Gourmet's Companion* by Cyril Ray. Copyright © by Cyril Ray.
Reprinted by permission of the author.

Paul R. Reynolds, Inc.
"The Brighton Belle" and "Brillat-Savarin" by Joseph Wechsberg which appeared in *Gour-
met* Magazine. Copyright © 1970, 1971 by Joseph Wechsberg. Reprinted by permission of
Paul R. Reynolds, Inc., 599 Fifth Avenue, New York, N.Y. 10017.

Waverley Root:
From "An Epicure's Memoirs of a New England Boyhood" by Waverley Root, published
in *Gourmet* Magazine July, 1972. Copyright 1972 by Waverley Root. Reprinted by permission of the author.

Rothco Cartoons Inc.
"Petit Tour de France" by E. S. Turner. © Punch/Rothco.

Russell & Volkening, Inc.
"Just Enough Money" from *Between Meals* by A. J. Liebling. Copyright © 1959, 1962 by A. J. Liebling. Reprinted by permission of Russell & Volkening, Inc. as agent for the author. From "The Supreme Table" by William Sansom, published in *Holiday* Magazine. Copyright 1959 by Curtis Publishing Company. Reprinted by permission of Russell & Volkening, Inc. as agent for the author.

Charles Scribner's Sons:
From *A Movable Feast* by Ernest Hemingway. Copyright © 1964 by Ernest Hemingway, Ltd. From *Cross Creek* by Marjorie Kinnan Rawlings. Copyright 1942 by Marjorie Kinnan Rawlings, renewal copyright 1970 by Norton Baskin. From *Cross Creek Cookery* by Marjorie Kinnan Rawlings. Reprinted by permission of Charles Scribner's Sons.

Mimi Sheraton:
From *The Seducer's Cook Book* by Mimi Sheraton. Copyright 1962, 1963 by Mimi Sheraton. Reprinted by permission of the author.

Simon & Schuster, Inc.
From *The Guide to Inexpensive Wines* by Alexis Bespaloff. Copyright © 1973 by Alexis Bespaloff. Reprinted by permission of the author and Simon & Schuster, Inc.

The Society of Authors:
"A—Apple Pie" from *The Complete Poems of Walter de la Mare.* Copyright © 1969 by The Literary Trustees of Walter de la Mare. Reprinted by permission of The Literary Trustees of Walter de la Mare and The Society of Authors as their representatives.

Taplinger Publishing Co., Inc.:
From *The George Bernard Shaw Vegetarian Cook Book* by Alice Laden and R. J. Minney. (Taplinger, 1972) Copyright © 1971 by R. J. Minney. Reprinted by permission of Taplinger Publishing Co., Inc.

Robert Lewis Taylor:
From *W. C. Fields, His Follies and Fortunes* by Robert Lewis Taylor. Copyright 1949 and 1967 by Robert Lewis Taylor. Published by Doubleday. Reprinted by permission of the author.

Time-Life Books Inc.:
From Food of the World/*A Quintet of Cuisines.* Copyright © 1970. Courtesy of Time-Life Books Inc., publisher.

University of California Press:
Adapted from *The Tukuna,* University of California Publications in American Archaeology and Ethnology, Vol. 45, 1952 (as cited in *The Raw and the Cooked* by Claude Levi-Straus.) Reprinted by permission of the University of California Press.

University of Oklahoma Press:
From *Ruxton of the Rockies,* edited by Leroy R. Hafen. Copyright 1950 by the University of Oklahoma Press. Reprinted by permission.

The Viking Press, Inc.:
From *End of the Affair* by Graham Greene. Copyright 1951 by Graham Greene. From *Charles Dickens, His Tragedy and Triumph* by Edgar Johnson. Copyright 1952, © 1977 by Edgar Johnson. "Ballad of Culinary Frustration" from *A Pocketful of Wry* by Phyllis McGinley. Copyright 1940 by Phyllis McGinley. From *The Pastures of Heaven* by John Steinbeck. Copyright 1932, renewed 1960 by John Steinbeck. From *Too Many Cooks* by Rex Stout. Copyright 1938, renewed © 1966 by Rex Stout. From *Nero Wolfe Cook Book* by Rex Stout and Viking Press Editors. Copyright © 1973 by The Viking Press, Inc. All rights reserved. Reprinted by permission of Viking Penguin Inc.

A. P. Watt Ltd. Literary Agents:
"My First Love" from *The World We Laugh In* by Harry Graham. Reprinted by permission of the Estate of Harry Graham. "Love Song" by A. P. Herbert. Reprinted by permission of the Estate of A. P. Herbert.

Rogers C. M. Whittaker:
A quotation from "The Old Curmudgeon" made in conversation. Reprinted by permission.

Every reasonable effort has been made to clear the use of material in this volume with the copyright owners. If notified of any omissions, the editor and publisher will be glad to make any proper corrections in future editions.

INDEX OF AUTHORS